Effective Data Protection

Managing information in an era of change

Mandy Webster

icsa.
Publishing

ALISTAIR MACKENZIE LIBRARY
Barcode: 3690289517
Class no: WA 950 WEB

WX 173 WEB

First published 2011
Published by ICSA Information & Training Ltd
16 Park Crescent
London W1B 1AH
© ICSA Information & Training Ltd, 2011

All rights reserved. No part of this publication may be reproduced, stored in a retrieval system, or transmitted, in any form, or by any means, electronic, mechanical, photocopying, recording or otherwise, without prior permission, in writing, from the publisher.

Typeset by Hands Fotoset, Mapperley, Nottingham

Printed by Hobbs the Printers Ltd, Totton, Hampshire

British Cataloguing in Publication Data
A catalogue record for this book is available from the British Library

ISBN   9781860724589

Contents

Alistair Mackenzie Library
Wishaw General Hospital
50 Netherton Street
Wishaw
ML2 0DP

Preface	vii
Table of cases	ix
Table of statutes	xi
Acronyms and abbreviations	xiii

Part 1: Towards Effective Data Protection	**1**
1 The legislative background	3
2 The changing legislative environment	14
3 Data protection basics: notification and exemptions, offences and penalties	38
4 The data protection principles	50
5 A strategic approach to data protection compliance	66
6 Personal information processing: risks and risk management	86
7 Conducting risk assessments	101
8 Avoiding and mitigating risk: tactics	132
9 Training and staff awareness	144

Part 2: Effective Data Protection: Q&A	**157**
Introduction	159
A Fair processing and marketing	160
B Record keeping	173
C Security	175
D CCTV	178
E Outsourcing	185
F Employment	190
G International transfers	197
H Websites	201
I Enforcement	203

Glossary	207
Directory	211
Index	217

Preface

The UK's first introduction to data protection law was the Data Protection Act 1984 required as part of Britain's ongoing commitment to Europe. Signing up to the Convention for the Protection of Individuals with regard to Automatic Processing of Personal Data in 1981 in Strasbourg enabled the UK to participate in European data sharing. To the extent that there was any appetite for data protection, it was to manage the abuse of personal information used for marketing purposes. Privacy was not a consideration; even to this day the courts regularly state that there is no general law of privacy in the UK.

Over the years since 1984 the perspective has changed, partly driven by technological developments like the internet and the massive increase in the amount of personal information organisations are able to hold and process and partly due to increasing fears of identity theft and fraud. There has been a rise in data security risk as the value of personal information has become clear and this has focused mainly on IT security. The latest trend is the increasing emphasis on information management, recognising that data security is more than just IT security.

The objective of this book is to capture the current legislative environment on the cusp of a raft of potential new data protection obligations and to map out the likely direction of changes in the law. It will consider the wider legal environment, how data protection interacts with other legislation such as Freedom of Information, Human Rights, Regulation of Investigatory Powers and regulations resulting from other EC Directives. This is the content of Part 1 of the book. However, it remains an essentially practical guide to the management of data protection compliance in the current environment, with suggested strategies and tactics, with explanations of what is involved, how they can be implemented, pitfalls to avoid and the likely benefits. Part 2 of the book addresses frequently asked questions in the context of everyday business activities.

Chapter 1 outlines the wider legislative background, the data protection regulatory structure in Europe and the national regulatory authority in the UK, the Information Commissioner. Chapter 2 considers how changes in UK data protection law are driven, exploring the UK's relationship with the European Commission over its implementation of the Data Protection Directive and how developments in Europe generally under the Lisbon Treaty are impacting on data protection law. It looks at lobbying powers internationally and those of the Information Commissioner and other regulators at home. Many of the key themes that emerge as likely developments in the law are highlighted throughout the remainder of the book.

Chapters 3 and 4 outline how data protection law has been implemented in the UK, looking at the offences under the Act, notification requirements and key elements of the data protection principles. They explain how the Information Commissioner's powers have been augmented in the last 12 months.

In a response to the pressure for better information management and to position organisations so that they can deal with prospective changes in the law, a strategic approach to data protection compliance is recommended and explained in Chapter 5. The weaknesses in current data protection management practices identified by industry commentators are considered and a risk management approach to compliance is outlined. Chapter 6 builds on the risk management approach identifying the key risks and relating them back to the data protection principles. Most compliance topics can be considered in terms of the implications of risk to the organisation, its directors, managers and employees. Failures in data protection carry implications for individual customers too and these are investigated.

Chapter 7 outlines how a risk assessment of data protection compliance risks may be made and is largely a series of case studies to illustrate the risks of different aspects of personal data processing operations. Various tactics to avoid data protection risks are examined in Chapters 8 and 9. Chapter 9 focuses on training as a tool to help avoid risks or mitigate those that cannot be avoided.

To provide a practical perspective on current data protection law, Part 2 of the book deals with frequently asked questions in the context of marketing, record keeping, security, outsourcing, data sharing, employment and staff monitoring, transfers of personal information to territories outside of the EEA, website compliance, data protection enforcement activity, and CCTV.

Mandy Webster
January 2011

Table of Cases

Bodil Lundqvist v Kammeraklagareu [2003] C101/01 ECJ6/11/2003   62, 76
Campbell v MGN Ltd [2004] UKHL   22, 24
CCN Systems Limited and CCN Credit Systems Limited v The Data Protection
    Registrar [Case DA/90 25/49/9]   36, 91
Douglas and others v Hello! Ltd and others [2005] EWCA Civ 595   24
Durant v Financial Services Authority [2003] EWCA Civ 1746   4, 14, 15, 16,
    20, 23
Equifax Europe Limited and the Data Protection Registrar [Case DA90/25/49/7]
    91
Innovations Mail Order v Data Protection Registrar [Case DA92 31/49/1]   22
MS v Sweden (1997) 28 EHRR 313   58
Murray v Big Pictures (UK) Ltd [2008] EWCA Civ 446   24
Peck v The UK 28 January 2003 (ECHR)   57
R v Hardy [2007] CA Crim Division   46
R (Bernard) v Enfield London Borough Council [2002] EWCA Civ 1726   5
S and Marper v The UK (Application nos 30562/04 and 30566/04)   5
Von Hanover v Germany (Application No 59320/00) 24 June 2004 (ECHR)   24
X and Y v The Netherlands, Judgment of 26 March 1985, Series A No. 91   5

Table of Statutes

Charities Act 2006

Charities Act (NI) 2008

Charity and Trustee Investment Act (Scotland) Act 2005

Contracts (Rights of Third Parties) Act 1999

Coroners and Justice Act 2009

Criminal Justice and Immigration Act 2008

Data Protection Act 1984

Data Protection Act 1998

Data Protection Directive 95/46/EC

Data Protection (Conditions under Paragraph 3 of Part II of Schedule 1) Order
2000 (SI 2000/185)

Data Protection (Jersey Law) 2005

Data Protection (Processing of Sensitive Personal Data) Order 2000
(SI 2000/417)

Data Retention (EC Directive) Regulations 2007 (SI 2007/2199)

European Convention for the Protection of Human Rights and Fundamental
Freedoms

Financial Services and Markets Act 2000

Freedom of Information Act 2000

Human Rights Act 1998 (HRA)

Interception of Communications Act 1985

Privacy and Electronic Communications Directive 2002/58/EC

Privacy and Electronic Communications (EC Directive) (Amendment) Regulations
2004 (SI 204/1039)

Privacy and Electronic Communications (EC Directive) Regulations 2003
(SI 2003/2426)

Regulation of Investigatory Powers Act 2000 (RIPA)

Reporting of Injuries, Diseases and Dangerous Occurrences Regulations 1995
(SI 1995/3163)

Representation of the People (England & Wales) (Amendment) Regulations 2002
(SI 1871/2002)

Telecommunications (Data Protection and Privacy) Regulations 1999
(SI 1998/3170)

Telecommunications (Lawful Business Practice) (Interception of Communications)
Regulations 2000 (SI 2000/2699)

Telecoms Directive 97/66/EC
Transfer of Undertakings (Protection of Employment) Regulations 1981
  (SI 1991/1794)
Unfair Terms in Consumer Contracts Regulations 1999 (SI 1999/2083)

Acronyms and Abbreviations

ASA	Advertising Standards Agency
BCR	Binding Corporate Rules
CIFAS	UK's Fraud Protection Service
CJIA 2008	Criminal Justice and Immigration Act 2008
CRM	Customer relationship management
DMA	Direct Marketing Association
DPA 1998	Data Protection Act 1998
EC	European Community
ECHR	European Court of Human Rights
ECJ	European Court of Justice
EDPS	European Data Protection Supervisor
EEA	European Economic Area
EU	European Union
FSA	Financial Services Authority
GRC	Governance, risk management and compliance software
HMRC	Her Majesty's Revenue and Customs
HR	Human resources
HRA 1998	Human Rights Act 1998
ICO	Information Commissioner's Office
MPS	Mailing Preference Service
NHS	National Health Service
PET	Privacy enhancing technologies
PIA	Privacy Impact Assessment
PIMS	Personal Information Management System
PNC	Police National Computer
RIPA 2000	Regulation of Investigatory Powers Act 2000
SIA 2001	Security Industry Act 2001
SIRO	Senior Information Risk Owner
TPS	Telephone Preference Service

Part 1

Towards Effective Data Protection

1   The legislative background

Introduction

One of the aspects of providing for and supporting a common market involved the harmonisation of European data protection law. The European Commission adopted Directive 95/46/EC in 1995 following on from the Convention for the Protection of Individuals with regard to Automatic Processing of Personal Data adopted within the Council of Europe in 1981.

Data protection is highly regulated within the European Community (EC) and it is viewed as part of a whole policy area to stimulate the information society and exploit its benefits as well as regulate its operation. There is a Commissioner for Information Society and Media who has responsibility for a range of activities and policy areas encompassing regulation and protection, such as data protection, electronic communications, digital rights management, the exploitation of public sector information and internet governance.

The EC Directive and the DPA 1998

The source of data protection law throughout the European Community is Directive 95/46/EC, which was adopted in 1995. Member States were required to introduce national law to enact the Directive within three years. The Data Protection Act 1998 (DPA 1998) implemented the Directive in the UK. It was introduced in October 1998 and provided a further three-year transitional period for any organisations processing personal information to comply with the new law.

The aim of the Directive is to safeguard the fundamental rights of individuals while also fostering consistency and closer relations between member states, ensuring economic and social progress etc.[1] In particular the Recitals to the Directive state: 'The difference in levels of protection of rights and freedoms of individuals, notably the right to privacy, with regard to the processing of personal data afforded in Member States may prevent the transmission of such data from the territory of one Member State to that of another Member State: whereas this difference may therefore constitute an obstacle to the pursuit of a number of economic activities at Community level, distort competition and impede authorities in the discharge of their responsibilities under Community law; whereas the difference in levels of protection is due to the existence of a wide variety of national laws "regulations and administrative provisions"'.[2]

Article 1 states the object of the Directive. Again it is two-fold: the protection of fundamental rights and freedoms (in particular the right to privacy with respect to the processing of personal data); and the removal of restrictions on the free flow of personal data between Member States. The two objectives do not naturally work together and in practice the free flow of personal data has to be balanced continually against the rights of individuals.

The DPA 1998 implemented the Data Protection Directive although there is some controversy as to whether or not the UK has adequately implemented the Directive. The European Commission is of the view that the powers of the national data protection supervisory authority, the Information Commissioner, are inadequate and are less than provided for in the Directive. Since the landmark legal case, *Durant v Financial Services Authority*,[3] the definition of 'personal data' adopted in the UK has also been criticised as being too narrow. In 2004 the European Commission started the formal process of taking action over what it considers to be inadequate implementation of the Data Protection Directive. For a number of reasons, a review of current European data protection law is underway with proposals for a new legal framework due to be published by mid-2011. However the European Commission has specifically indicated[4] that, despite the review, Member States are required to comply with their obligations to ensure the proper application of the Data Protection Directive.

Other relevant legislation

The Human Rights Act 1998

The DPA 1998 applies to all records containing personal information, but the right to privacy in Europe has grown beyond just records. The Human Rights Act 1998 includes a right to respect for an individual's private and family life, home and correspondence.[5] It is referred to in the Recitals to the Directive. Recital 10 provides: 'Whereas the object of the national laws on the processing of personal data is to protect fundamental rights and freedoms, notably the right to privacy, which is recognised both in Article 8 of the European Convention for the Protection of Human Rights and Fundamental Freedoms.'

The right is set out in Article 8 which reads:

8.1. Everyone has the right to respect for his private and family life, his home and his correspondence.

8.2. There shall be no interference by a public authority with the exercise of this right except such as is in accordance with the law and is necessary in a democratic society in the interests of national security, public safety or the economic well-being of the country, for the prevention of disorder or crime, for the protection of health or morals, or for the protection of the rights and freedoms of others.

Article 8 provides for respect for individual privacy, but this is a qualified right. It can be infringed in certain circumstances as set out in Article 8.2.

Article 8 has been interpreted as not only a requirement to protect rights from interference by a public authority, but also as imposing a positive obligation on public authorities to actively protect rights in certain circumstances. Human rights cases can be appealed from national courts to the European Court of Human Rights in Strasbourg (ECHR) so influential legal cases include those from other EU Member States.

In *R (Bernard) v Enfield London Borough Council*,[6] the Court held that the council had a duty to provide assistance to a disabled lady so that she could maintain her basic physical and psychological integrity.

In *X and Y v Netherlands*,[7] the ECHR held that the Netherlands should have taken steps to protect the applicants from sexual assault by their parents, as this assault was a grave breach of their right to respect for their private life.

In relation to data protection and privacy issues, 'private life' includes personal information. In particular, the protection of 'correspondence' is likely to include personal information in communications with others. Article 8 covers all forms of communication (e.g. telephone calls, e-mail and mail) and has been used to challenge the monitoring of telephone lines by the police and secret services. Monitoring is an intervention which gives rise to privacy issues.

As set out in Article 8.2, there are circumstances where an interference with Article 8 rights is justified. These must be:

- 'in accordance with the law', so there must be a clear legal basis for the interference;
- necessary in pursuit of at least one of:
  - national security;
  - public safety or the economic well-being of the country;
  - the prevention of disorder or crime;
  - the protection of health or morals; or
  - the protection of the rights and freedoms of others.
- 'necessary in a democratic society', meaning there must be good reason for the interference and that it must be proportionate to the problem perceived.

Information retention periods have been considered in connection with the Article 8 right. In *S and Marper v the UK*[8] the ECHR held that police databases of DNA samples of individuals they had arrested but later either acquitted or brought no charges against was a violation of their Article 8 rights. This underlines Data Protection Principle 5 that personal information shall be held for no longer than is required for the purposes for which it is processed.

Bearing in mind the positive obligations of Article 8 (i.e. the obligation on public authorities to actively protect rights in certain circumstances) there is also a link between data security and human rights. In a Finnish case, a lady working in an eye clinic was receiving treatment for AIDS. Her colleagues discovered her condition after one or more of them accessed her medical records. The ECHR[9] found that the medical data should have been properly protected and the failure of the eye clinic to follow national privacy laws had resulted in a breach of her human rights under Article 8.

The Court ruling means that public bodies and governments breach Article 8 (implemented in the UK as the Human Rights Act 2000) if they do not maintain security for personal data. Note, however, that the circumstances of the case involved an individual in a relationship with the public body as both employee and patient to whom a duty of confidentiality was owed in both relationships. Also, note that the information that was disclosed was medical information, 'sensitive data' under the EC Directive.

Freedom from unsolicited marketing

Directive 97/66/EC (known as the 'Telecoms Directive') and Directive 2002/58/EC (the 'Privacy and Electronic Communications Directive') led to the Privacy and Electronic Communications (EC Directive) Regulations 2003. These Regulations restrict unsolicited marketing via privately subscribed telecommunication channels like home telephone landlines, mobile phones and e-mail and support the right set out in the DPA 1998, s 11 to prevent the use of personal information for the purposes of direct marketing.

Controls on the use of CCTV

The Regulation of Investigatory Powers Act 2000 (RIPA) specifies those public bodies that are authorised to conduct surveillance where private space is invaded (e.g. surveillance which captures images either wholly or partly inside cars or homes).

RIPA also prohibits the interception of electronic mail although there is an exemption for commercial organisations, for example, using spam filters under a legitimate business purposes contained in the Lawful Business Practices Regulations 2000.

This is an area where further regulation is likely following comments made by the Deputy Prime Minister, Nick Clegg, after the May 2010 election in response to the growing public debate on the 'surveillance society'.

The regulatory structure in the EC

The Commissioner

Viviane Reding is currently the EU's Commissioner for Justice, Fundamental Rights and Citizenship and is responsible for data protection. Ms Reding is also Vice-President of the European Commission. Prior to July 2010 she was the European

Commissioner for Information Society and Media with an input to data protection in that role.

The European Data Protection Supervisor

The regulatory structure in the European Community works on two levels serving separate jurisdictions. There is a European supervisor who regulates European Community authorities and national supervisory authorities that regulate national government agencies, public bodies and commercial organisations. Peter Hustinx is the European Data Protection Supervisor (EDPS). He has been appointed for a term of five years by a joint decision of the European Parliament and the Council pursuant to Article 286 of the Treaty establishing the European Community. His work is that of an independent supervisory authority ensuring that EC institutions and bodies respect their data protection obligations. He has no supervisory powers over the processing of personal data by individuals, private companies or national authorities in Member States.

The key elements of the EDPS role are supervision, consultation and cooperation. Supervision of personal data processing by the European institutions and bodies is based on notifications of processing operations presenting specific risks that require prior checking by the EDPS. The EDPS website[10] notes that: 'In most cases, this exercise leads to a set of recommendations that the institution or body need to implement so as to ensure compliance with data protection rules.' However the EDPS also investigates complaints about the mishandling of personal data by a European institution or body. It may also carry out inquiries on its own initiative. All European institutions and bodies are required to appoint Data Protection Officers who have a reporting line to the EDPS. Notably the EDPS ensures the supervision of the central unit of Eurodac, the EU-wide electronic system to identify asylum seekers

The EDPS advises EU institutions and bodies on data protection issues relating to proposals for new legislation. He also monitors new technologies that may have an impact on data protection. He may issue an opinion to establish a consistent policy on data protection issues and administrative measures related to data protection adopted by European institutions or bodies (e.g. the EDPS gave an opinion on the new central exclusion database established to protect the financial interests of EU institutions when procuring work or issuing grants funded by EU funds). The central exclusion database allows institutions to exclude entities from procurement or grant procedures. The EDPS had been involved in the development from an early stage and, in May 2010, gave an opinion that there was no reason to believe that there had been any breach of the provisions of data protection.

In terms of cooperation, the central forum for international cooperation in the EU is the Article 29 Working Party. This forum allows national data protection authorities to meet and exchange views on current issues, discuss interpretation of data protection law and to give expert advice to the European Commission. The EDPS participates in the working party and in EC 'third pillar' activities covering police and judicial cooperation.

National Supervisory Authorities

Article 28 of the Data Protection Directive provides for Member States to provide one or more public authorities to be responsible for monitoring the application of provisions implementing the Directive in its jurisdiction. It goes on to state that the authorities shall act with 'complete independence in exercising the functions entrusted to them'.[11] The national supervisory authorities have jurisdiction over data processing in the relevant Member State and must be 'consulted when drawing up administrative measures or regulations relating to the protection of individuals' rights and freedoms with regard to the processing of personal data'.[12]

The powers of the supervisory authorities are outlined in Articles 28.3 to 28.5 and include:

- investigative powers and powers to obtain the information it needs to carry out its supervisory duties;
- effective powers of intervention, such as publication of opinions, ordering data to be blocked, erased or destroyed, warning measures and the right to refer issues to national parliaments;
- the power to commence legal proceedings where there have been breaches of national laws implementing the Data Protection Directive;
- the power to hear complaints from data subjects and to investigate these and report back to the individual;
- the right to publish its reports.

Representatives from the national supervisory authorities participate in the working party established under Article 29 of the Data Protection Directive.

The Article 29 Working Party

The Article 29 Working Party is another independent body, set up to achieve several primary objectives:[13]

- to advise the European Commission on any Community measures affecting the rights and freedoms of natural persons with regard to the processing of personal data and privacy;
- to cooperate and examine issues relating to the application of the Data Protection Directive that impact on the uniformity of its interpretation across Member States;
- to provide the European Commission with an expert opinion on the level of protection in the Community and in third countries (those outside the Community);

- to provide an opinion on codes of conduct drawn up by bodies that operate at Community level;
- to make recommendations to the Commission on matters relating to the protection of rights and freedoms with regard to the processing of personal data and privacy in the EC.

Pursuant to Article 15 of Privacy and Electronic Communications Directive,[14] the Article 29 Working Party also has jurisdiction to advise, opine and examine issues that relate to the protection of rights, freedoms and legitimate interests in the electronic communications sector.

The national supervisory authority in the UK

The Data Protection Act 1984 provided for an official, the Data Protection Registrar, to carry out duties prescribed in the Act. Directive 95/46/EC required the appointment of a 'Commissioner' for data protection and the title of the Registrar was first changed to Data Protection Commissioner and then again to Information Commissioner when responsibility for the implementation of the Freedom of Information regime was accorded to the role.

The Information Commissioner is an independent official appointed by the Crown and he reports annually to parliament. His role and responsibilities in relation to data protection are set out in Parts V and VI of the DPA 1998. The Information Commissioner has a duty to:

- promote the following of good practice and the observance of the requirements of the Act by data controllers;
- provide information to the public about the operation of the Act and about good practice. This is achieved by publication of information in leaflet form, video and CD-Rom, publication of information on the ICO website,[15] participation in public events and speaking engagements;
- develop codes of practice after consultation with trade associations and data subjects. The Commissioner also has a duty to encourage and assist trade associations in the development of codes of practice, which they can then publicise to their members. This duty also specifically includes the development and publication of a data-sharing code.[16] The aim of the code is to provide practical guidance in relation to compliant sharing of personal data and the promotion of good practice in the sharing of personal data. The code is to be admissible in evidence in any legal proceedings but failure to act in accordance with any provision of the code does not of itself constitute an offence;
- inform data controllers and the public of any developments in data protection law arising in the EC and to provide information about the protection of data protection rights in countries and territories outside the European Economic Area (i.e. the EC and Norway, Iceland and Lichtenstein);

- carry out assessments of data processing for best practice. Initially these were specified to be with the consent of the data controller, but recent changes brought about by the Coroners and Justices Act 2009[17] mean that the Information Commissioner's Office (the ICO) may carry out an assessment of any government department or public body specified by the Secretary of State. Assessments are basically an investigation of circumstances surrounding a complaint or issue brought to the attention of the Information Commissioner by a data subject or some other party. An assessment notice may involve a direction to assist the ICO, provide specific information, allow the ICO access to premises, equipment and or staff;
- maintain a register of notifications made by data controllers (the 'Data Protection Register') under DPA 1998, s 19;
- enforce data protection law under DPA 1998, Part V. The Commissioner can enforce data protection law using a variety of enforcement tools including enforcement notices, assessment notices, information and special information notices. Failure to comply with a notice is an offence under DPA 1998, s 47.

The Office of the Information Commissioner's website can be found at www.ico. gov.uk. It says of itself:

> The Information Commissioner's Office is the UK's independent authority set up to uphold information rights in the public interest, promoting openness by public bodies and data privacy for individuals.

The Information Commissioner is supported by the following departments:
- a strategic policy group, which develops data protection guidance;
- a freedom of information group;
- a compliance department which includes an enquiry line;
- a legal department;
- an investigations department;
- a notification department (responsible for maintaining the register of data controllers);
- a marketing department.

In addition, the Information Commissioner is the designated authority in the UK for international cooperation on data protection matters. International obligations result in the Commissioner being:

- the supervisory authority in the UK for the purposes of the EC Directive on Data Protection;
- the point of contact for international initiatives on data protection;

- the conduit for communication with the European Commission and EC Member States on matters pertaining to data protection, including participation in the Article 29 Working Party.

The ICO has published a Data Protection Strategy which explains that the Office will take a risk-based approach to regulation 'in line with good regulatory practice'. The issues on the ICO agenda are:

- stopping unlawful trade in confidential personal information;
- the monitoring and regulation of public security and surveillance;
- the monitoring and regulation of increased information sharing;
- promoting privacy by design;
- monitoring security and integrity of personal information; and
- providing effective data protection supervision.

Other legislation relevant to the role of the Information Commissioner

Enhanced powers of the Information Commissioner

The powers of the Information Commissioner have recently been enhanced, taking effect in 2010. The Criminal Justice and Immigration Act 2008 introduced a new power for the Information Commissioner to impose significant fines[18] for data protection breaches as well as potential custodial sentences[19] for the s 55 offence of unlawfully obtaining or disclosing personal data. The new maximum fines for breaches of the Data Protection Act has been set at £500,000, but it should be noted that breaches in the financial services sector have attracted higher fines from the Financial Services Authority (FSA). The power to impose penalties only applies to serious breaches of the Act that have the potential to cause substantial damage or distress. Offences have to be committed knowingly or recklessly where the perpetrator either knew, or ought to have known, that there was a risk that a contravention would occur, which would be likely to cause substantial damage or substantial distress, but failed to take reasonable steps to prevent it.

The power to impost custodial sentences is not yet in force.[20]

The Coroners and Justice Act 2009 gives the Information Commissioner a new power to audit government departments by way of 'assessment notices'.[21] It also contains a provision to extend these powers by Order to designated public bodies[22] and private organisations.[23]

David Smith, Deputy Commissioner with responsibility for the data protection supervisory functions of the ICO, when asked to comment on the enhanced powers that the ICO required to operate effectively replied to the effect that penalties for data protection breaches needed to be strengthened; this is now happening. He also referred to the need for a power to audit organisations without consent; this has been partly implemented, but it seems clear that it is something the ICO will continue to campaign for.

Conclusion

This overview of the current legal and regulatory structure of data protection in the UK highlights that there are several regulatory bodies with high level input into the development of data protection rights and freedoms. Several of these, as we would expect, are European, rather than national bodies, data protection law being driven out of the European Community. These bodies are all forces for change and are remarkably active in promoting issues and highlighting concerns.

It is also clear that data protection law in the UK is in a state of transition, particularly in respect of the powers of the Information Commissioner.

The next chapter considers the issues the regulators are highlighting, the introduction of potential changes to data protection law and how pressure in the recent past from the regulators (particularly the recent changes to the powers of the ICO) has impacted on UK law.

Notes

1 Recitals 1 to 5 of Directive 95/46/EC.
2 Recital 7.
3 [2003] EWCA Civ 1746.
4 Communication from the Commission to the European Parliament, the Council, the Economic and Social Committee and the Committee of the Regions, a comprehensive approach on personal data protection in the European Union, published 4 November 2010.
5 Human Rights Act 1998, Art 8.
6 [2002] EWHC 2287 (Admin).
7 Judgment of 26 March 1985, Series A no 91.
8 Application nos 30562/04 and 30566/04.
9 Affaire Erdal Aslan c. Turquie *(Requêtes n°s 25060/02 et 1705/03)*.
10 See www.edps.europa.eu.
11 Article 28.1.
12 Article 28.2.
13 Article 30.
14 Directive 2002/58/EC of the European Parliament and of the Council of 12 July 2002 concerning the processing of personal data and the protection of privacy in the electronic communications sector.
15 See www.ico.gov.uk.
16 DPA 1998, s 52A as amended by the Coroners and Justice Act 2009.
17 Section 173 amending DPA 1998, s 41.
18 Criminal Justice and Immigration Act 2008 (CJIA), s 144.
19 CJIA 2008, s 77.
20 As at April 2010.
21 DPA 1998, s 41A(2)(a).

22 Section 41A(2)(b) of the Data Protection Act 1998 provides for the Secretary of State to provide by Order public bodies to be subject to the section.

23 Section 41A(2)(c) of the Data Protection Act 1998 provides for the Secretary of State to provide by Order any category of 'persons' to whom s 41(A) will apply.

2   The changing legislative environment

The forces behind legislative change

Undoubtedly the European Union (EU) has been the main driving force behind data protection law in the UK. The Data Protection Acts of 1984 and 1998 were implemented to meet our obligations under European Directives. As well as setting out the standards for data protection in Directives, the European Commission monitors the implementation of directives and informs Member States if national law is non-compliant. This activity has also impacted on UK data protection law.

Since the implementation of the Data Protection Act 1998 (DPA 1998) there has been evidence that the European Commission does not consider that the UK has met its obligations under Directive 46/95/EC (the Data Protection Directive).

In 2004 the European Commission issued a formal notice to the UK Government setting out areas where it felt that UK law did not meet the standards required by the Directive.

In the notice the Commission claimed that a significant number of articles in the Directive had not been implemented properly in the UK including the definition of personal data as interpreted by the UK Courts in *Durant v Financial Services Authority*.[1] The powers of the Information Commissioner were judged to be inadequate and criticism was levelled at subject rights and enforceability, fair processing, information given to data subjects, the conditions for fair processing, sensitive categories of personal data and the conditions for transfer of personal data outside of the EEA, all key parts of data protection law.

Indirect but pointed criticism was also levelled at the UK's Data Protection Act when an adequacy finding was sought by the State of Jersey. Countries outside the EU can apply to the Commission for a ruling on the adequacy of data protection law in that country. Without an adequacy finding the country would be a prohibited territory for the export of personal information from EU Member States pursuant to Article 25,[2] (the Eighth Data Protection Principle in the UK). Consequently countries with regular commercial links with EU Member States apply for a ruling as to the adequacy of their internal protection for the rights and freedoms of individuals in relation to data protection.

The Article 29 Working Party advises the European Commission on data protection matters and assesses the adequacy of data protection in third countries to enable the free transfer of personal data from Member States to those countries.

Opinion 8/2007 on the level of protection of personal data in Jersey notes that the Data Protection (Jersey) Law 2005 (the Jersey law) is based on the UK Data

Protection Act 1998 and secondary legislation adopted pursuant to it. The Opinion criticises the narrow definition of personal data in the Jersey Law. The Jersey definition restricts personal data to information which identifies an individual or information which, taken together with other information in the possession of the data controller, will identify that individual. The definition in the Directive is wider and includes information that allows another party to identify the individual, and is not restricted to the data controller. In addition the effect of the *Durant* case on English data protection law is specifically considered. The following statement is made: 'In so far as such interpretation restricts the definition of personal data of the Directive, this may compromise the extent to which the Jersey legislation protects personal data.'

Another criticism relates to the powers of the Jersey Data Protection Commissioner. Commenting on the procedural and enforcement mechanisms of the Working Party he notes that 'the Commissioner's powers appear more limited than those set out in Article 28 of the directive'. A particular weakness is that the exercise of investigative powers must be supported by a warrant which a data controller may oppose, thus hampering the investigation. The Working Party deduces that this also means that the Commissioner cannot carry out random checks on data controllers. The Working Party states that its 'concerns about the lack of sufficient powers of the Commission therefore casts some doubt about the suitability of the Commissioner as an instrument to deliver a good level of compliance'. By implication, the Working Party also cast doubts on the ability of the Information Commissioner in the UK to deliver a good level of compliance because, at the time, the Commissioner's powers were similarly restricted.

The conclusion of the Article 29 Working Party was that the protection offered to personal data under the Jersey law was adequate but, crucially, the view was expressed that the Jersey law would not meet the higher standards required for compliance with the EC Data Protection Directive. The Working Party was satisfied that, because adequacy does not mean complete equivalence with the level of protection set by the Directive, the level of protection offered in the State of Jersey was adequate. But where does this leave the UK? A finding of adequacy is not sufficient to conform with the Directive for Member States. They are subject to the much higher requirement of equivalence with the provisions of the Directive.

The issues raised by the Jersey adequacy finding – the overly restrictive definition of personal data and the lack of real powers of the Information Commissioner – were not new issues. However the Article 29 Working Party made a public statement criticising the Jersey Law and, by implication, the DPA 1998 as implemented in the UK.

Behind the scenes, correspondence dating back to 2004 shows that the Article 29 Working Party was less than convinced that the UK statute met the terms of the 1995 Data Protection Directive. The *Durant* ruling in December 2003 was followed, in the summer of 2004, by a formal notice to the UK government from the

European Commission setting out the areas in which it was felt the UK law did not meet the standards required by the Directive. The notice was an invitation to respond to the issues raised; however it was not made public by either the Commission or the government. The legal community tried to require disclosure of the letter and the UK government's response under freedom of information legislation but was initially unsuccessful. The Information Commissioner gave a view supporting the government's refusal to disclose the information stating:[3]

> The correspondence that you have requested relates to potential action against the UK Government by the European Commission. You will appreciate that our letter also closely reflects the matters contained in the other correspondence and to reveal this would also reveal the substance of the other letters. We understand that the European Commission have informed the UK Government that they would not expect to release such details under their own access to information regulations (EC Regulation 1049/2001) nor would they expect the UK to release such details where infraction proceedings are contemplated. The UK Government has taken the view that taking a line different from the Commission's position could adversely affect their relations with them.

This statement indicates the seriousness of the UK position in relation to the conformity of its data protection laws with the underlying Directive. However the government had decided to keep the details of the Act's supposed non-conformity secret and details were not to emerge until 2007.

One law firm, Pinsent Masons, continued to lobby for access to the letter from the Commission and the UK government's response. Finally in September 2007 Pinsent Masons released an exclusive news story based on the letters. The news was surprising. The Commission claimed that a significant number of Articles in the Directive had not been implemented properly in the UK. They referred to definitions in the powers of the Information Commissioner as expected, but also to deficiencies in subject rights and enforceability, fair processing information given to data subjects, the conditions for the fair processing of sensitive categories of personal data and the conditions for transfer of personal data outside of the EU.

The European Commission constantly assesses the implementation and effectiveness of data protection law in Member States and this is likely to be what initiated the correspondence with the UK government. It may well be engaged in similar correspondence with other Member States. However the timing of the *Durant* ruling certainly seemed to act as a trigger to the first round of correspondence. The views expressed and implicit in the Jersey adequacy finding indicate that the exchange was being taken to a new level. It created an expectation that further developments would emerge. This came in 2009 when the European Commission launched infringement proceedings against the UK over privacy rights and data protection. Matters came to a head in the telecoms sector over the use of 'Phorm'. Phorm is internet behaviour mapping technology which allows Internet Service Providers (ISPs) to target advertising based on the activity of internet users.

In April 2008 BT admitted that it had tested Phorm in 2006 and 2007 without informing customers. This led to a number of complaints to the Information Commissioner's Office (the ICO). The European Commission has been in correspondence with the UK government about the use of Phorm in the UK and has not been satisfied with the answers it has received.

The infringement proceeding is based on perceived problems with the UK implementation of the Directive on Privacy and Electronic Communications (2002/58/EC) and the Data Protection Directive. The European Commission is calling on the UK authorities to change the law to ensure that the Information Commissioner has the appropriate enforcement powers to deal with the emerging challenges to privacy presented by new technology.

The second step in the enforcement proceedings was taken by the European Commission in June 2010. The Commission wants the ICO to have the power to carry out random audits of organisations. The enforcement process is a three-stage process. In its statement the Commission says:[4]

> The case concerns the implementation of the EU's 1995 Data Protection Directive both in UK law (the Data Protection Act of 1998) and its application by UK courts. It continues: The Commission has worked with UK authorities to resolve a number of issues, but several remain, notably limitations of the Information Commissioner's Office's powers:
>
> - it cannot monitor whether third countries' data protection is adequate. These assessments should come before international transfers of personal information;
> - It can neither perform random checks on people using or processing personal data, nor enforce penalties following the checks.
>
> Furthermore, courts in the UK can refuse the right to have personal data rectified or erased. The right to compensation for moral damage when personal information is used inappropriately is also restricted.
>
> These powers and rights are protected under the EU Data Protection Directive and must also apply in the UK. As expressed in today's reasoned opinion, the Commission wants the UK to remedy these and other shortcomings.

The first stage of the Commission's formal process when taking Member States to task is to send a Letter of Formal Notice. If the response to that is unsatisfactory then a Reasoned Opinion is sent. Member States have two months in which to comply with the Reasoned Opinion. If they do not, then the Member State is referred to the European Court of Justice (ECJ), Europe's highest court.

'However, in over 90% of infringement cases, Member States comply with their obligations under EU law before they are referred to the Court', said a Commission explanation of the process. 'If the Court rules against a Member State, the Member State must then take the necessary measures to comply with the judgment.'

These are specific criticisms levelled at the implementation of the Data Protection Directive in the UK. This means that the UK DPA 1998 is open to legal challenge in the ECJ from both the European Commission and from a UK litigant under the Act because the UK is under an obligation to implement the Directive properly and it is clear that the European Commission does not consider that it has done that. Despite signs of impending wholesale changes to data protection law in Europe, the criticisms leveled at the Act in the UK are still being pursued. In a Communication from the Commission to the European Parliament and others,[5] the Commission stated that it would continue to ensure the proper monitoring of the correct implementation of Union law in this area, by pursuing an active infringement policy where EU rules on data protection are not correctly implemented and applied. It goes on to point out that the current review of the state of data protection law does not affect the obligation of the Member States to implement and ensure the proper application of the existing legal instruments on the protection of personal data. In practice changes to data protection law may still overtake problems with implementation at national level.

Lobbying power in the UK

The Information Commissioner has a role in lobbying for changes in data protection law enshrined in the Data Protection Directive. The Information Commissioner is an independent official appointed by the Crown reporting annually to parliament, therefore he is not just a bureaucrat following legal rules, but a lobbyist with a key input to legislative developments. As noted in Chapter 1, his role and responsibilities in relation to data protection include a duty to inform both data controllers and the public of any developments in data protection law arising in the EC, but stop short of specifying lobbying power. The Data Protection Directive specifically requires Member States to consult with the national supervisory authority when 'drawing up administrative measures or regulations relating to the protection of individuals' rights and freedoms with regard to the processing of personal data'.[6]

In 2008 the government announced a strategy of increasing data sharing opportunities in the public sector and, to identify the privacy issues, Richard Thomas (then Information Commissioner) and Dr Mark Walport, Director of the Wellcome Trust, were invited to carry out a Data Sharing Review.[7] Based on the recommendations in the Review, in November 2008 Jack Straw (then Justice Secretary) put forward proposals[8] to enable the Information Commissioner's Office to:

- impose monetary penalties on data controllers for deliberate or reckless loss of data;
- inspect central government departments and public authorities' compliance with the Data Protection Act without always requiring prior consent;
- require any person, where a warrant is being served, to provide information required to determine compliance with the Data Protection Act;
- impose a deadline and location for the provision of information necessary to assess compliance;
- publish guidance on when organisations should notify the ICO of breaches of the data protection principles;
- publish a statutory data sharing code of practice to provide practical guidance on sharing personal data.

By mid-2010 the powers of the Information Commissioner had been significantly enhanced in most of these areas.

Joint initiatives conducted in the early part of the 2000's between the ICO and government agencies revealed the extent to which there was a flourishing illegal trade in personal data. The IC submitted a report, *What Price Privacy?* in 2006 calling for the introduction of custodial sentences for data protection offences and, since then, successive Information Commissioners have continued to lobby for more severe penalties for data protection offences. This area is explored more fully in Chapter 3.

Reacting to criticism

By the end of 2008 therefore, it was clear that the UK government would enact legislation to remedy some of the perceived flaws in data protection law to meet EC requirements and in response to lobbying by the Information Commissioner. The Criminal Justice and Immigration Act 2008, s 144 contains provision for significant fines to be levied for breaches of data protection. Consultations and discussions throughout 2009 resulted in recommendations that the level of fines should be subject to a maximum of £500,000 (formerly fines on summary conviction were limited to £5,000) and were brought into force in the second quarter of 2010. Even this perceived higher level of monetary penalty is relatively low in comparison with fines levied in the financial services industry by the Financial Services Authority (FSA) for data protection breaches affecting its members.

The Criminal Justice and Immigration Act 2008 also included enabling provisions for custodial sentences for data protection offences to be introduced. Their commencement was made subject to further discussion in parliament. However there has still been pressure from the Information Commissioner for custodial sentences for the criminal offences of unfairly obtaining and unfair disclosure of personal information in circumstances where parties deliberately break the law for profit or other advantage.[9] The Commissioner recognises that unscrupulous traders in personal data would not be deterred by fines alone, for example those individuals knowingly involved in the recent trafficking of details of T-Mobile customers.[10]

The Information Commissioner (ICO) has lobbied long and hard for powers to audit organisations without their consent. This is one of the main areas where the European Commission believes the UK's implementation of the Data Protection Directive is inadequate. The Coroners and Justice Act 2009 affords the Information Commissioner a new power to carry out assessments of data processing for best practice. Section 41 of the Data Protection Act 1998 (amended) gives the ICO the power to carry out an assessment of any government department or public body specified by the Secretary of State. An assessment notice may involve a direction to the organisation to assist the ICO, to provide specific information, or to allow the ICO access to premises, equipment and/or staff. Clearly these are the basic tools of investigative audit work.

Prior to the Coroners and Justice Act 2009 coming into effect, the Prime Minister had instructed government departments to cooperate in spot check audits undertaken by the ICO. In evidence to the Justice Select Committee,[11] Richard Thomas said his Office was about to conclude its first government department spot check and would carry out more audits throughout the year than ever before.

Continuing to lobby for future changes

The Information Commissioner has already expressed concern that the new audit powers are too restrictive, pointing out that many functions of public bodies are actually carried out by, for example, charities. His office receives a high level of complaints of unfair data processing and breaches of the Data Protection Act relating to the activities of the private sector.

The Coroners and Justice Act also contains a provision to extend these assessment powers by Order to public bodies and private organisations. Introducing audit powers to the business world in general is only a short step away.

Influencing interpretation and application of data protection

In the courts

As well as legislative change, data protection law is influenced by changes in interpretation and application by the courts as well as by regulatory authorities. The main legal case is *Durant v Financial Services Authority*[12] when the Court of Appeal considered crucial legal issues resulting in a major change in the interpretation of the definition of 'personal data' in the DPA 1998. The Court concluded that personal data is information that is significantly biographical in relation to the data subject or information which has the data subject as its main focus. This was a significant narrowing of the definition of personal data; guidance from the Information Commissioner prior to the case was that all information relating to a living individual was within the scope of data protection law.

In the same case the Court of Appeal also considered the meaning of a 'structured filing system' which is a 'relevant filing system'[13] under the Act. It decided that a two-tier test should be applied to determine if a filing system was structured:

- such a system would allow the identification at the outset whether or not a file or set of files contained information relating to a specific data subject. It would be referenced, structured or indexed to allow the relevant information to be located quickly;
- having identified which file or set of files contained information relating to a specific data subject, the structure of the individual file(s) should be such as to allow easy identification of the piece of information sought.

The Information Tribunal

The First-tier Tribunal (Information Rights) (formerly the Information Tribunal, and before that, the Data Protection Tribunal) hears appeals from Notices issued by the Information Commissioner under the Freedom of Information Act 2000, the DPA 1998, the Privacy and Electronic Communications Regulations 2003 and the Environmental Information Regulations 2004. It has generally confirmed the position of the Information Commissioner when hearing appeals and has been influential in the developing interpretation of the DPA 1998.

There have been cases involving the Police National Computer (PNC) in which the police authorities (represented by relevant Chief Constables) wanted to keep information about criminal convictions without any time restrictions. In a number of appeals[14] the guidelines for the Association of Chief Police Officers were refined to require automated 'weeding' of information, deletion of certain records and sophisticated access rights so that some information would still be available to the police but not to third parties, such as prospective employers, on the Criminal Records Bureau.

Other cases before the Tribunal have involved claims of unfair processing where customer details are used for marketing purposes without some form of consent, particularly in industries where there has been a monopoly situation in the past (e.g. the supply of gas and electricity) thereby further reducing the data subject's choice when selecting a supplier and negotiating how his or her personal information will be used.[15]

In *Innovations Mail Order v Data Protection Registrar*,[16] the Tribunal supported the Information Commissioner's (the then Data Protection Registrar) position that the provision of fair processing information is subjective (i.e. depends on what the data subject understood at the time), it has to be established in every case for processing to be fair. It also established that fair processing information had to be provided at the time the personal information was obtained, although it was good practice to follow this up with reminders of how personal data was to be used.

The Tribunal also had significant influence in the development of proper guidelines for the credit reference industry where data extraction methods were insufficiently refined to be fit for purpose resulting in damage and distress to innocent individuals whose credit records were tarnished by information linked erroneously to their record.[17]

The Information Commissioner's influence

The prescribed duties of the Information Commissioner include the provision of information to the public about the operation of the Act and about good practice. There are also specific requirements for him to develop industry codes of practice and encourage industry bodies to develop codes of practice to support data protection compliance. This guidance and codes of practice are vehicles for influencing the interpretation and application of data protection law.

The Employment Practices Code, developed with input from industry over several years to 2003, gives insight into how the Information Commissioner's Office interprets the data protection principles in the human resources (HR) context. For example, applying the Third Principle (personal information to be adequate, relevant and not excessive) to job application forms, the requirement for a National Insurance number is considered excessive on the grounds that a number of applicants will supply this information, but it will be relevant in only one case, that of the successful candidate. It also raises the question about the purpose for which personal information on a job application form will be processed. Ostensibly the information is required to assess the applicant's suitability for employment, but often the information is used for employment administration purposes. This illustrates how the principles are being interpreted and how they work together in practice.

The CCTV Code of Practice published by the Information Commissioner's Office applies and interprets the data protection principles in the context of CCTV images. To meet the requirements of the Third Principle in this context, the cameras should be fit for purpose and record sufficiently clear images to allow them to be used to identify wrongdoers where that is the stated purpose of the CCTV Scheme. In applying the Fifth Principle (personal information only to be retained for as long as necessary for the purpose for which it is obtained) it was suggested in the first edition of the CCTV Code that 28 days would be an appropriate period for the retention of CCTV recordings unless they were to be used in court as evidence of wrong doing. Twenty-eight days has been adopted as the standard retention period for most digital and video CCTV recordings. Again this illustrates how the principles are to be interpreted in context and the fact that the Information Commissioner influences practice.

There have been occasions when the interpretation put on data protection law by the Information Commissioner has been challenged and overturned by the courts. In the *Durant* case the court referred to the wide interpretation placed on 'structured filing system' a key element in deciding which paper files are subject to the DPA 1998. The Information Commissioner (then Elizabeth France) had said that even an individual's messy desk was a structured filing system within the meaning of the Act and that all paper files held by or on behalf of an organisation were therefore subject to the Act. The court rejected this view and set new criteria for deciding whether or not paper files met the 'structured filing system' test.

Initially, information made available to the public about the operation of the Act took the form of educating the public about their rights, but lately the focus has been on raising awareness of key privacy issues such as the privacy implications of online social networking, the management of credit ratings, how information on the electoral register may be used, how information relating to health and housing may be used, identity theft and how to avoid, or at least reduce, junk mail. Public interest can be a powerful tool for influencing organisations so that they change their behaviour and the media has a part to play in this.

The Information Commissioner also has a role in the development of data protection law at the European level. In a keynote speech at the European Privacy and Data Protection Commissoners' conference in Edinburgh, on 24 April 2009[18] Richard Thomas, then UK Information Commissioner outlined the strengths of the current Data Protection Directive: that it is comprehensive and sets high standards, and that the data protection principles are flexible in approach and have stood the test of time. However he also outlined the weaknesses. These included that technology has developed in the past 20 years, and he described the Directive as a 'Mainframe Directive' (i.e. one that catered for the state of IT development at the time which was based around mainframe computers not personal computers). Mr Thomas said:

I fear that the Directive has insufficiently clear objectives and insufficient focus on detriment, on risk and on enforcement in practice.

It is also widely seen as excessively bureaucratic and burdensome, and too prescriptive. Detailed rules tell organisations 'How' to do things, with less attention to 'What' they should be achieving or their own responsibility for achieving it.

In particular he criticises the data export rules, describing them as no longer fit for purpose and unwieldy, especially in a world where globalisation is having a major impact. Notification is heavily criticised for not delivering transparency and Mr Thomas suggests that the term 'registration' be restored. Any attempt to undertake prior checking or prior approval of processing is no longer workable as it is too slow. The conditions for fair processing are likewise criticised on the grounds that they have become a rigid control mechanism.

Concluding his speech Mr Thomas outlined themes to signpost the way to 'better data protection'. These include understanding the risks of adverse effects from personal data processing both to individuals whose personal information they process and society as a whole. The principle of accountability is aired, organisations should be held to account if they get it wrong and data protection must become a top-level governance issue managed at senior levels within the organisation.

Pressure from the media

Over the last ten years there has been significant awareness of privacy issues in the UK with several high profile, celebrity confidentiality cases such as *Douglas and others v Hello! Ltd and others*,[19] *Campbell v Mirror Group Newspapers*,[20] and privacy cases brought by Princess Caroline of Monaco,[21] and JK Rowling.[22] At the same time, there has been growing awareness of the crimes of identity theft and fraud and its implications. It is probably fair to say that the general public has started to realise that information is a valuable asset that needs to be protected.

Developments in online networking mean that more personal information is held in electronic form, largely outside of our direct control, than ever before. So the risk posed by data security breaches has increased. The media has sensationalised data security issues, reporting and highlighting new cases. It only takes a couple of laptops to be disposed of without due care revealing bank details or details of vulnerable children to outraged purchasers on ebay for stories to make the headlines and for discussion forums and articles to pick up the topic.

Given that the subject matter of media attention is primarily data security breaches, this is one area where there is media pressure for change, specifically the introduction of a data security breach notification law. In the US a number of states have adopted such a law, requiring organisations that suffer a data security breach to publicise the event and the steps that they have taken to avoid or redress any potential harm.

At the time of writing it is still voluntary to report breaches of data protection law to the Information Commissioner's Office in the UK. The ICO has said that there will be no breach notification law in the UK and that organisations should decide as a matter of good practice whether or not to blow the whistle on a data management breach depending on the numbers affected and the severity of the likely impact on individuals.[23]

However the pressure continues to be in favour of introducing a data security breach notification law and there are developments which suggest that such a law will be introduced. In November 2009 the European Commission adopted the Telecoms Reform package, which requires telecoms firms to notify data security breaches to the 'competent authority'. This would apply in situations like the one that affected T-Mobile in 2009 when staff were found to have been selling customer lists to competitors in breach of their employment contracts, the duty of commercial confidentiality and the DPA 1998. The ICO is likely to be the competent authority in the UK for telecoms companies to report data security breaches. Outside of the telecoms sector, the ICO has warned that organisations may face tougher sanctions if they fail to report security breaches which later come to its attention. Although there is no law requiring notification of data security breaches in the UK, organisations should report significant incidents to the regulator as part of their breach management process. If, as seems likely, the ICO gains the power to audit private organisations for data protection compliance, breach notification will be a key element in enforcement and selecting which organisations to audit.

Independent of developments in the rest of Europe, the Republic of Ireland is considering a data breach notification rule. Again this indicates the pressure on governments and regulators to introduce a data security breach notification requirement when serious breaches of data protection occur.

Other influences

In recent years the Financial Services Authority (FSA) has taken action against its members for data protection breaches. In February 2007 the FSA fined Nationwide £980,000 when a laptop was stolen from an employee's home. The laptop had names and account numbers of some 11 million customers held in unencrypted form. Nationwide was accused of failing to train staff adequately and not having procedures in place to promote data minimisation techniques or to encrypt laptops (the appropriate standard to secure personal information against loss or unauthorised access per the Seventh Data Protection Principle).

In December 2007 Norwich Union was fined £1.26 million by the FSA for system failures which resulted in personal information relating to over 3 million customers being stolen and used in fraudulent attacks on customer accounts. HSBC was fined by the FSA in July 2009 for data security breaches at its financial services operations. The fines, levied on several subsidiaries, totalled in excess of £3 million after a discount for cooperating with the regulator.

In August 2010 Zurich Insurance plc was fined by the FSA. Zurich used outsourced data processing services provided by a sister company based in the RSA. The service provider had lost an unencrypted back up tape during a routine transfer to a data storage centre. The breach had been covered up for a year, at least in part because there were no formal reporting lines in place for such an occurence. In the event the FSA fine related primarily to Zurich's failure to put effective systems and controls in place to manage the security risks around personal information being processed under the outsourcing arrangement. This was seen as a failure of systems which resulted in, and was brought to light by, a data security breach. In a press release dated 24 August 2010 the FSA said:

> The Financial Services Authority (FSA) has fined the UK branch of Zurich Insurance plc (Zurich UK) £2,275,000 for failing to have adequate systems and controls in place to prevent the loss of customers' confidential information. The fine is the highest levied to date on a single firm for data security failings.

The Information Commissioner took action over the data security breach, which had occurred in August 2008. He required Zurich to make a public announcement about the loss of the data and, in March 2010, the UK Branch Manager of the Zurich gave an undertaking to ensure that appropriate data security measures would be put in place, together with procedures and training for staff and subcontractors to ensure that they understood security procedures.

The level of fine the FSA can and does impose contrasted sharply with the maximum fine that the courts could impose for breaches of data protection. Cases brought by the ICO typically resulted in fines of a few thousand pounds, as fines were restricted by the maximum set under the DPA 1998. This all changed with the implementation of the Criminal Justice and Immigration Act 2008, which provides for significant fines to be levied in respect of s 55 offences (unfair obtaining and disclosure). After consultation the maximum level of financial penalty has been set at £500,000 for serious breaches of s 55. The significant fines levied by the FSA played a part in the setting of the new maximum fine for data protection offences[24] although it falls well short of the significant fines the FSA can impose.

The future – the international perspective on data protection

The thirty-first International Conference of Data Protection and Privacy held in Madrid in November 2009, approved the Joint Proposal on International Standards for the Protection of Privacy (the 'Madrid Resolution'). The Madrid Resolution has been approved by data protection authorities from more than 50 countries, spanning all five continents.

The Madrid Resolution affirms that privacy is a fundamental human right and reminds all countries of their obligations to safeguard the civil rights of their citizens, residents and international human rights law.

It anticipates the strengthening of rights to privacy and data protection in the EU and sets out current privacy concerns. In particular it notes 'with alarm' the increase of secret and unaccountable surveillance, collaboration between governments, new strategies to pursue copyright and unlawful content investigations as it considers that these pose a substantial threat to privacy of communication, intellectual freedom and due process of law. It also expresses concern at the growth and consolidation of internet-based service providers, which is resulting in some organisations gathering vast amounts of personal data.

It warns that the privacy laws have failed to take full account of new surveillance practices and that this failure jeopardises associated freedoms (i.e. freedom of expression, freedom of assembly, access to information, non-discrimination and ultimately the stability of constitutional democracies).

Having rehearsed the arguments for robust data protection laws, the basic principles of the Madrid Resolution largely mirror the requirements of the Data Protection Directive. There are principles requiring lawfulness and fairness when processing, including legitimacy based on the conditions for fair processing. There is also a principle requiring transparency when processing, including the provision of information to the data subject before his or her personal data is obtained or processed. Proportionality is another key principle requiring that personal information should be adequate, relevant and not excessive for the purpose for which it is being processed and requiring data minimisation as a standard. A further principle concerning data quality requires that it should be accurate, sufficient for the purpose and kept up to date when necessary, be kept for no longer than is necessary for the purpose and then deleted or rendered anonymous.

There is a new principle which introduces the principle of accountability, specifically:

The responsible person[25] shall: (a) Take all the necessary measures to observe the principles and obligations set out in this Document and (b) in the applicable national legislation, and have the necessary internal mechanisms in place for demonstrating such observance both to data subjects and to the supervisory authorities in the exercise of their powers, as established in section 23.[26]

The Accountability principle is picked up in the Article 29 Working Party Opinion 3/2010 referred to below. Basically it means making the data controller more responsible for compliance with data protection obligations and answerable to national data protection supervisory authorities. States are also required to encourage better compliance by introducing (*inter alia*) requirements for:
- procedures to prevent and detect breaches, based on information security governance and/or management;

- appointing one or more data protection officers with the qualifications, resources and power to exercise adequate supervisory functions;
- the periodic implementation of training, education and awareness pro- grammes;
- audits by qualified and, preferably, independent parties;
- Privacy Impact Assessments to be conducted.

Clause 20 of the Working Party Opinion sets the standard for appropriate security for personal information and includes a data security breach notification require- ment. The duty to notify data subjects of a data security breach falls on all of those involved in the processing of the data, not just on the data controller, although the data controller is the party ultimately liable to the data subject.[27] There is a specific duty of confidentiality set out in clause 21 which also requires all 'those involved at any stage of the processing' to maintain the confidentiality of personal data.

These are the new themes emerging at the international level but they have already been widely circulated within Europe.

Current themes

Consultation by the European Commission on reform of the Data Protection Directive is planned. In the UK the Ministry of Justice issued a Call for Evidence[28] on current data protection legislation, asking for views on how the European Directive and the Data Protection Act are working. It included a survey on the cur- rent powers and penalties of the Information Commissioner and whether these could be strengthened. This precedes negotiations on a new EU data protection instrument.

In October 2010 the Information Commissioner published his response to the Call for Evidence. In the Commissioner's opinion, an effective new data protection framework must:

- be clear in its scope, particularly in the context of new forms of individual identification;
- protect the rights and freedoms of individuals whilst permitting the free flow of data;
- place clear responsibility and accountability on those processing personal data, throughout the information life cycle;
- ensure obligations for those processing personal data are focused on process- ing that poses genuine risk to individuals or society, rather than focusing on particular categories of data; and
- give individuals clear, effective rights and simple, cost-effective means of exercising them.

As with other commentators the Commissioner recommended retaining the data protection principles, not only on the grounds that they are sound and are still applicable, but also because they are familiar and any wholesale revision could cause confusion and undermine the historical continuity of data protection law, therefore limiting its effectiveness. In common with other commentators, the Commissioner recommends adopting new principles to cover the topics of privacy by design and accountability. Suggested wording for the principle of Accountability is outlined, requiring data controllers to:

> take appropriate and effective measures to implement data protection principles; and be able to demonstrate, on request, that such measures have been taken.

Commenting on the need for a data security breach notification law, the Commissioner is of the opinion that notification of serious security breaches to the Commissioner is both appropriate and good practice for organisations as part of their breach management procedure. However, if any new legislative framework is to be introduced to require notification of security breaches, the Commissioner feels that this must not be too prescriptive. There needs to be a sensible definition of what constitutes 'serious breaches' taking a risk-based approach.

The Commissioner continues to call for greater powers of enforcement, in particular for custodial sentences for individuals who knowingly or recklessly obtain or disclose personal data. He also highlights a current problem where information notices can only be served on data controllers. This can impede investigations where a third party is believed to hold pertinent information which is currently inaccessible to the ICO. Lastly the Commissioner argues in favour of ICO audit rights being extended to the private sector.

In Europe, consultation meetings were held with the European Data Protection Supervisor, Member States and law enforcement agencies in June 2010 and with data protection authorities in July 2010, organised by the European Commission's Directorate General for Justice.

Written contributions have also been made. In December 2009 the Article 29 Working Party issued a press release announcing the adoption of the Joint contribution to the Consultation of the European Commission on the legal framework for the fundamental right to protection of personal data of the Article 29 Working Party and the Working Party on Police and Justice (*The Future of Privacy*).[29] In the paper the Article 29 Working Party expressed the view that the 'present legal framework has not been fully successful in ensuring that data protection requirements translate into effective mechanisms that deliver real protection'. The paper discusses data protection in the light of new technologies and globalisation and in the perspective of the Lisbon Treaty.

The central message of all the Article 29 Working Party opinions and papers is that main principles of data protection are still valid despite important challenges. To deal with the issue of globalisation, there are recommendations that initiatives be taken towards the further development of global standards regarding the protection of personal data. It suggests that the adequacy process (the process by which third countries can ask for a decision by the EC as to the adequacy of data protection law in that country) be redesigned. The Binding Corporate Rules regime should also be given higher priority.

Raising the stakes to deal with the technological challenges, the recommendation is the adoption of a principle of Privacy by Design. This involves privacy impact assessments at the planning stage of IT systems and procedures not only to maintain security but to avoid or minimise the amount of personal data processed. The principle would be binding on data controllers, technology designers and producers. Examples given by the Working Party of Privacy by Design in operation include:

- biometric identifiers being stored in devices under the control of the data subject (i.e. in smart cards rather than in databases);
- video surveillance in public transport being designed so that the faces of traced individuals are not recognisable unless they are suspected of committing a criminal offence;
- patient names and other personal identifiers in hospital IT systems being separated from data on the health status and medical treatment except as is necessary for medical or other reasonable purposes in a secure environment;
- where appropriate, functionality should be included facilitating the data subject's right to revoke consent to process his or her personal information resulting in data deletion.

Recognising that changes in the behaviour and role of data subjects calls for a stronger position or empowerment of the data subject, the Working Party recommends the improvement of redress mechanisms and the introduction of a procedure for class actions. Critically the Working Party recommends the introduction of a general privacy breach notification rule. The wording is key; here the recommendation is for a 'general privacy breach notification'[30] which covers more situations than simple data security breaches. The rationale for the US data security breach notification rule is that individuals need to know when their personal details have been compromised so that they can take action to mitigate their exposure. What the Working Party is suggesting is a requirement to report a wider range of data protection and privacy breaches.

The Working Party also advises strengthening the role of the data controller and increasing his responsibility for compliance, introducing a principle of Accountability for data controllers to carry out the necessary measures to ensure substantive principles and obligations are observed when processing personal data. The Accountability principle would also require data controllers to have the necessary internal mechanisms in place to demonstrate compliance to external stakeholders including data protection authorities. This tends towards supporting a regime where the national data protection authority has the right to audit organisations to check their data protection compliance. In a press release covering the Working Party's adoption of the opinion on accountability[31] it said:

> The Accountability principle aims at strengthening the role of the data controller and increasing his responsibility for compliance. Nowadays, there is an increasing need and interest for data controllers to ensure that they take effective measures to deliver real data protection. Building and maintaining a good reputation, ensuring the trust of citizens and consumers, and minimising the legal, economic and reputational risks that are likely to derive from poor data protection practice are becoming more crucial for data controllers in all sectors ... A statutory accountability principle would explicitly require data controllers to implement appropriate and effective measures to put into effect the principles and obligations of the Directive and demonstrate this on request. In practice this should translate into effective scalable compliance programs aiming at implementing the existing data protection principles, and controllers should be able to demonstrate to data protection authorities, upon their request, that their program fulfils the requirement of accountability. The type of procedures and mechanisms would vary according to the risks represented by the processing and the nature of the data.

The Article 29 Working Party makes recommendations for stronger and clearer roles for the national data protection authorities, noting that currently there are large divergences between Member States regarding the position, resources and powers of national authorities. The Working Party emphasised the need to guarantee uniform standards concerning independence, effective powers and the advisory role of national data protection authorities in the legislation-making process and their ability to set their own agenda by setting priorities regarding the handling of complaints.

On 15 July 2010 a press release[32] quoted EC Vice-President Reding, the EU's Justice Commissioner, recommending that data protection authorities should be strengthened and they should have the necessary sanction and enforcement powers. VP Reding also emphasised the need for one legal framework on data protection at EU level, for the private and public sectors, including police and judicial cooperation (in line with the Treaty of Lisbon). The Vice-President wants to see a framework to ensure a high level of protection for individuals, regardless of where their data are being processed and by whom.

The European Data Protection Supervisor, Peter Hustinx, has also called for an urgent review of the relationship between Freedom of Information and data protection. Commenting on the 'Bavarian Lager' case,[33] Mr Hustinx said:

The judgment of the Court confirms the importance of the review of how to reconcile two fundamental rights: access to documents and data protection in the light of the Lisbon Treaty. We will continue to provide advice to the EU legislator with a view to ensuring the protection of privacy, but also to ensure that this right is exercised within the context of the greatest possible transparency of EU public activities.

European Commission consults on data protection law in Europe

Against this background the European Commission is consulting on the development of data protection law in Europe. The agenda has largely been set by international data protection initiatives and current thinking and likely changes in the law are heralded by the Article 29 Working Party. Based on this background, these are the areas and changes which seem likely to be the focus of developments in European data protection law.

Vice-President Reding has outlined a timetable for new data protection law at European level. The Commission will present a Communication on data protection in the autumn of 2010, followed by a legislative proposal in the first half of 2011.

One legal framework

Data protection was introduced as an internal market-related issue. The Data Protection Directive was designed to be a general legal framework which could be complemented by specific regimes for data protection for specific sectors. In practice only one specific regime has been adopted, for e-Privacy (Directive 2002/58/EC). The European Data Protection supervisor, Peter Hustinx, recommends new laws to regulate specific areas of technology. These are social media, RFID and targeted advertising where consumer behaviour is profiled with the objective of being able to direct products and services that are considered appropriate to them.

The Data Protection Directive does not cover processing by EU institutions or processing falling outside the former first pillar (internal market). Since 9/11 the exchange of personal data between Member States is an essential part of police and judicial cooperation and it is not subject to the current data protection regime. So there is a patchwork of different data protection regimes. Also data protection is now recognised as a general concern of the EU not necessarily linked to the internal market. A comprehensive and consistent data protection framework is needed. The Lisbon treaty provided for a new approach to data protection, paragraph 14 stating that: 'The main safeguards and principles should apply to data processing in all sectors, for an integrated approach as well as a seamless, consistent and effective protection.'

Dealing with the effects of globalisation

The position of the European Commission is that data protection is a fundamental right pursuant to Article 8 of the Charter of Fundamental Rights of the European Union. Therefore the European Union (EU) should guarantee this fundamental right for everyone, in so far as they have jurisdiction, including when data is processed outside the EU.[34]

Article 4 of the Data Protection Directive provides that the Directive applies to data processing anywhere, including outside the EU when the controller is established in the EU, or is established outside the EU but processes personal information on equipment in the EU. There is a specific regime for the transfer of personal data to third countries pursuant to Article 25 of the Directive (the Eighth Principle in UK law); however it is not always clear when national or EU law should apply. Also the Directive does not apply to organisations located in third countries who target EU nationals, a practice particularly prevalent on the internet.

The next step for the European Commission might be the adoption or endorsement of the Madrid Resolution.[35] This was adopted by the International Conference of Data Protection and Privacy Commissioners from all five continents on 6 November 2009. It includes a draft global standard and brings together all the approaches possible in the protection of personal data and privacy. It also includes a set of principles, rights and obligations that could be the basis for data protection in any legal system all over the world. Although the Madrid Resolution has yet to be adopted by the European Commission, it has been strongly recommended by the Article 29 Working Party.

Most commentators agree that changes are required to streamline the adequacy process so that third countries can progress their case for a ruling on adequacy of data protection in their territory more quickly. Changes are also recommended to the Binding Corporate Rules regime so that a multinational organisation can apply for approval to the national data protection supervisory authority in one Member State and then have the same Binding Corporate Rules more easily recognised by other EU Member States.

Dealing with technological changes

The European Commission may adopt 'Privacy by Design' as a new data protection principle. The framework of existing principles are considered to have dealt with the influx of new technologies because the principles are clear and wide-reaching and use concepts that are sound and technologically neutral. The existing framework supports the addition of a new principle; Article 17 of the Data Protection Directive requires appropriate technical and organisational measures to protect data. Recital 46 of the Directive also calls for security measures to be taken, both at the time of the design of the processing system and at the time of processing. Privacy by Design is considered in Chapter 8.

Empowering the data subject

Recognising that the full potential for empowering the data subject has not been utilised, and in an environment where the data subject is increasingly aware of the need for protection of personal data, suggestions include:

- improving the mechanisms for redress either through administrative or judicial procedures;
- increased transparency so that data subjects can understand what processing of their personal data is to be undertaken, by whom and in what circumstances;
- revisiting the rules around consent. There are many cases where consent cannot be given freely, especially when there is a clear imbalance between data subject and data controller, (e.g. in the employment context or when personal data must be provided to public authorities). Consent must be informed as currently consent is often cited inappropriately when there may be other more suitable authorities to rely on. The new legal framework should specify when consent is an appropriate justification and clarify what does, and what does not, constitute consent.

Embedding data protection in organisations

The Article 29 Working Party, the signatories to the Madrid Resolution and commentators agree that action needs to be taken to make organisations more responsible for meeting their data protection obligations. Proactive measures for national governments to consider are suggested, their objective to improve data protection compliance and force management to take responsibility for compliance. The introduction of the principle of Accountability is seen as a necessity. The recommendation is for a two-fold obligation, first to establish controls to manage data protection and second to be able to demonstrate those controls, probably to the national supervisory authority. A mandatory data security breach notification requirement is also recommended requiring organisations to report significant breaches of data security, although this is not absolutely clear and the obligation may extend to other data protection breaches. Above all there is a call for transparency of such adopted measures both to data subjects and the public in general.

Other changes we might expect

In November 2010 the Commission published a Communication regarding a comprehensive approach on data protection in the European Union.[36] As expected the Communication picks up the need for harmonisation and consistency of data protection law in EU Member States, and extending the law to cover former third pillar activities, policing and judicial cooperation in criminal matters. In addition to the themes already identified such as providing a framework that will demand improved transparency, accountability and contributing to the development of a standard set of universal data protection principles, the Commission highlighted other specific areas of concern (e.g. the processing of personal data relating to children and how consent is defined and established in data processing). Issues around processing sensitive data are to be revisited as are the grounds for international data transfers where personal data is exported beyond the borders of the European Economic Area. Potential developments include the mandatory appointment of Data Protection Officers within organisations that process personal data and the introduction of a mandatory data security breach notification law.

Conclusion

This chapter has considered the current political and legal environment affecting data protection law. It has highlighted the growing pressure, both nationally and internationally, for change in data protection and how it is regulated. The pressure is now such that change is inevitable and the changes can largely be predicted based on current debate. The authorities are unanimous in calling for greater accountability for organisations and their management and it is likely that a variety of measures will be brought in to try to achieve this, including a data security breach notification law.

In subsequent chapters the impact of these impending and wide-reaching changes is considered, with the particular objective of how to manage data protection so that compliance with the new requirements will not be onerous. Principally this can be achieved by switching to a strategic view of data protection management, employing risk management techniques to identify and manage data protection compliance risks and implementing compliance tactics appropriate to the organisation as well as the problem it is seeking to overcome. These aspects are considered in following chapters.

Notes

1 [2003] EWCA Civ 1746, Court of Appeal (Civil Division) (8 December 2003).
2 Article 25 of Directive 95/46/EC.
3 ICO Disclosure Log – Response to Request. Request Ref: FOI/040 Date of Response: 8 March 2005.
4 Data protection: Commission requests UK to strengthen powers of national data protection authority, as required by EU law, IP/10/811, Brussels, 24 June 2010.
5 Communication from the Commission to the European Parliament, the Council, the Economic and Social Committee and the Committee of the Regions, a comprehensive approach on personal data protection in the European Union, published 4 November 2010.
6 Article 28.2.

7   Data Sharing Review Report available on the Information Commissioner's website: www.ico.gov.uk.

8   Response to the Data Sharing Review Report, a publication available on Ministry of Justice website: www.justice.gov.uk

9   DPA 1998, s 55.

10 In November 2009.

11 In January 2009.

12 [2003] EWCA Civ 1746.

13 DPA 1998, s 1(1).

14 *The Chief Constables of West Yorkshire, South Yorkshire and North Wales Police and the Information Commissioner.* Also Information Tribunal Appeal Numbers: EA/2007/0096, 98, 108, and 127. *The Chief Constables of Humberside, Staffordshire Police, Northumbria Police, West Midlands Police and Greater Manchester Police and the Information Commissioner.*

15 *Midlands Electricity plc and the Data Protection Registrar*, Appeal decision by the Information Tribunal 7 May 1999. Also *British Gas Trading Limited and the Data Protection Registrar* DA98/ 3/49/2.

16 *Innovations Mail Order Ltd v Data Protection Registrar* 1997 DA92 31/49/1.

17 *CCN Systems Limited and others v the Data Protection Registrar* DA/90 25/49/8 and 9. See also *Equifax Europe Limited and the Data Protection Registrar* DA/90 25/49/7 and *Infolink Limited and the Data Protection Registrar* DA/90 25/49/6.

18 Data Protection in the European Union - Promising Themes for Reform.

19 *Douglas and others v Hello! Ltd and others* [2005] EWCA Civ 595.

20 *Campbell v MGN Ltd* [2004] UKHL 22.

21 *Von Hanover v Germany* (Application no. 59320/00) 24 June 2004 (ECHR).

22 *Murray v Big Pictures (UK) Ltd* [2008] EWCA Civ 446 (7 May 2008).

23 ICO guidance on data security breach management, available in the document library at www.ico.gov.uk.

24 The Data Sharing Review Report published by Mark Walport and Richard Thomas in 2008 called for 'the maximum level of penalties ... to mirror the existing sanctions available to the Financial Services Authority ...'.

25 Clause 2 defines a 'responsible person' as any natural person or organisation, public or private which, alone or jointly with others, decides on the processing.

26 Section 23 is concerned with the establishment of national data protection supervisory authorities.

27 See Clause 25 'Liability'.

28 See www.justice.gov.uk/consultations/call-for-evidence-060710.htm.

29 *The Future of Privacy* (WP 168) of December 2009.

30 Page 3 of the document.

31 See http://ec.europa.eu/justice/policies/privacy/news/docs/pr_15_07_10_en.pdf.

32 See http://ec.europa.eu/justice/policies/privacy/news/docs/pr_15_07_10_en.pdf.

33 The case involved an attempt to discover the identities of individuals at a meeting. The ECJ ruled that surnames and forenames are personal data and the communication of such data is within the definition of 'processing' for data protection purposes. The Court also held that data protection applies in all circumstances where the right of access to a

public document is exercised not just in those situations where the privacy or integrity of the individual would be infringed per Article 8 as the lower court found.

34 The Future of Privacy Joint contribution to the Consultation on the Legal Framework for the Fundamental Right to Protection of Personal Data.

35 The Joint Proposal on International Standards for the Protection of Privacy.

36 Communication from the Commission to the European Parliament, the Council, the Economic and Social Committee and the Committee of the Regions, a comprehensive approach on personal data protection in the European Union, published 4 November 2010.

3 Data protection basics: notification and exemptions, offences and penalties

Introduction

This chapter considers those provisions of the DPA 1998 (the Act) that impact on the operation and administration of business other than compliance with the data protection principles which are considered in Chapter 4. The principal requirements on a business, other than compliance with the principles, are the duty to notify processing activities to the Data Protection Register and the duty to avoid the commission of offences under the Act.

What is notification?

The Data Protection Directive[1] includes a requirement[2] for data controllers to notify the relevant supervisory authority[3] before carrying out any data processing activity involving personal information. Part III of the Data Protection Act 1998 sets out the framework for notification in the UK. It starts with a prohibition on processing personal information unless and until a data controller is registered with the Commissioner.[4] The terminology changes in s 18 of the Act; this sets out the details required to be notified to the Commissioner. The terminology has caused problems, but 'notification' is interchangeable with 'registration' in this context.

As well as differences in terminology, the Act approaches registration from the negative angle (i.e. that it is an offence for an organisation to fail to register if it is required to do so). Similarly any changes in activities must be notified to avoid committing an offence.

The requirement to notify

All data controllers are required to notify unless their activities are exempt. When considering the exemptions, the safe route is to register if in doubt. There are a number of exemptions covering domestic use of personal information, National Security and so on, but the key exemption for businesses and charities is the 'Core Business Exemption'. This applies where an organisation does not process personal information except client or customer records for administration and marketing and processing its own staff records. Processing activities outside of that narrow exemption must be notified.

Certain business activities must be notified. These are:

- accountancy and auditing;
- the provision of legal services;
- credit referencing, debt administration and factoring;
- crime prevention and the prosecution of offenders;
- training and education;
- financial services, including mortgage and insurance services;
- health administration and provision of health services;
- journalism and media;
- provision of professional services such as consulting, advice and intermediary activities;
- pastoral care;
- pensions administration;
- private investigations; and
- property and estate management.

All these activities have one thing in common: the processing of personal information is an essential part of the work undertaken. The Core Business Exemption only applies to manufacturing-type activities where personal information, other than client or customer administration, the marketing of own goods or services and staff administration, is not processed.

A business whose core activities are exempt from notification may still have to register if it is involved in any of the following activities:

- the use of credit reference information;
- trading and/or sharing of personal data, including sharing within a group of companies; this means that all corporate groups need to be registered unless they can demonstrate an 'arm's length' relationship with each other;
- marketing goods and services using personal data obtained from a third party;
- marketing goods and services on behalf of a third party.

In practice, it is difficult to establish that individual trading companies within a group of companies do not need to notify, because there is an assumption that some personal information will be shared or held in common. The filing fee for small and medium-sized businesses is £35 and it may not be worth management time worrying about whether companies are sufficiently autonomous to meet the exemption criteria. If in doubt, notify.

Organisations with a turnover exceeding £25.9 million and more than 249 employees are subject to a higher notification fee of £500. Public authorities and charities (as defined[5]) are always subject to the lower fee of £35.

Who can notify?

Companies can be registered, as can sole traders, unincorporated associations, partnerships, trustees, charities and individuals.

The registration process involves supplying basic details and the process can be done by telephone or online. Company registration details are required for limited companies and it is useful to include any trading names because they assist anyone searching the register to find the organisation's details. A contact name and address will be required and the type of business to be undertaken identified.

For online registration, go to www.ico.gov.uk and select 'Register of Data Controllers' from the website menu. Scroll down and select 'Register Online' and follow the instructions. Registration entries are based on a standard template for each industry which is helpful, but the details need to be checked to ensure that the registration covers all of the organisation's processing activities involving personal information (e.g. 'Crime prevention and prosecution of offenders' will need to be added to any template if the organisation is responsible for CCTV).

Although the categorisation seems clumsy, companies in a trading group should also register 'Trading in or sharing personal information' as a processing activity. This covers the inevitable sharing of personal information within the group. Note that data protection law does not recognise trading groups of companies (e.g. subsidiaries of a single holding company); each company is viewed as a separate legal entity and requires a separate notification. Commerce between companies within a group has to be registered, in the same way as between any independent companies.

The registrant also has to give an overview of security measures to protect personal information in its custody or control. These are high-level indications, not detailed information.

If the registration process is done online, the actual registration forms will be sent out by post. The registration details should be checked, the form signed and returned together with a cheque for the filing fee. Fees may be paid by cheque or direct debit, however, at the time of writing there is no facility to pay the £500 large organisation filing fee by direct debit.

The notification is renewable annually. The Information Commissioner's Office (the ICO) sends out reminders and automatically renews entries if they are paid by direct debit. There is a continuing obligation to keep the register entry up to date and the annual renewal provides an opportunity to make any amendments required. A quick tip is to check the registration entries of other companies in the industry or to check against ICO templates to check that your organisation's entry is complete and as up to date with industry standards as possible. Forms to amend registrations can be downloaded from the ICO website.[6] Select 'Register of Data Controllers' from the menu then scroll down to select ''Form to Alter or Remove a Register Entry' or, if a new processing purpose needs to be added, 'Purpose Form – to Add a Purpose to a Register Entry'.

What next for notification?

The requirement to notify is embodied in the EC Directive on Data Protection and the current registration details are taken directly from those prescribed in that Directive. Currently all that is required are contact details and a description of processing purposes, categories of data subject and likely disclosures.

If we consider what the purpose of notification is, there are options to alter the content of the register going forward. Currently the purpose of notification is to meet a statutory obligation which aims for transparency in processing activities.

Given that the purpose of notification is to increase transparency, it is arguable that, in the future, notification of data security breaches should be included on the register. The Information Commissioner currently publishes formal undertakings by organisations on a separate part of its website, but provision could be made to allow this information to be entered on the register. Data subjects would then be able to access an organisation's data security breach record. A section of the general public is already familiar with accessing reviews and rating statistics of prospective products and suppliers before undertaking a transaction online. Transactional websites such as ebay and Amazon make customer reviews a key part of their service offering. In future, its security breach record could significantly impact the credibility of a business. The move to include additional information on the register would further the aim of empowering the data subject and would also provide transparency about organisations' data processing record.

There is also a potential impact for public authorities that publish their security breach record, although generally service users in the public sector have a limited choice of provider. There may also be benefits in publishing security breach statistics. The NHS East of England Strategic Health Authority publishes an overview of data security incidents on its website.[7] It provides details of the incident including the date, a summary of the circumstances, the outcome and the number of patients affected. Although there are relatively significant numbers of fairly minor breaches, this Health Authority is able to identify and log when they have occurred and has a monitoring control to allow it to follow up issues and report findings. This voluntary publication illustrates that this particular Health Authority has a system of control for data protection compliance that highlights breaches, so remedial action can be taken. How many organisations can make that claim? Certainly not those criticised by the Financial Services Authority (FSA),[8] where the theme is that penalties were imposed because of failings in systems of control and risk management rather than as punishment for data security breaches. In the case of Nationwide Building Society the FSA said:[9]

The systems and controls were such that, when the laptop was stolen, Nationwide was not aware that it contained confidential customer information. For a period of three weeks after the theft of the laptop Nationwide failed to take any steps to investigate whether it contained such information.

In a recent investigation involving Orbit Heart of England Housing Association based in Stratford-upon-Avon, Staffordshire a data security incident reported to the Information Commissioner involved the loss of 57 paper files during an office move. The data loss was only discovered when a third party found some of the files in a second-hand filing cabinet. There had been no inventory of files prior to the office move so staff did not know how many files they should have had. Following the move, some of the packing cases had not been unpacked after six months, even though the Housing Association admitted that the files contained 'a significant amount of personal data relating to each tenant and, in some cases, members of his or her family'.

In each of these examples, it is not the fact of the security breach that is damning but the failure (or lack) of systems to control compliance and to highlight when things have gone wrong. So voluntarily publicising details of data security breaches, as NHS East of England Strategic Health Authority has done, both helps an organisation to demonstrate the strength of its internal reporting and risk management systems and informs the public about its security breach record. A statutory requirement to notify breaches, on the other hand, is likely to focus attention only on the negative aspects of the issue.

Other information that might be usefully recorded on the register would be information about international transfers of personal information. Currently the purpose registration form features an entry confirming whether or not there are any international transfers and, if there are, which countries are recipients of the data; this includes an option to record that transfers are made 'worldwide'. This information is of little use as it stands, but requiring registrants to supply details of how they authorise transfers outside the EEA could be informative and useful to data subjects. If the company is a multinational, does it rely on Binding Corporate Rules or does it have contracts in place to meet EU standards? The inclusion of this information would at least force organisations to consider how they will legitimise transfers to third countries (those outside the EEA) at the time of registration and annually at renewal thereafter.

If an Accountability principle is introduced to European data protection law, again details of the system of control adopted by the registrant could be included on the register, even if the record is relatively high level (e.g. current security questions). Registration and annual renewal provide prompts to organisations to think about their data processing activity and record the status of security provisions and the breadth of data, data subjects and disclosures. Systems of control for data protection compliance is another area where their attention might usefully be focused

As the Information Commissioner is likely to be given increased powers to audit organisations, could the register be used to indicate which organisations should be targeted? Certainly the details on the register would allow the regulator to build up a picture of the risk presented by an organisation's processing activities. Even the sparse details currently on the Register will be used by the ICO when conducting an assessment of data processing. Additional information about the organisation's security breach record, its international transfers and its chosen system of control for data protection compliance would be useful indicators as to the level of risk the operation presents.

As well as enhancing the content of the Data Protection Register, access could also be improved. The Register might be more accessible to the general public if there were more signposts from data controllers towards their registration entry. Data protection registration information could form a useful addition to online privacy policies or company status disclosure information. Many companies already include brief details of their data protection registration, or the fact of it, in their terms and conditions.

Penalties for failing to notify

Personal information cannot be processed until a business is registered.[10] Failure to observe the prohibition and notify when required to do so is an offence under s 21 of the Act to which there is no defence. Further, it is an offence[11] not to keep registered details up to date; that comprises details of the names and addresses of the business and the person to contact regarding the registration, the intentions of the data controller with respect to the processing of personal information and the general description of security measures currently being taken. It is a defence for a person charged with the offence of failing to keep a registration entry up to date to show that all due diligence was exercised to comply. Showing that an annual check on activities is carried out to identify changes for the renewal would help to establish that all due diligence was exercised.

The penalty for failing to notify is a fine, imposed in either the magistrates' or the Crown court. To give examples of the level of fines imposed, in November 2009 two recruitment firms were ordered to pay fines and costs in excess of £2,500 for failing to notify for data protection. The fines were £300 and £500 respectively, the balance being made up of costs. In October 2009 an accountancy firm was prosecuted for failing to register. The firm and its director were each fined £500 and had to pay costs of £776.40.

Generally, non-compliant operations tend to be small businesses. Presumably there will be an increase in the level of fine if a large organisation is found not to have a current register entry as a fine of £300 to £500 provides a commercial advantage over the new annual filing fee of £500.

Obtaining or disclosing personal information unfairly (the s 55 offence)

Under s 55 of the DPA it is a criminal offence to knowingly or recklessly obtain or disclose personal information. This is an offence that may be committed by the organisation but, in practice, is more likely to be committed by individual staff members.

An example of institutional breaches is the continuing case involving a Sunday newspaper accused of condoning the practice of its reporters of accessing the telephone records of members of the royal family. In the past the offence has been reported in relation to private investigators and tracing agents falsely representing themselves as data subjects to gain access to personal information held on government agency records. Up to March 2002 the Information Commissioner participated in the Baird Project, a joint initiative run in conjunction with the Department for Work and Pensions and HM Revenue & Customs. Its objective was to identify persons and organisations that systematically obtain personal details from those government agencies unlawfully and sell the information on to clients. A number of cases were brought to trial and were successfully prosecuted.

Operation Motorman was a similar initiative which began in November 2002. It uncovered an organised and large-scale trade in personal information involving private investigators and corrupt officials who had access to personal information held by the DVLA and the police. Documents seized during Operation Motorman and other investigations enabled the ICO to build up a picture of how personal information is traded as a commodity. In *What Price Privacy? The Unlawful Trade in Confidential Personal Information*[12] the Commissioner notes that:

On the demand side, the customers come from the following main groups:
- the media, especially newspapers;
- insurance companies;
- lenders and creditors, including local authorities chasing council tax arrears;
- parties involved in matrimonial and family disputes;
- criminals intent on fraud, or seeking to influence jurors, witnesses or legal personnel.[13]

The investigation showed that personal details, often (but not exclusively) relating to celebrities, which could be obtained illegally included criminal records, details of registered keepers of vehicles, driving licence details, ex-directory telephone numbers, itemised telephone bills and mobile phone records including telephone numbers designated 'Friends and Family'.

The Commissioner took action, not only against the criminals who obtained the personal information unlawfully but also against those identified as illegal recipients of the information. The point was made that the persons who commissioned the reports on individuals must have been aware that personal information in those reports had been obtained unlawfully as, by the very nature of the information, it could not have been obtained lawfully. Since 2002 the ICO has been working with industry bodies, The Press Complaints Commission, the Law Society, the Association of British Insurers to underline for their members that this activity is unlawful and unacceptable.

Successive Information Commissioners have repeatedly raised the issue and continue to be concerned by the illegal trade in personal data. In *What Price Privacy?* the Information Commissioner called for custodial sentences to be introduced as a penalty for s 55 offences saying:

> The fact that prison is not currently an option for persons convicted of section 55 offences belittle the offence and masks its true seriousness, even to the judiciary.

The Information Commissioner has lobbied long and hard[14] for custodial penalties for s 55 offences. In his response to the Ministry of Justice consultation on the provision of custodial sanctions for those found guilty of offences under DPA 1998, s 55, the Commissioner said that he was in favour of custodial sentences on the grounds that they are necessary 'if the law is to provide an effective deterrent against the illegal trade in personal data'.[15]

The Information Commissioner makes the case for increased penalties, highlighting a 'steady stream of complaints from individuals who have reported that their privacy has been breached'. In response to its first report on the illegal trade in personal data *What Price Privacy?* a consultation was set up which reported in *What Price Privacy Now?* and consultation by the government on the introduction of custodial sentences. The Criminal Justice and Immigration Act 2008, s 77 gives the Secretary of State the power to introduce custodial sentences for s 55 offences. The Secretary of State may, by order, introduce custodial sentences for offences under DPA 1998, s 55 for a term, on summary conviction, of 12 months and two years in the case of conviction on indictment.

Where custodial sentences already apply

There have already been cases involving individuals convicted of an offence under s 55 being given a custodial sentence. In 2007, the Court of Appeal ruled that custodial sentences should be mandatory for police officers who abused their position to unlawfully obtain information on the Police National Computer. In *R v Hardy*[16] a police officer had accessed and downloaded information on three people who were witnesses in a court case from the PNC. The information was unlawfully disclosed to the defendant whose record included violent offences. The police officer knew that the defendant wanted the information so that he could take action against those persons he considered had committed offences against himself or a friend. The Court surmised that it was clear that there was a serious risk that physical violence would be used against those named. The Court of Appeal held that the offence was so serious that it demanded immediate imprisonment saying:

Police officers had to realise that accessing the police national computer for an improper purpose was an offence that required an immediate prison sentence.

Fines as penalties for data protection offences

In general, data protection offences carry fines. Until recently, the maximum fine that could be imposed on summary conviction was £5,000; on indictment (in the Crown court) theoretically the fine could be unlimited. However the level of fines actually imposed was very low. In November 2006, in Huntingdon magistrates' court a husband and wife were convicted of unlawfully obtaining and selling personal information. The man was fined £3,300, his wife £4,200 and both were ordered to pay a contribution to prosecution costs of £3,694. The defendants had committed numerous s 55 offences; the man asking for a further 46 to be taken into account and the woman for a further 51 offences to be taken into consideration. Unlawfully obtaining personal data was part of their routine business as private investigators.

In December 2006, at Kingston-upon-Thames magistrates' court, a man was sentenced to an 18-month community penalty (150 hours of community service) after pleading guilty to 16 counts of illegally obtaining and selling personal information. He was also ordered to pay costs of £2,000. Again the defendant was a repeat offender.

In April 2007, Infofind Limited, a private investigation business based in Kingston-upon-Thames, was found guilty of unlawfully obtaining personal data. Its proprietor was fined £3,200 and ordered to pay costs of £5,000 for unlawfully obtaining personal data from the Department of Work and Pensions.

There has been constant criticism that the level of fines imposed for data protection offences is derisory. The Information Commissioner has lobbied for increases in penalties in *What Price Privacy?*, and in other reports and evidence given to Parliament select committees. In September 2009, in an interview with BBC Radio

4's Today programme, Christopher Graham (the current Information Commissioner) said that penalties under the DPA were 'pathetic'. Commenting in connection with the case involving the publication of BNP membership on the internet he said:

> There is a very lively trade in confidential personal data and if the only thing you are going to get as a private investigator is a pathetic fine in the magistrates' court and even the judge is embarrassed to impose it, it is simply not enough.

In court, Judge John Stobart said:

> It came as a surprise to me, as it will to many members of the party, that to do something as foolish and as criminally dangerous as you did will only incur a financial penalty.

The individual found guilty of publishing details of the BNP membership was fined £200 and ordered to pay £100 towards costs.

The Criminal Justice and Immigration Act 2008 introduced a new power for the Information Commissioner to set the appropriate level of a monetary penalty for offences under s 55 (unfair obtaining and disclosure). This was implemented in 2010. Section 144 allows a penalty to be levied by the Commissioner in cases where he feels there has been a serious offence under s 55 of a kind likely to cause substantial harm or distress. In such cases, the necessary mental intent to commit the offence is either:

- deliberate; or
- the perpetrator:
  - knew or ought to have known that there was a risk that the contravention would occur; and
  - knew that such a contravention would be of a kind likely to cause substantial damage or substantial distress, but failed to take reasonable steps to prevent the contravention.

The ICO has issued a Code of Practice on the imposition of monetary penalties.[17] Factors that will be taken into account when determining the amount of a monetary penalty include the size, financial and other resources of the data controller and the sector in which it operates. The ICO accepts that 'there may be wide variations in the amount of the monetary penalty depending on the circumstances of each case'.

A monetary penalty notice will only be appropriate in the most serious situations. The factors determining the perceived seriousness of a contravention include the nature of the personal data concerned, the duration of the contravention, its extent, the number of data subjects affected, the severity of the damage caused and whether the contravention was due to deliberate or negligent behaviour on the part of the data controller. The attitude of the data controller is likely to be important too; a cooperative data controller who submits to an assessment is less likely to have a significant monetary penalty imposed.

Conclusion

The notification regime could be significantly enhanced by adding other categories of information to the register (e.g. more information about international transfers of personal data, a history of any reported security breaches and a history and summary of an organisation's chosen system of control for data protection compliance). All of these additions would be consistent with the stated objectives in the Madrid Resolution, endorsed by a number of privacy groups including the Article 29 Working Party for:

- increased transparency and openness in data processing activities;
- increased accountability for data controllers; and
- empowering individuals.

Penalties for offences under the DPA 1998 have long been regarded as derisory and, recognising the disparity between the lucrative trade in illegally obtained personal information and the penalties, successive Information Commissioners have lobbied for increased penalties.

Some of the recommendations made by the Information Commissioner have been adopted. In 2010 the Commissioner was granted powers to levy significant monetary penalties in the most serious cases involving breach of s 55. The power to introduce custodial sentences for offences under s 55 is available to the Secretary of State and the Commissioner continues to lobby in favour of this penalty. The European Commission has made it clear that the UK's implementation of the Data Protection Directive is inadequate in key areas including penalties for data protection offences. It is likely that changes will continue to be made, although they may well be increased suddenly and dramatically if new legislation in Europe forces the issue.

Notes

1   Directive 95/46/EC.
2   Art 18 of the Directive.
3   The Commissioner in each jurisdiction.
4   DPA 1998, s 17.
5   Defined in the Charities Act 2006(a), s 1 or a body entered in the Scottish Charity

Register under the Charity and Trustee Investment (Scotland) Act 2005(a), s 3 or as defined in the Charities Act (Northern Ireland) 2008(b), s 1.

6   See www.ico.gov.uk.

7   See About us – Publications – Information Governance: NHS Data Security Incidents.

8   See Chapter 2 page 18 and Chapter 7.

9   Final Notice to Nationwide Building Society, para 2.3(c).

10 DPA 1998, s 17.

11 Section 21(2).

12 Published by the ICO in May 2006.

13 See para 5.5.

14 See *What Price Privacy?*, *What Price Privacy, Now?* and other ICO publications.

15 See *Knowing or Reckless Misuse of Personal Data – Introducing Custodial Sentences*, 16 November 2009, response to question 1.

16 CA March [2007] CA Crim Div.

4 The data protection principles

Introduction

The principles are the backbone of data protection law. They are eight statements of do's and don'ts for processing personal information. The principles are set out in the Data Protection Directive and were copied directly into Sch 1 of the Data Protection Act 1998.

Summary of the principles

1. Personal data shall be obtained and processed fairly and lawfully.
'Lawfulness' means in accordance with an up-to-date registration with the Data Protection Register (part of the Information Commissioner's Office (ICO)). It also means processing within the organisation's legal authority and in accordance with any legal duties, such as the duty of confidentiality. An employee's work activities are covered by the business' authority and are therefore lawful as long as activities are restricted to proper business purposes.

'Fairness' means processing in accordance with information provided to the individual before the personal data was obtained and the 'privacy notice'. Consent is not generally required to process personal information, the requirement is to provide information before the personal information is collected. Individuals should be advised the name of the business seeking the information, the purposes for which it will be processed and any other information relevant in the circumstances, such as any disclosures or other sources of information.

'Fairness' also means meeting one or more specific conditions for fair processing as set out in the DPA 1998. The conditions for fairly processing personal data are set out in Sch 2 to the Act, those for fairly processing sensitive categories of data are set out in Sch 3.

2. Personal data shall be obtained only for one or more specified and lawful purposes and shall not be processed in any manner incompatible with that purpose or those purposes.
Again, work activities are covered by the organisation's authority as long as they are restricted to proper business purposes. If the organisation moves into new activities it may be restricted by what it told its data subjects in its privacy notice and may have to seek specific authority from individuals to use their personal data in connection with these new activities. It would probably also need to register the new purposes for which personal information is being processed.

3. Personal data shall be adequate, relevant and not excessive in relation to the purpose or purposes for which they are processed.
This means checking the questions on forms and other documents and in scripts that seek personal information and thinking about the reasons for which the information is required. Personal information should never be obtained on a 'nice to have' or 'it might be useful in future' basis.

4. Personal data shall be accurate and, where necessary, kept up to date.
On advice that personal information is inaccurate, the information should either be corrected or, if the organisation is unable or unwilling to amend the information, a note should be made of the details, the date and the person who advised that the information was inaccurate.

5. Personal data processed for any purpose or purposes shall not be kept for longer than is necessary for that purpose or those purposes.
This principle requires both regular purging of files to remove personal information that is no longer required and a clear document retention policy specifying how long files and documents will be retained before disposal.

6. Personal data must be processed in accordance with an individual's rights under the Act.
Individuals are granted specific rights under the Act and this principle requires that data controllers observe those rights.

7. Appropriate technological and organisational measures shall be taken against unauthorised or unlawful processing of personal data and against accidental loss or destruction of, or damage to, personal data.
As well as protecting computer systems, this means having appropriate physical security for business premises and measures to protect personal information when working from home or using a laptop.

There is a requirement to ensure that staff whose role involves handling personal information are reliable and there are technical requirements where outsource service suppliers are used.

8. Personal data shall not be transferred to a country or territory outside the European Economic Area unless that country or territory ensures an adequate level of protection for the rights and freedoms of data subjects in relation to the processing of personal data.
If an organisation has to transfer personal information outside the European Economic Area (EEA) (e.g. sending personal information to the US or Australia) steps must be taken to ensure the adequacy of protection for the personal information in the hands of the recipient.

There are several useful publications on the Information Commissioner's website including the 2009 plain English *Data Protection Guide*.[1] This guide clearly explains key definitions and the principles and gives guidance on how they apply in practice. Given the standard of this guidance, it is not proposed to cover the basics about the principles in this chapter. Instead we will focus on some of the practical implications and some aspects of the principles that are not covered in the Commissioner's Guide.

The First Principle

Keeping people informed

The Information Commissioner's guide to the first data protection principle cross-refers to specific guidance, again from the Information Commissioner's Office (ICO), relating to privacy notices.[2] A few other aspects of compliance with the First Principle are worth a specific mention at this point however. The First Principle requires personal information to be fairly and lawfully obtained and processed. Fair processing includes keeping individuals informed about who is collecting and using their personal information and the purposes for which it will be used ('fair processing information' or in the Commissioner's new terminology 'privacy notice'). Such communication with data subjects presents the organisation with the opportunity to manage expectations and to give any comfort messages such as the fact that personal information is never sold to third parties or that it will be held in confidence. The explanation needs to be as clear as possible including details of the purposes for which personal information will be processed, the organisation's intentions regarding sharing the information, if any, and generally informing the data subjects so that they may consider and accept the uses to which their personal information will be put.

Having clearly explained the identity of the organisation and its intended processing activity, that explanation or statement becomes the organisation's authority to process personal information obtained subsequently. Note, however, that the authority is restricted to the processing activity described in the statement, which is why it is essential that privacy notices are drafted carefully to include all intended processing including likely disclosures.

As long as these simple rules are observed there is no requirement for consent to process personal information. The whole issue of consent is quite fraught. If you seek consent you must consider how you will deal with data subjects who decline to consent. This may mean that you cannot provide goods or a service as it is not possible, for example, to deliver a sofa if the data subject declines to allow you to hold and process his address details. In an opinion published in 2001,[3] the Article 29 Working Party pointed out several weaknesses in relying on consent to justify personal data processing. If there is apparent inequality in bargaining power between the parties then it is difficult to demonstrate that consent was freely given, without duress. This was particularly referenced in the relationship between employer and employee. There is also the problem of how consent can be evidenced. The usual method is to obtain consent in writing, generating another paper document which must be retained and filed so that it is accessible.

When is consent needed?

If an organisation has a clear and complete privacy notice defining its authority to process personal information, individuals' consent to the processing of their details will not be required.

There are limited circumstances when an organisation would still seek consent.

The primary example is where the privacy notice is incomplete, which means that the authority to process is inadequate. For example, this might arise where a new use of the personal information is intended and the original privacy notice did not specify the intended new use. In the context of what constitutes a 'new use' of personal information, the Commissioner's Guide talks about compatibility of the new purpose with existing purposes as a test. Referring back to the concepts of 'keeping people informed' and 'managing expectations', an appropriate test would be whether or not the data subject would be surprised at the intended processing or if he would view it as part of the same processing activity as was disclosed to him in the privacy notice. If an existing privacy notice does not cover planned processing then the organisation may seek the positive consent of individuals. Where no response is received, then effective consent has not been obtained; consent in this context involves a positive indication of agreement that cannot be inferred from silence.

Another circumstance when consent to processing might be sought is in relation to the transfer of personal information to a territory outside the EEA. The Eighth Principle prohibits the export of personal information outside of EU Member States, Norway, Iceland and Lichtenstein, but consent of the individual concerned can remove any barrier to transferring the data.

Fair and lawful processing in accordance with the First Principle also requires that the processing meet one or more conditions for fair processing set out in the Data Protection Act 1998 Sch 2 (the Act). One of the conditions is that the processing is undertaken with the consent of the data subject. The Information Commissioner's guidance on this point[4] is that consent should be sought only as a last resort when all the other conditions for fair processing have been considered and rejected. Similarly the processing of sensitive categories of data (information relating to health, sex life, race, religion, politics, criminal record and allegations of criminal offences) should only be undertaken on the basis that the processing meets one or more of the conditions in Sch 3 to the Act in addition to the conditions in Sch 2. The same considerations apply; the data controller should consider whether or not any of the other conditions can be met before resorting to the consent of the subject.

Probably the most vexed area where consent may need to be sought is in relation to marketing activity. The standard of consent required is an opt out for direct marketing by mail, fax or telephone and an opt in for marketing via text or email. The opt out is the preferred option for marketers because the default position, where someone does not tick the box, allows marketing to proceed, thereby capturing the inertia vote. The opt in, where the box has to be ticked to allow marketing, obviously gets fewer takers. However the rules about presentation must make the choice clear; either the individual is being asked to positively indicate consent to the use of their personal information for marketing, the opt in, or they are being asked to take positive action only if they want to object to such use of their personal information.

The Article 29 Working Party commented on the use of consent to authorise aspects of data processing in *The Future of Privacy*[5] stating:

> 'Consent' is an important ground for processing which could under certain circumstances empower the data subject. However, at the moment, it is often falsely claimed to be the applicable ground, since the conditions for consent are not fully met. Therefore the new framework should specify the requirements of 'consent'. Furthermore, harmonisation needs to be improved, as the empowerment of the data subject is currently being undermined by the lack of harmonisation amongst the national laws implementing Directive 95/46/EC.

The 'conditions for consent' are as specified in Art 2(h) of the Data Protection Directive:[6]

> (h) 'the data subject's consent' shall mean any freely given specific and informed indication of his wishes by which the data subject signifies his agreement to personal data relating to him being processed.

'Freely given' consent means there should be no duress and the fact that the Directive refers to an 'indication' means that silence cannot be construed as consent, it requires some positive action on the part of the subject.

Aspects of consent are likely to continue to exercise the Article 29 Working Party and this is an area where further rules of law, guidance and opinion can be expected.

Data sharing

One aspect of managing data subjects' expectations is informing them of the likely disclosures of the personal information being collected. Even where a disclosure is foreseeable it is best practice to draw the attention of the data subject to any data sharing activity.

There are a number of good reasons why organisations want to share data (e.g. the government has a stated objective of providing seamless services to individuals and, as different government agencies may be involved in the care of any one data subject, some degree of data sharing is required to make any handover processes seamless). Take, for example, a patient being discharged from hospital. To ensure that his care is handled in the community, his doctor will need to be informed, social services may need to be informed so that appropriate support can be arranged and home visits may be required to tend to dressings or administer medication. Each agency involved in this process is likely to be a separate legal entity with separate data protection registrations and procedures. The compliant sharing of personal information in this context is a sound objective, but there are issues around the First Principle. Data sharing can also make government services more accessible to users. This is an example of fully justifiable data sharing, directed to the benefit of the data subject and the proper advancement of a defined objective. How to differentiate this from the 'big brother database' scenario is a two-fold exercise; first the data sharing must be fully justifiable and in the interests of advancing a defined and legitimate objective, and second, it must be communicated to data subjects as such.

In 2007 the government asked Mark Walport of the Wellcome Foundation and Richard Thomas (then Information Commissioner) to undertake a review of the framework for the use of personal information in both the public and private sectors with a view to facilitating data sharing while at the same time ensuring that data sharing was transparent and accountable. The recommendations made in the *Data Sharing Review Report* published on 11 July 2008 were that the culture that influences how personal information is viewed and handled needed to be changed. A principal recommendation was that organisations handling or sharing personal information should use their corporate governance provisions to clarify the ownership and accountability for personal information in their custody or control. Steps were also recommended for regular review of governance arrangements and improved transparency to be achieved by publication of the organisations' privacy notices and details of data sharing practices and schemes.

As already noted, the report also called for a Data-Sharing Code of Practice to be developed and published by the Information Commissioner. The framework code of practice for sharing personal information to enable organisations to develop their own code of practice was published in 2007, which placed a legal requirement on the Commissioner to publish a new data sharing code. A consultation on a draft code for data sharing was launched in October 2010.

A preliminary step to data sharing is to consider the reasons why it is to be undertaken and the benefits that will accrue. A realistic appraisal of the likely effect of data sharing on data subjects is recommended together with a consideration of alternatives to data sharing which might achieve the same objective. Identifying the privacy and data protection implications in a data sharing initiative can be achieved by conducting a Privacy Impact Assessment (PIA), which is a review of the data protection principles and how these might apply to the proposed activity (PIAs are covered more fully in Chapter 7). The Information Commissioner describes a PIA as an assessment of 'any benefits that the information sharing might bring to society or individuals. It also involves assessing any negative effects, such as an erosion of personal privacy, or the likelihood of damage, distress or embarrassment being caused to individuals. It should help to avoid or minimise the risk of any detriment being caused.' The principles of data minimisation (using the minimum amount of data required to achieve the objective) and proportionality (only relevant information should be shared) are paramount.

Article 8 of the Human Rights Act 1998 (HRA 1988) also applies in data sharing undertaken by public bodies or by bodies undertaking certain functions considered as those of a public body. Finally the Commissioner recommends that public bodies publish their data sharing practices and policies as part of their Freedom of Information publication scheme.

There is a useful Ministry of Justice publication *Public Sector Data Sharing: Guidance on the Law* (the Guidance) which was published November 2003.[7] It starts by rehearsing the reasons why public bodies need to share personal information and why they have concerns that data protection hampers them in meeting their obligations to meet policy objectives and improve service delivery.

The Guidance outlines the steps to be taken when considering data sharing. These are to consider if:

- the public body has the authority or power, or if it is *ultra vires*;
- the proposed data sharing activates the Human Rights Act 1988, Art 8;
- the proposed data sharing would be in breach of confidence at the point of disclosure; and
- the proposed data sharing would be in accordance with the Data Protection Act and the principles.

The problem of ultra vires
The public body must check that any proposed data sharing is in accordance with any relevant statutory duty to which it is subject or which is within the normal authority of its routine activities before making any disclosure. The disclosure should only be made for normal business purposes and in the normal course of

business. Disclosures that are *ultra vires,* or outside the public body's authority are unlawful.

Interaction with the Human Rights Act 1998

Article 8.1 of the Human Rights Act states that: 'Everyone has the right to respect for his private and family life, his home and his correspondence.'

Article 8.2 applies specifically to public authorities and bodies that exercise the functions of a public body:

> There shall be no interference by a public authority with the exercise of this right except such as is in accordance with the law and is necessary in a democratic society in the interests of national security, public safety or the economic well-being of the country, for the prevention of disorder or crime, for the protection of health or morals, or for the protection of the rights and freedoms of others.

Article 8.2 is a qualified right. The interference may be in accordance with the law, in the pursuit of a legitimate aim and necessary in a democratic society. The question is whether or not the activity can be described as the activity of a public body. If it can, data sharing may engage the Human Rights Act. Where the HRA is involved, then the data sharing must be in accordance with the law, in pursuit of a legitimate aim and necessary in a democratic society.

The courts have considered the application of Article 8.2 in practice and had some of their decisions referred to the European Court of Human Rights (ECHR). In *Peck v UK*,[8] Brentwood Borough Council was deemed to have breached the human rights of Mr Peck when it disclosed to the media CCTV images of him carrying a knife. It transpired that Mr Peck was suffering from depression and considering suicide, but the images of him were later used to illustrate the fight against violent crime in the area and the usefulness of CCTV in that fight. The images should not have been retained beyond the Council's CCTV image retention guideline of 90 days, but in fact were retained and used long after the expiry of that period. The High Court found that the Council's disclosure of the CCTV material was in breach of its own privacy guidelines.

The ECHR said that monitoring the actions of an individual in public does not give rise to an interference with the individual's private life but the situation is different where a record is maintained or disclosed. It was not in accordance with the law or with the Council's own guidelines. The use of the images misrepresented Mr Peck's involvement in the incident, leaving him embarrassed. The Council had failed to protect Mr Peck's privacy and had breached his Art 8 rights. In determining whether Art 8 was engaged it was necessary to consider both the information disclosed and the anticipated use to which it would be put.

In *MS v Sweden*, the ECHR stated that the sharing of personal data will inevitably give rise to human rights issues:[9]

> Government must show that any proposal for data sharing is both justifiable and proportionate

Breach of confidence

Some information is held under a duty of confidentiality. This is a common law duty arising from the type of information held, or the circumstances in which it was obtained. Organisations involved in data sharing need to be clear that there is no duty of confidentiality attaching to the information to be shared and that it is not likely to be used in an unlawful way.

The consent of the individual concerned to the data sharing will remove any breach of confidentiality.

Data protection issues

Establishing the legal grounds for data sharing before considering any data protection aspects is imperative as the first data protection principle requires that processing (which is defined to include disclosure) must be fair and lawful. If the data sharing is unlawful it will automatically be unfair in accordance with the first principle.

The fair processing aspects of the First Principle also apply. The disclosure must be open and transparent, within the expectations of the data subject. Ideally any data sharing activity should have been fully explained in the privacy notice provided to the data subject at the time the personal information was obtained. Fair processing in accordance with the First Principle also involves meeting one or more conditions for fair processing set out in Sch 2 to the DPA 1998 unless any exemptions apply. If the data to be shared includes sensitive categories of data, then one or more conditions in Sch 3 to the DPA 1998 must be met unless any exemptions apply. All these requirements are covered in depth in the Commissioner's Data Protection Guide.

The Fifth Principle[10]

Problems around the retention of electronic records

The Fifth Principle requires personal information to be retained only for as long as is necessary to fulfil the purpose for which it was obtained. This means establishing a set of information retention periods and purging and deleting records against that standard. Also understood is the fact that various different time periods will be appropriate for records created for different purposes based on legal requirements; for example, information relating to a contract and the performance of it should be kept for six years from date of termination of the contract and accounting records should be kept for seven years for tax purposes.

Most organisations purge and delete paper records as part of their archive and document management system, but some overlook electronic records, especially spreadsheets set up to manage an event for example. Computer systems have not always included strict document management protocols whereby the expected life of the document is required to be stated at the outset and most staff do not undertake routine housekeeping to remove old and unwanted files. Indeed old files may be used as a template for the following year's records.

A further problem is caused by the automated back up of electronic records, particularly e-mail, where there is no facility to delete a document once created. A user may 'delete' the document from his work drive, but the IT system ensures that it is retrievable at need, therefore it is not truly deleted. The ICO is aware of this problem and recognises that it is a block on the effective implementation of the Fifth Principle. However the wording of the Principle gives no room for manoeuvre; the requirement is absolute – personal information should not be held for longer than is necessary for the purpose. Computer systems need to be specified to include document or information deletion capabilities.

Holding on to personal data outside of a defensible retention period gives rise to potential breaches of other data protection principles. Older data is more likely to need updating, it is likely to be irrelevant and excessive for current processing purposes. Generally it can be seen that holding records longer than is necessary for the purpose for which they were obtained will increase the risk profile presented by the organisation in respect of its data processing activities. Risk in the context of data protection compliance and governance is a subject that is covered in detail in Chapter 5.

The Seventh Principle

A new definition of data controller and data processor[11]

Early in 2010, the Article 29 Working Party published an opinion on the concepts of 'controller' and 'processor'[12] in the Directive. This is new guidance on these definitions, which may not yet be covered elsewhere, so an explanation is included here.

The key role of the concept of controller is to determine who shall be responsible for compliance with data protection rules and how data subjects can exercise their rights in practice. It is also a key element in determining which national law applies to a particular processing operation. The concept of processor is important in the context of confidentiality and security of processing. The applicable law for security of processing is the national law of the Member State where the processor is located.

The definitions of controller and processor impact on the statutory obligation to put contracts in place with contractors which include specific data protection terms and to carry out compliance checks.[13] The Data Protection Directive defines a data controller as:

- the natural or legal person, public authority, agency or any other body;
- which alone or jointly with others;
- determines the purposes and means of the processing of personal data.

The data controller is the 'determining body'. It may have control stemming from explicit legal authority such as appointment by law (e.g. a public body might have a statutory duty to process personal data). There may be control from implicit authority, stemming from legally appointed duties such as employment law. Alternatively, control may stem from factual influence, involving an assessment of the actual relations between different parties. Identifying the party which determines the purposes and means of processing personal data is a factual decision arising from circumstances of the case. The Working Party notes that this may be different to what is set down in the contract, but the key is to consider the factual circumstances of the processing. It also considers that the concept of a controller needs to be interpreted by reference to data protection law and not by reference to other potentially conflicting laws such as intellectual property. It is purely a data protection definition.

In circumstances involving joint control it may be that in practice some of the data controller obligations can be more easily met by other data controllers, however that does not prevent a data controller from fulfilling its data protection obligations. The Working Party surmises that joint and several liability for all parties involved is a means of removing uncertainty. It should be applied only where an effective, clear allocation of obligations and responsibilities has not been provided for by the parties involved by contract, or where it does not clearly follow from the factual circumstances.

Processors

The definition of 'processor' involves two basic conditions: first, a data processor is a separate legal entity to the data controller and second, it must be involved in processing personal data on his behalf. 'On behalf of' means serving someone else's interest and recalls the legal concept of 'delegation'.

The Article 29 Working Party, in its Opinion, notes that many service providers specialise in processing data (e.g. the payment of salaries). These service providers will normally set up standard contracts for clients. Although the service provider is determining the contractual side of the relationship, this does not alter the fact that the service provider is the data processor and the client retains all the rights and obligations of a data controller.

The Working Party recognised that some parties are exercising a professional function and are therefore data controllers; the example used was a barrister in court, who is acting as a data controller although he is processing on behalf of his client. The example applies equally to an insurance broker acting on behalf of a client; he brings his own professional standards into play and is a data controller.

Acting as a repository for information from a number of sources is considered by the Working Party as likely to give rise to data controller status, as no individual data processing source can be held responsible for the whole process of data collection. When data from different sources are brought together there is a particular threat to data protection. This is best countered by interpreting the collation and holding of that information as the function of a data controller, not a data processor.

The Eighth Principle

Publication of material on websites

The Eighth Principle generally prohibits the transfer of personal information to territories outside the EEA unless certain conditions are met, or the transferor takes steps to authorise the transfer. The Information Commissioner has issued guidance on what constitutes a 'transfer' of personal information,[14] but it is possible to make an unintentional, or at least an uninformed, transfer which breaches the data protection principles (e.g. when promoting a blog site or asking members of the public to create an online profile which will be visible to visitors to the website no matter where they are located in the world).

International transfers – legal guidance

This guidance, published by the ICO in April 2010, replaces the preliminary analysis on international data transfers published in July 1999. It outlines an approach to the transfer of personal data outside the EEA. This is new guidance which may not yet be covered elsewhere so for completeness it is discussed here.

The ICO notes that it will look for evidence that exporters of personal data have followed the steps outlined for compliant data transfers. The order in which exemptions and authorising activities are considered in the guidance differ from the order previously set out for data controllers.

Step 1

Consider whether there will be a transfer of personal data to a third country (i.e. those territories located outside of the EEA which is made up of EU Member States, Norway, Iceland and Liechtenstein).

This first step includes analysing whether or not an actual transfer has taken place; a transfer is not the same as mere transit through a territory. It also deals with the difficult decision of the European Court of Justice (the ECJ) in *Bodil Lindqvist v Kammaraklagaren*[15] where it was held that simply loading information onto an internet page in a Member State did not constitute a transfer of personal data, but that the transfer was effected when someone else downloaded that information in a third country. In practice the ICO advises that if the intention is to allow access to the data in a third country then a transfer will have taken place because the download cannot be prevented in these circumstances.

Step 2

Consider whether the third country and the circumstances surrounding the transfer ensure an adequate level of protection for that data. The finding of adequacy may be made by the European Commission, which makes rulings on applications by third countries as to the adequacy of their protection for personal information. Adequacy findings have already been made in relation to Andorra, Argentina, Canada, the Faroe Islands, the Isle of Man, Israel, Guernsey, Jersey, Switzerland and Uruguay. In the US, Safe Harbor is a finding of adequacy in favour of organisations which subscribe to it. Where Safe Harbor (applicable in the US only) is relied upon, the data controller must check that the intended transferee of the personal data has signed up to the protocol.

The finding of adequacy may also be made by the data controller on all the relevant facts of the intended transfer. When conducting an investigation into the adequacy of protection for personal data in a third country the data controller should consider the criteria in two categories, general adequacy criteria and legal adequacy criteria. The general adequacy criteria are:

- *The nature of the personal data.* This is a risk-based approach dependent on the type of risk posed to the rights and freedoms of individuals.
- *The purpose(s) of the proposed transfer and processing.* Again this is to be a risk-based approach.
- *The period during which the data is intended to be processed.* The ICO makes the point that where it is intended to process the personal information once, or only for a short time and then destroy it, the risks may be less than if personal data is being processed on a longer term basis.
- *Any security measures taken in respect of the data in the third country.* This includes technical measures such as encryption or the adoption of information security standards similar to ISO 17799.

- *The country of origin of the personal data.* Where this is the same as the country of final destination it will be a relevant factor to consider because the data subject will enjoy the same level of data protection in his home territory.
- *The country of final destination of the personal data.*

The legal adequacy criteria are:

- the law in force in the third country;
- the international obligations in that third country;
- any relevant codes of conduct or other rules which are enforceable in that country or territory.

The ICO states:[16]

> Even in those cases where they do not conduct an exhaustive analysis, exporting controllers will be expected to be able to recognise countries where there would be real danger of prejudice because of, for example, instability in the third country at the time of the transfer, and they will be expected to assess this danger in light of the general adequacy criteria.

Step 3

This is followed where the third country and the circumstances surrounding the proposed transfer do not establish an adequate level of protection for the personal information and consideration is then given to what safeguards can be put in place to protect it. The model contract clauses approved by the European Commission between data controller and data controller or between data controller and data processor include clauses for the protection of personal information as well as clauses establishing responsibility between the parties and providing an enforcement mechanism for data subjects.

Binding Corporate Rules (BCR) are internal codes of conduct, technical and organisational standards adopted by multinational organisations for the purposes of enabling international, intra-group transfers of personal information. They are designed to be a global solution for multinational organisations and have to be approved by the relevant national data protection supervisory authority. There is some movement towards the mutual recognition of approval by national supervisory authorities so that organisations established in more than one EU Member State may cite the approval of one authority as part of the process of gaining the approval of another.

Step 4

This is followed if model clauses or BCR are not appropriate in the context of the intended transfer. The prohibition on the transfer of personal information to third countries is qualified by the conditions set out in Sch 4 to the DPA 1998. In the legal guidance the point is made that these conditions are used when there is not necessarily any protection in place for the personal information being transferred. This is why the Sch 4 conditions are only considered as a last resort.

This order of considering how transfers of personal information to a third country may be authorised is different to the order suggested in the 1999 legal guidance when the adequacy test was the recommended last step, so this marks a change in the way international transfers of personal information should be dealt with.

When to report breaches of the data protection principles

We have already seen that there is currently no statutory duty to report breaches of the data protection principles, although pressure is growing for at least a data security breach notification law. However, in serious circumstances, data controllers are expected to report breaches and there is guidance on the ICO website on deciding when an incident is sufficiently significant to warrant being reported.[17] The potential harm to data subjects is the main consideration. The ICO outlines ways in which harm can occur:

- exposure to potential identity theft through the release of non-public identifiers such as passport numbers; and
- information about private aspects of someone's life becoming public knowledge, such as their financial circumstances.

Both the volume of personal data and its sensitivity will also be key factors.

The guidance provides examples of incidents the ICO would expect to be reported (e.g. the theft or loss of an unencrypted laptop holding names and addresses, dates of birth and National Insurance numbers of 1,000 or more individuals would be reportable. Alternatively the ICO would not expect a report to be made concerning the theft or loss of a marketing list of 500 names and addresses where there is no particular product sensitivity.

Where sensitive personal data[18] is lost or stolen it should be presumed that a report to the ICO will be required even where smaller numbers of individuals or data are involved. As an example, the ICO would expect a report for a manual paper-based filing system holding personal data relating to 50 individuals and their financial records. They would not expect a report for a similar system holding member subscription records where there were no special circumstances surrounding the loss.

When reporting a breach, the following information should be included:

- the type of information and the number of records;
- the circumstances of the loss;

- any action taken to mitigate the effect on individuals involved, including whether they have been told of the loss;
- details of how the breach is being investigated;
- the involvement of any other regulatory body;
- remedial action taken to prevent future occurrences; and
- any other information that might assist the ICO to make an assessment.

The ICO might simply record the breach and take no further action against the organisation, depending on the circumstances. It might investigate the circumstances of the breach and require the data controller to take specific steps to avoid further breaches or it might instigate formal enforcement action and require a legal undertaking by the organisation to comply with the law in future. The ICO also has the power to fine organisations. In 2010 the maximum financial penalty is £500,000. The Commissioner has the power to bring criminal prosecutions in the most intransigent cases.

Notes

1   See www.ico.gov.uk.
2   See www.ico.gov.uk/upload/documents/library/data_protection/detailed_specialist _guides/privacy_notices_cop_final.pdf.
3   Opinion 8/2001.
4   See *Legal Guidance*, para 3.1.5, published by the ICO, December 2001.
5   Joint contribution to the Consultation of the European Commission on the legal framework for the fundamental right to protection of personal data adopted 1 December 2009.
6   Directive 95/46/EC.
7   See www.justice.gov.uk.
8   28 January 2003 (ECHR).
9   *MS v Sweden* (1997) 28 EHRR 313 para 41.
10 Data protection principles 2, 3 and 4 are adequately covered by the Information Commissioner's *Data Protection Guide*.
11 The Sixth Data Protection Principle is adequately covered in the Information Commissioner's *Data Protection Guide*.
12 Opinion 1/2010 adopted on 16 February 2010 Ref. 00264/10/EN WP 169.
13 Seventh Data Protection Principle.
14 *International Transfers – Legal Guidance*, published April 2010.
15 (2003) (Case C-101/01).
16 *International Transfers – Legal Guidance*, published April 2010, para 2.5.3.
17 *Notification of Data Security Breaches to the Information Commissioner's Office*, published July 2010.
18 Sensitive personal data is information relating to physical or mental health, sex life, political opinions or beliefs, trade union membership, religious or philosophical beliefs, race or ethnicity, criminal convictions or allegations of criminal activity.

5 A strategic approach to data protection compliance

Introduction

In September 2010 a Housing Association gave an undertaking to comply with the Data Protection Act 1998 (DPA 1998) after it lost paper files during an office move. The data loss was only discovered when a third party notified the Housing Association that it had found some of the files in a secondhand filing cabinet. The files contained 'a significant amount of personal data relating to each tenant and, in some cases, members of his or her family'.[1]

There had been no inventory of files prior to the office move so staff did not know how many files they should have had. Some of the removal packing cases had not been unpacked some six months after the office move. The incident highlights how data protection needs to be managed from the top down rather than by simply reacting to crises. It also shows that the problem needs to be defined before solutions can be sought.

On the BBC news website, in an article entitled 'Ministers attacked over lost laptop',[2] the following exchange is recorded:

In a written Commons answer, Mr Woolas said that 29 Home Office laptops and two mobile phones had either been lost or stolen in 2007.

Earlier this year, Lord West put the figure at 15 for missing laptops and 47 for missing phones.

The Home Office said the figures given by Mr Woolas were 'unfortunately' wrong and would be corrected since they included information from areas no longer part of the department.

But opposition parties said the confusion was symptomatic of the government's complacent attitude to data handling.

'Not only does the government not have a grip of the problem, it does not even know the scale of the problem', said shadow home secretary Dominic Grieve.

'The government cannot combat the threat of data loss if it cannot even measure it.'

A strategic approach involves taking an overview of the subject, identifying strengths, opportunities, weaknesses and threats and then managing them. A strategic approach necessarily commits the most senior management of the organisation; they are best placed to take an overview and the only ones who can commit the resources, time and money to resolve or manage the issues identified.

Risk management is a useful tool in assessing the gravity of weaknesses and the likelihood and extent of any damage resulting from a threat or weakness. Most senior managers are familiar with the concept of risk management – this involves identifying risks and taking action to avoid the risk where possible or mitigate it where it cannot be avoided. Ordinarily risk management is employed to identify and manage operational threats (e.g. risks to service delivery). However, the principles of risk management can also be applied to identify and manage risks associated with compliance failures.

The strategic approach recommended for data protection compliance

Over recent years, various regulators and industry commentators (the Information Commissioner, the European Data Protection Supervisor, the Financial Services Authority (the FSA), Deloitte Consulting *et al*) have recommended a strategic approach to data protection compliance, particularly the information security aspects. Commentators criticise the current approach in many organisations whereby senior management take no leadership role on data protection compliance and instead try to manage issues as they arise and in a piecemeal fashion.

In 2007, Deloitte expressed the view that there is a need for organisations to have a strategy to manage information security, a key aspect of data protection. Their report *The Shifting Security Paradigm*[3] recommends adopting a risk-based approach to compliance. There was concern that, even though information security incidents are grabbing the headlines, executives and directors do not take ownership of the problems. Deloitte's research shows that senior managers think that information security is solely within the remit of IT. This is not an accurate assumption because the Seventh Principle requires 'appropriate technical and organizational measures' to safeguard personal information. The IT controls only meet part of the requirement. This error is further compounded by the fact that most security failings are due to staff not following procedures or not being trained and made aware of risks or the procedures to manage them, rather than IT security failures. A lot of work has been done in the area of IT controls for information security. There are international standards against which IT directors can check the standards in operation within their organisation. Notably ISO27001 is couched in terms of having a system of control for information security management; this allows the organisation to identify and manage risk. A key element of ISO27001 is the requirement to monitor and check that the system of control works in practice.

The attitude of senior managers, unwilling to take ownership of data protection compliance, delegating information security to IT instead of seeing it as a company-wide issue, typifies the piecemeal approach to data protection compliance.

Issues are commonly dealt with from the bottom up rather than adopting a top-down approach; this is a basically flawed attitude because it only addresses the problems that have already arisen, not those that may arise in the future.

Other industry commentators have levelled the same criticisms at UK senior management. In July 2007 the Information Commissioner said:[4]

Business and public sector leaders must take their data protection obligations more seriously. The majority of organisations process personal information appropriately – but privacy must be given more priority in every UK boardroom.

The same concerns were voiced by the FSA in its report, *Data Security in Financial Services*, published in April 2008. The report was based on investigative work carried out by the FSA on a number of firms in the financial services sector. The objective of the FSA's investigation was to highlight how financial services firms in the UK are addressing the risks around customer data being lost or stolen and then being used to commit fraud or other financial crime.[6] Its report has some interesting insights into where ultimate responsibility for compliance lies. The FSA's view is that responsibility lies with the senior management. In its *Principles for Businesses*,[7] the organisation's senior management are held 'responsible for making an appropriate assessment of the financial crime risks associated with their customer data'. In practice the FSA found that firms had not allocated ultimate accountability for data security to a single senior manager. The FSA concluded, that this resulted in significant weaknesses in otherwise well-controlled firms.

The FSA also understands the need for systems of control and an overarching strategy to manage compliance issues. Rule 3.2.6R in the FSA's *Senior Management Arrangements, Systems and Controls* sourcebook requires firms to:

Take reasonable care to establish and maintain effective systems and controls for compliance with applicable requirements and standards under the regulatory system and for countering the risk that the firm might be used to further financial crime.

A key element of the strategy to manage compliance outlined in the FSA report is risk management. It identifies three main reasons in the failure to identify all aspects of the data security risk presented by an organisation. The firm either does not appreciate the gravity of this risk, it does not have the expertise to make an assessment of the main risk factors and find ways of mitigating them, or it simply fails to allocate and supervise resources appropriately to address the risk. It notes that many firms do not undertake any risk assessment and only a few continuously monitor the effectiveness of their information security controls. These are major failings in implementing an effective system of control.

In summary, the systemic failures included:

- the failure of senior management to take responsibility for data security;
- the tendency to think of data security only in terms of IT security and to focus on IT security to the detriment of organisational controls;
- failing to train staff appropriately and regularly and to test how well any training has worked. In medium and small firms, there was a lack of awareness that customer information is a valuable asset to criminals;
- failing to carry out risk assessments of the risk posed by information management or, where these are undertaken, too much focus on the risks to the firms themselves, without considering the wider risks of identity fraud and the potential impact on customers.

The FSA concluded that 'it is good practice for firms to conduct a risk assessment of their data security environment and implement adequate mitigating controls'.

The *Data Sharing Review Report*[8] comments that the culture of organisations who collect and use personal information needed to change. The recommendations made in the report include references to accountability and the need for senior managers to take responsibility for data protection compliance.

> Recommendation 1: As a matter of good practice, we therefore recommend that all organisations handling or sharing significant amounts of personal information should clarify in their corporate governance arrangements where ownership and accountability lie for the handling of personal information. This should normally be at senior executive level, giving a designated individual explicit responsibility for ensuring that the organisation handles personal information in a way that meets all legal and good-practice requirements. Audit committees should monitor the arrangements and their operation in practice.

Given the problems identified by industry commentators, a strategic approach including some form of risk assessment and risk management is generally recommended. To help focus resources and to give data protection issues the high profile they merit, general opinion is that responsibility for data protection compliance falls at the highest levels within the organisation.

The likely impact of the principle of accountability

Chapter 2 considered how the law of data protection may develop. One aspect in particular, favoured by most of those involved at international, European and national level, is the introduction of a principle of Accountability. The Article 29 Working Party notes[9] that EU data protection principles and obligations are often insufficiently reflected in the internal measures and practices of organisations. It considers that, without data protection being embedded in the values and practices of an organisation, with responsibility expressly assigned, effective compliance is at risk and data protection 'mishaps' are likely to continue. Additional tools are required to achieve this embedding of data protection principles and acceptance of responsibility at senior levels within organisations and the Working Party is advising that a new principle of Accountability be adopted.

The suggested wording for such a principle is:

Article X – Implementation of data protection principles

1. The controller shall implement appropriate and effective measures to ensure that the principles and obligations set out in the Directive are complied with.
2. The controller shall demonstrate compliance with paragraph 1 to the supervisory authority on its request.

Thus there are two key elements to the principle: first that the data controller will have a system of control and second, that it should be able to demonstrate that control to the supervisory authority.

The principle of Accountability was endorsed in the Madrid International Standards developed by the International Conference of Data Protection and Privacy Commissioners. It states that the responsible person (i.e. the organisation responsible for personal information processing) shall:

a. Take all the necessary measures to observe the principles and obligations set out in this Document and in the applicable national legislation, and b. have the necessary internal mechanisms in place for demonstrating such observance both to data subjects and to the supervisory authorities in the exercise of their powers.

While the wording is different, the Madrid Resolution's proposal for a principle of Accountability contains the same two elements as the proposal put forward by the Article 29 Working Party. The organisation would be required to take appropriate and effective measures to implement data protection principles and it would have to be able to demonstrate upon request that those measures have been taken.

The requirement to demonstrate that appropriate and effective measures have been taken to implement data protection principles begs the question: 'demonstrate to whom?' National data protection supervisory authorities seem to be the natural choice. However the national authorities will require meaningful powers of sanction, including the possibility of imposing precise instructions upon data controllers regarding their compliance system, for the control to be effective.

Article 22 of the International Standards adopted in Madrid by data protection authorities suggested internationally consistent measures that member states could adopt to encourage accountability among organisations, including:

- national data protection breach notification law;
- the requirement to appoint one or more data protection officers adequately qualified and with resources and powers for exercising their supervisory functions;
- a requirement to undertake periodic audits using qualified and preferably independent parties to verify compliance;
- the adoption of privacy by design techniques;
- the adoption of privacy impact assessments as a mandatory measure; and
- the adoption of binding codes of practice with penalties for non-compliance.

These recommendations are mirrored in the Madrid Resolution on Privacy. They suggest the options for elements in a system of control for data protection compliance.

The British standard on data protection

The British Standards Institute has published a standard on data protection compliance: BS10012: 2009 *Data protection – Specification for a personal information management system (PIMS)*. It promotes a strategic approach to data protection compliance with the aim of enabling organisations to:

- identify the risks presented by processing personal information;
- manage those risks through processes and procedures; and
- monitor the effectiveness of their risk identification and management processes and amend the systems appropriately.

Published in May 2009, BS 10012 provides a framework for maintaining and improving compliance with data protection law and good practice. It specifies that organisations should adopt a personal information management system or 'PIMS', a system of control for data protection compliance. Recognising that the directors and leaders at the top of the organisation set the compliance level, there is an emphasis on responsibility and accountability at a senior level. A senior management team is to be tasked with issuing and maintaining a policy that sets a clear framework for managing compliance with data protection law and good practice. Flowing from the policy, the PIMS brings together many of the elements of a system of control for data protection compliance.

The elements of a system of control for compliance

BSI 10012 outlines the scope of the PIMS to take account of the relevant legal requirements, the organisation's objectives and obligations, its acceptable level of risk and the interests of individuals and other key stakeholders. The PIMS structure requires a senior manager or managers to be identified with responsibility for data protection compliance with a key worker, suitably qualified or experienced, to handle day-to-day enquiries and issues. It suggests that, in some organisations, it may be appropriate to identify local data protection representatives. It requires that an inventory of categories of personal information processed is maintained. It also requires the establishment of a cycle of continuous improvement for procedures and processes in a 'Plan-Do-Check-Act' cycle. This means planning procedures for compliance, putting them in place, auditing and monitoring to check their effectiveness and taking remedial action to improve the PIMS.

The Article 29 Working Party in its Opinion on the principle of Accountability gave illustrations of how organisations might meet the requirement for accountability by introducing 'common accountability measures' or elements of a system of control. It described these as follows:

- *Procedures*: the establishment of internal procedures before commencing any new personal data processing operations based on internal review and assessment. This would be akin to the current recommended practice of conducting a Privacy Impact Assessment (PIA).
- *Policies*: establishing written and binding data protection policies to be considered and applied to data processing operations to encourage compliance with data quality requirements, fair processing or privacy notice requirements, the security principles and data subject rights.
- *Inventory of data processing operations*: mapping procedures to ensure proper identification of all data processing operations and maintaining an inventory of data processing operations. This approaches the concept of an Information Asset Register and links into audit and risk assessment measures.
- *Identifying data protection officer or officers*: appointing a data protection officer and/or other individuals with responsibility for data protection compliance within the operation.
- *Staff training*: offering adequate data protection training and education to staff members. This should include those processing, and those responsible for processing, personal data including operational staff and support functions such as human resources (HR), health & safety, facilities management etc as well as IT managers and developers.
- *Subject rights procedures*: setting up procedures to manage subject rights including access, correction and deletion requests. The procedures should be transparent to data subjects.
- *Complaints management*: establishing an internal complaints handling mechanism.
- *Internal security breach reporting*: setting up internal procedures for the effective management and reporting of information security breaches;
- *Monitoring and audit*: implementing and supervising procedures to ensure that procedures are documented and that they are implemented and work in practice. This can be achieved by internal or external audits.

Establishing a system of control for data protection compliance may involve several of the elements identified. These elements are considered in more detail below and some of the practical implications are identified.

Senior accountability

Commentators agree that senior management must be engaged in data protection compliance. Good leadership is the key to embedding data protection compliance in an organisation. Senior management sets the agenda for operational colleagues and it controls access to finance and resources, key to prioritising compliance. Without these elements compliance is unlikely to be either achieved, or even taken seriously.

Clear leadership and communication cascading from the board will communicate to staff the organisation's ideals and values and help to convince its employees to accept and work to further them. Having employees who understand their place in the order of the organisation, what they are responsible for and to whom, significantly reduces risks to the business from security and other data management breaches.

Good leadership throughout the organisation is also important. Managers at all levels need to understand and communicate the need for training and procedures to manage the risks associated with handling personal information. Managers should agree with the ideals and values of the organisation and demonstrate commitment to work towards them. Training and procedures can be seriously undermined by managers who criticise or flout procedures. Managers should set a good example in this area as in many others.

As an example of how this might work in practice, in the National Health Service (NHS) sector the issue of senior accountability for data protection compliance has been addressed. Information governance rules require the appointment of a senior official designated the 'Senior Information Risk Owner' (SIRO). There is also a requirement in relation to clinical or patient records to appoint a 'Caldicott Guardian', whose role is similar to that of a data protection officer in other organisations and is considered further below. However it is worth noting that the requirement is that:

> A senior person, preferably a health professional, should be nominated in each health organisation to act as a guardian, responsible for safeguarding the confidentiality of patient information.

Both the SIRO and the Caldicott Guardian are concerned with ensuring NHS data is protected and is not handled inappropriately. In practice, the roles are different. The SIRO should be a board member or equivalent, concerned with identifying and managing information risks across the board. The Caldicott Guardian is primarily concerned with the protection of patient information.

Appointing data protection officers

Appointing an in-house data protection officer demonstrates a commitment to data protection compliance only in so far as the individual has sufficient power to enforce compliance. The individual, who must be highly trained in the technical aspects of data protection compliance, should have the backing of senior management in carrying out the role. He or she will need access to all parts of the organisation and the cooperation of the management team. The data protection officer also needs access to what could be confidential corporate information to be able to identify new developments and other initiatives which could have an impact on privacy so that compliance input can be provided at an early stage and not after the event. Access to senior management is a key requirement at all times both to inform the data protection officer and to facilitate clear reporting of issues directly to those ultimately accountable. Ideally this should be a two-way process, with senior management consulting with the data protection officer as a matter of course.

On a positive note, centralising the role gives other employees an identifiable source of information and guidance on data protection, both through *ad hoc* approaches and by providing technical training to colleagues. The role of the data protection officer then largely becomes that of internal auditor for data protection compliance. Informed by a risk assessment, a system of control is established partly by an annual schedule of reviews to cover all key risks and the development of risk management tools appropriate to the organisation and its activities.

In a diverse organisation, it may be more appropriate to designate a data protection officer in each operational area resulting in a team of suitably trained data protection officers tailored to support the operation. These individuals are less likely to spend all of their time on data protection issues, but may have a dual role in the organisation. This makes it even more important to ensure that this type of data protection officer has the backing and support of senior managers as they may have to prioritise their data protection role over their other responsibilities if these conflict. One benefit of designating more than one data protection officer is that they can support each other in the role, exchanging views and experiences, keeping each other up to date with developments in data protection law and practice.

The disadvantage of appointing multiple data protection officers is that it may take time to establish and communicate the responsibilities of the role. Ongoing training will be required to cope with leavers and vacancies. Succession planning will have to be managed to ensure sustainability. A further disadvantage is that centralising responsibility for data protection compliance in a designated officer may lead other employees (wrongly) to consider that it is not an issue for which they are personally responsible.

One advantage of an in-house data protection officer (or officers) is that employees have easy access to tailored, specific advice on data protection as it affects their work, in addition to monitoring and review activities undertaken by the data protection officer.

To give an example of a data protection officer role in practice, following the recommendations in the Caldicott Report,[10] the role of the Caldicott Guardian is to:

- develop local protocols governing the disclosure of patient identifiable information to other organisations;
- restrict access to patient information within each organisation by enforcing strict need to know principles;
- regularly review and justify the uses of patient information;
- improve organisational performance across a range of related areas: database design, staff induction, training, compliance with guidance etc.

Although the Caldicott Guardian is a senior official within an NHS organisation, he is not required to implement a system of control at the highest level; that is the role of the SIRO. The role of the Caldicott Guardian is more operational, akin to that of a data protection officer.

Register of personal information

This element of systems of control involves the creation of a register of all databases in use in the organisation, highlighting those that contain personal information. It meets the BSI 10012 requirement for an inventory of categories of personal data processed and takes it a step further. For each database a 'responsible person' should be identified to be both the point of contact for enquiries concerning that database and with responsibility for its data protection compliance.

The type of information that might be required initially to establish the register would include the purpose of the database, the department(s) it serves, the individual with day-to-day responsibility, an outline of the access controls, the type of data subject, whether or not 'sensitive' categories of data are held and how long the information on the database is typically held for.

The register would need to be supplemented with new material and audited on a continuing basis. This would require some degree of central control and coordination. Therefore, as a system, it fits well with designated data protection officers in the business.

The disadvantage of the approach is the requirement for a central controller to manage compliance on a continuing basis using reports and updates from those responsible for databases. Many senior managers wrongly identify data protection as the responsibility of the IT department, so, ideally, the IT manager should not be the one tasked with initiating and managing the register.

The advantage of a register is that the persons 'responsible' for databases on the register become *de facto* data protection officers. With responsibility comes accountability, a spur to understanding and managing the risks.

Again the NHS provides an example of how a register might work in practice. All databases are registered centrally within each NHS entity under the control of the SIRO. The SIRO is supported in his role by one or more Information

Asset Owners who have assigned responsibility for the information assets of the organisation. Regular audits and monitoring may then be undertaken against the Information Asset Register.

Job-related risk management

Another system of control for organisations that handle a lot of personal information focuses compliance activity on those employees whose work involves using personal information. The first step is to identify which roles have a significant exposure to personal information and risk-rate them appropriately, taking into account the amount and type of personal information, the number of data subjects likely to be affected by any misuse or data breach and the current level of training and awareness of the staff who access that information. This is effectively applying risk management techniques to job roles.

High-risk roles require special procedures at selection interview and throughout the life cycle of the employee. Appropriate competence-based questions can be put at interview to highlight whether or not the candidate has an appreciation of privacy issues and has already identified that confidentiality will be a keynote of their work. This understanding can be built upon with appropriate training fitting into existing training matrices, professional development and key performance indicators.

The aim of this type of control mechanism is to empower and inform individual employees so that they can take more responsibility for compliance issues related to their work. It involves fundamental agreement and alignment with the organisation's ideals and values. A precursor to this 'buy-in' is the organisation's ability to communicate its ideals and values clearly and to ensure that individual employees understand their place in the organisation, where their authority devolves from and to whom they are responsible in turn. In this type of framework members of staff become more accountable for their choices and actions rather than relying wholly on procedures.

This system of control is particularly effective in organisations that still rely heavily on paper files rather than electronic records. Its disadvantage is that it involves keeping most of the workforce up to date with risk awareness and data protection training. There will be a heavy initial investment and ongoing support will be required. The advantage is that data protection compliance is integrated into the work of all relevant employees rather than being the responsibility of an individual data protection officer. There are no issues with leavers and succession management as the system of control is integrated with continuing professional development and personal targets.

Governance, risk management and compliance software

The role of a data protection officer can be supported by governance, risk management and compliance software (GRC) available from a number of providers. Each aspect of each compliance subject is identified together with the required actions to ensure compliance. Responsibility for each action can be allocated to an individual manager or level of managers who are required to report back, via the software, when actions have been taken. The software gives compliance officers evidence that the organisation is compliant and that it is not at immediate risk of a compliance breach.

Managing data protection compliance in projects

The identification of potential data protection issues in a new development or initiative is a useful step both to demonstrate control over new personal information processing activities and in effective project management. Potential issues highlighted at an early stage of a development are generally easier and cheaper to resolve than those identified towards the end of a project when the issue may have become entrenched in systems or administration.

Privacy Impact Assessments (PIAs) are in use in a variety of jurisdictions worldwide and are currently being heavily promoted by European and national data protection regulators. The term can be applied to any process which attempts to identify potential privacy risks in a given project, new venture or development. The aim is to inform the project team so that further advice can be taken to address the issues during development so that the project is compliant at completion.

At its simplest a PIA might be the one question: 'Will we be using personal information as part of this development or as a result of this development?' If the answer is 'yes', either seek input from a data protection specialist or work through the eight data protection principles to identify how these will impact on the project.

Chapter 9 considers how to conduct a PIA.

Audit

An audit of an organisation's data protection compliance should identify compliance risks and recommend tactics to avoid or mitigate them. However an audit is not a 'system of control' for data protection compliance, it is a check that the system of control is operating effectively. Nevertheless it might be a good starting point for introducing a system of control.

The success of an audit depends on the organisation's commitment to compliance in implementing the audit recommendations. An audit presents the compliance picture at a given point in time and will have to be repeated periodically to keep up to date with developments within and outside of the organisation. The advantage of conducting an audit is that the work is readily outsourced to a data protection specialist or auditor and it is a quick way to identify the current data protection risks to which the organisation is exposed.

In all likelihood an audit report will recommend implementing a system of control for data protection compliance and suggest how this might be achieved based on the auditor's knowledge of the organisation and its culture. In the medium term audit is therefore a complementary tool rather than a substitute for a system of control.

A system of control must include a form of checking to ensure that policies and procedures are being followed and that they are effective in practice. Accepted checking procedures involve audit, review and monitoring.

What is an audit?

Wikipedia says:

> The general definition of an *audit* is an evaluation of a person, organization, system, process, enterprise, project or product. The term most commonly refers to audits in accounting, but similar concepts also exist in project management, quality management, and for energy conservation.

The term tends to be associated with a financial audit, which is an examination of records or financial accounts to check and verify their accuracy. It also applies to compliance activities. Whatis.com defines a compliance audit as:

> A comprehensive review of an organization's adherence to regulatory guidelines. Independent accounting, security or IT consultants evaluate the strength and thoroughness of compliance preparations. Auditors review security policies, user access controls and risk management procedures over the course of a compliance audit.

What the ICO says about data protection audit

The Information Commissioner's Office (the ICO) defines an audit as:

> A systematic and independent examination to determine whether activities involving processing of personal data are carried out in accordance with the organisation's data protection policies and procedures, and whether this processing meets the standards of the Data Protection Act 1998.

The key feature of the role of an auditor is that of checking current compliance status, assessing staff's awareness of their data protection obligations and assessing whether the rights of the data subject are adequately protected. It involves identifying non-compliance and agreeing suitable corrective action to remove those non-compliances.

The *Guide to Data Protection Auditing* goes on to recommend that any person who conducts an audit must do so with the full authority of the executive management otherwise their recommendations will not be followed. The audit should be independent of the functions being audited and the auditor should be objective when undertaking the audit.

What does a data protection audit deliver?

A data protection audit is a critical review of current systems, policies, procedures and, most importantly, practices. It aims to identify:

- any aspects of the organisation's culture and management that could increase the risk of a data management breach;
- any training needs including specific training for specialist areas to general privacy and confidentiality awareness for staff engaged in general administrative work;
- the need for risk awareness training to help avoid data security breaches;
- whether or not a system of control for data protection compliance is in place and working effectively;
- areas where the organisation is not compliant with current data protection law;
- areas where the organisation is not meeting best practice guidelines; and
- potential value-added aspects of improved compliance.

An audit report will highlight these issues and will make recommendations to improve compliance and demonstrate how compliance can provide added value to the business; for example, a service provider can be encouraged to include data protection policies in responses to tender and 'beauty parades' when pitching for new business. This will show that the service provider understands that a potential client is bound by the Seventh Data Protection Principle to seek assurance about appropriate security measures when selecting a service provider. It also provides reassurance on privacy and confidentiality issues.

In addition to the benefits of identifying issues and addressing them, an audit is a way of ensuring that an organisation is compliant and functions as a basis for the annual renewal of the organisation's data protection registration.

The practicalities of a data protection audit

The audit process commences by scoping and agreeing the objectives of the audit. The DPA 1998 is not the only legislation that is relevant to privacy and confidentiality; the Human Rights Act 1998 (HRA 1998) also applies in certain circumstances and e-commerce issues also impact on privacy, especially in relation to the use of personal information for marketing purposes. The operations of the organisation need to be considered; should all areas should be audited or just specific areas (e.g. should the audit exclude finance where there is usually limited access to personal information and instead focus on HR activities which involve handling large amounts of confidential information relating to employees?). Alternatively a data controller may conduct an audit of its service providers to ensure that they are meeting appropriate security standards in IT and as an organisation generally.

The organisation's compliance history will be relevant. Has it been the subject of enforcement action or investigation by the ICO or any other regulator? Have any data protection breaches been reported in the media? Does its complaints history show a trend of data protection issues? It is important to identify what has triggered the decision to undertake an audit. Is it in response to a data protection breach, to satisfy service users' demands for audit or to allay general concerns that the organisation is not on top of the issues?

The conduct of the audit needs to be scoped and agreed. Usually it will involve access to managers and other staff to discuss data management and map data flows around the organisation. The key questions are set out in Chapter 7. This outlines the risks inherent in processing personal information.

There will also be an element of checking policies and procedures against accepted standards to ensure that they:

- exist;
- adequately cover the risks presented by the organisation;
- are communicated effectively to all relevant staff on a continuing basis;
- are being adhered to in practice;
- are effective at countering the risk presented; and
- are being monitored.

This process will also identify any further amendments and additions to existing policies and procedures.

What is a review?

The standard definition of a review describes it as going over or restudying material, particularly in the context of review for a final exam. It involves looking over again, considering material retrospectively and looking back on work done.

A definition of 'peer review' is also useful:[12]

Peer review is a process used for checking the work performed by one's equals (peers) to ensure it meets specific criteria. Peer review is used in working groups for many professional occupations because it is thought that peers can identify each other's errors quickly and easily, speeding up the time that it takes for mistakes to be identified and corrected. ... Generally, the goal of all peer review processes is to verify whether the work satisfies the specifications for review, identify any deviations from the standards, and provide suggestions for improvements.

The term 'review' in the context of data protection compliance refers to someone double checking a report of audit findings or revisiting the recommendations made in an audit report after a period of months has passed to check if they have been implemented.

Monitoring

Monitoring is the process of checking for proper conduct. In the work context this means checking that employees are following agreed policies and procedures when doing their job. Monitoring can help to identify if additional policies and procedures are required to deal with specific issues that arise regularly. In the employment context, monitoring is often linked to performance management. An employee is monitored to ensure they are doing their job properly and following procedures. They are also monitored to identify any training needs.

Example of a monitoring checklist

The NHS has been used as an example throughout this chapter because it has adopted a framework for a system of control for confidentiality, information security and data protection compliance – it calls this 'Information Governance'. The Information Governance Toolkit provides a checklist of the elements that make up the system of control; this illustrates the appropriate level of detail required. There are several versions; the one reproduced here is the NHS Business Services Authority Version 8, as it is more generally applicable than the versions that relate to specific NHS trusts.

Information Governance Management
1. There is an adequate Information Governance Management Framework to support the current and evolving Information Governance agenda.
2. There are approved and comprehensive Information Governance Policies with associated strategies and/or improvement plans.
3. Formal contractual arrangements, that include compliance with information governance requirements, are in place with all contractors and support organisations.
4. Employment contracts which include compliance with information governance standards are in place for all individuals carrying out work on behalf of the organisation.
5. Information Governance awareness and mandatory training procedures are in place and all staff are appropriately trained.

Confidentiality and Data Protection Assurance
1. The Information Governance agenda is supported by adequate confidentiality

and data protection skills, knowledge and experience, which meet the organisation's assessed needs.

2. Staff are provided with clear guidance on keeping personal information secure and on respecting the confidentiality of service users.
3. Consent is appropriately sought before personal information is used in ways that do not directly contribute to the delivery of care services and objections to the disclosure of confidential personal information are appropriately respected.
4. Individuals are informed about the proposed uses of their personal information.
5. There are appropriate procedures for recognising and responding to individuals' requests for access to their personal data.
6. There are appropriate confidentiality audit procedures to monitor access to confidential personal information.
7. Where required, protocols governing the routine sharing of personal information have been agreed with other organisations.
8. All person identifiable data processed outside of the UK complies with the Data Protection Act 1998 and Department of Health guidelines.
9. All new processes, services, information systems and other relevant information assets are developed and implemented in a secure and structured manner, and comply with Information Governance security accreditation, information quality and confidentiality and data protection requirements.

Information Security Assurance
1. The Information Governance agenda is supported by adequate information security skills, knowledge and experience which meet the organisation's assessed needs.
2. A formal information security risk assessment and management programme for key Information Assets has been documented, implemented and reviewed.
3. There are documented information security incident/event reporting and management procedures that are accessible to all staff.
4. There are established business processes and procedures that satisfy the organisation's obligations as a Registration Authority.
5. Monitoring and enforcement processes are in place to ensure NHS national application Smartcard users comply with the terms and conditions of use.
6. Operating and application information systems (under the organisation's control) support appropriate access control functionality and documented and managed access rights are in place for all users of these systems.
7. An effectively supported Senior Information Risk Owner takes ownership of the organisation's information risk policy and information risk management strategy.
8. All transfers of hardcopy and digital person identifiable and sensitive information have been identified, mapped and risk assessed; technical and organisational measures adequately secure these transfers.

9. Business continuity plans are up to date and tested for all critical information assets (data processing facilities, communications services and data) and service-specific measures are in place.

10. Procedures are in place to prevent information processing being interrupted or disrupted through equipment failure, environmental hazard or human error.

11. Information Assets with computer components are capable of the rapid detection, isolation and removal of malicious code and unauthorised mobile code.

12. Policy and procedures are in place to ensure that Information Communication Technology (ICT) networks operate securely.

13. Policy and procedures ensure that mobile computing and teleworking are secure.

14. Unauthorised access to the premises, equipment, records and other assets is prevented

15. All information assets that hold, or are, personal data are protected by appropriate organisational and technical measures.

16. The confidentiality of service user information is protected through use of pseudonymisation and anonymisation techniques where appropriate.

Clinical Information Assurance

1. The Information Governance agenda is supported by adequate information quality and records management skills, knowledge and experience.

Corporate Information Assurance

1. Documented and implemented procedures are in place for the effective management of corporate records.

2. Documented and publicly available procedures are in place to ensure compliance with the Freedom of Information Act 2000.

3. As part of the information lifecycle management strategy, an audit of corporate records has been undertaken.

This detailed checklist illustrates how widely data protection impacts on an organisation and the breadth of controls, policies, procedures and training that are required for compliance. It is specific to the NHS and its operations, but many of the check points are generally applicable to commercial businesses and other public bodies.

Conclusion

The response to the compliance requirements of the DPA 1998 has tended to be a piecemeal approach. Organisations send a member of staff on a training course and then deal with issues as they are brought to the attention of management, dealing with data protection on a reactive basis and taking a limited view of the issues rather than looking at the 'big picture'. In so far as risk assessments are undertaken, it is an informal assessment of how likely it is the organisation will be 'found out' and its data processing activities challenged. This may be partly fuelled by the low level of penalties formerly applicable to data protection breaches.

Increasingly though it is clear that a reactive policy to any governance issue is basically flawed as it does not allow for management of the issues in advance of problems arising. It is also obvious that risk management principles can be equally applied to compliance issues as to threats to service delivery and business operations. Identifying and managing risk is the key to a system of control for data protection compliance as it is with any other risk. From the outside it is apparent that senior management is not engaging with data protection compliance although the regulatory structure increasingly demands a system of control to allow reporting (at least) on governance issues.

There is increasing pressure on organisations from regulatory authorities to comply openly with data protection measures and the press is quick to highlight any data protection breaches. Meanwhile the legal requirements are still evolving: the Telecoms sector will soon be subject to a data security breach notification law and government departments have recently been opened up to audit by the ICO, an initiative that may well be extended to include private organisations in due course.

Against this macro environment a piecemeal approach to compliance will not suffice to protect organisations from exposure to data protection risks. A strategic approach is required to introduce a system of control for data protection compliance. The actual approach taken will depend on what is appropriate for the type of organisation, its culture and the demands of the sector in which it operates.

BSI 10012 has been produced to enable organisations to demonstrate compliance with data protection legislation and good practice to its clients and to facilitate assessment of compliance with data protection legislation and good practice. It also provides a standardised benchmark for audits and process reviews. It outlines, at high level, a strategic approach to data protection compliance.

A strategic approach requires senior ownership of the issue, clear leadership and communication cascading from the board or senior management. Risk management processes will help to identify the issues particular to the organisation and prioritise them for allocation of resources. Training and risk awareness are always instrumental in developing both personal accountability for staff and awareness of the risks inherent in managing personal information. All of these elements need to be monitored and reviewed to ensure that they are working effectively.

Some systems of control have been considered above, but these are not mutually exclusive; a data protection officer is an ideal controller for the information asset register and all organisations should have some form of privacy impact assessment tool for ensuring that projects and new developments recognise and manage their compliance issues. Organisations implementing a system of control for data protection compliance should identify and implement the elements that work best in their environment and with the culture of the organisation.

Notes

1   Wording of the Enforcement notice.
2   13 November 2008.
3   Deloitte 2007 Global Security Survey (the Shifting Security Paradigm).
4   Press release on 11 July 'CEOs urged to raise their game following unacceptable privacy breaches'.
5   *Ibid.*
6   Paragraph 1.1.1 of the report
7   Paragraph 1.1.4 of the report.
8   Report by Mark Walport and Richard Thomas, published in July 2008.
9   See *The Future of Privacy.*
10 *Report on the Review of Patient-Identifiable Information*, Department of Health, The Caldicott Committee – Chair: Dame Fiona Caldicott, published December 1997.
11 *Guide to Data Protection Auditing*, Information Commissioner, published December 2001. This has been withdrawn.
12 See www.searchsoftwarequality.com.

6 Personal information processing: risks and risk management

Why risk management?

Risk management is a topical and relevant approach to compliance as well as to business continuity. It can help to communicate the core compliance issues to business leaders who can understand and relate to the risks facing their business and it helps level the playing field so compliance risks can be addressed and prioritised along with other risks facing the organisation.

A risk-based approach is also a 'big picture' approach. Data protection law applies to a sub-set of information, but businesses process other commercially sensitive information such as trade secrets, business information, skills and know how. Risk management can take a holistic approach to considering risks inherent in information management generally. It is a wider remit than simply considering data protection and is potentially more valuable to the organisation.

Chapter 5 considered the elements of a strategic approach to data protection compliance. A key element of that approach is to apply risk management techniques to the processing of personal information. It is an approach that is endorsed by the regulator. The Information Commissioner has adopted a risk-based approach in his annual strategy since 2007 on the basis that limited resources must target the most high risk areas.

What risks are inherent in processing personal information?

Underlying trends in a number of high profile cases reported in the media can be identified.

Lost data

In June 2010 Lampeter Medical Practice were found to have breached the Data Protection Act 1998 (DPA 1998) following the loss of an unencrypted memory stick containing details of 8,000 patients. The database had been downloaded in contravention of practice policy. The memory stick was lost in the post, although it had been sent by recorded delivery.

In March 2010 Zurich Insurance plc was castigated for losing an unencrypted back-up tape containing the financial details of 46,000 policyholders. The tape was lost in transit between group companies based in South Africa. The loss was hidden from Zurich in the UK for over a year.

In July 2009 HSBC was fined more than £3m by the Financial Services Authority (the FSA) for inadequate data security. HSBC's financial services companies had lost customer data in the post. Large amounts of customer details had been sent via post or courier to third parties without encrypting the information. Two key incidents involved the loss of a floppy disk with name, address, dates of birth and NI number details of nearly 2,000 pension scheme members in April 2007 and the loss of a CD-Rom containing the details of 180,000 policyholders in February 2008.

In 2008 a memory stick found in a pub car park was found to contain the names and confidential sign-on information for individuals who use the Government Gateway. The government contractor, Atos Origin, was found to have been responsible for its loss.

In the same year, the Ministry of Defence revealed that CD-Roms containing the personal details of around 100,000 serving troops had been lost by contractor EDS. In a separate incident, data relating to thousands of prospective soldiers had also been lost.

In November 2007 HMRC admitted that it had lost CD-Roms containing personal data including the names, addresses, NI numbers and bank account details of 25 million child benefit recipients in the UK.

It is significant how many of these incidents actually involve third-party data processors who failed to take adequate security measures to protect the personal information they were processing on behalf of their principal. However it is the principal, the data controller, who carries the ultimate responsibility in law and who is castigated in the press.

It is also noticeable how vulnerable personal information is when in transit. In June 2008 a senior intelligence officer from the Cabinet Office was suspended when he left confidential papers on the train.

Lost and stolen laptops

In July 2010 Birmingham Children's Hospital NHS Foundation Trust was found to be in breach of the DPA 1998. The breach occurred when two unencrypted laptops were stolen. The laptops contained personal data relating to 17 patients, including sensitive personal data such as diagnoses and video recordings.

In March 2010 Warwickshire County Council was found to be in breach of the DPA 1998 when laptops and a memory stick containing personal data were stolen. The laptops were not encrypted. The information included sensitive data relating to pupils and staff at two local schools. In the same month, St Albans City and District Council were found to be in breach of the DPA 1998 when a laptop was stolen. The laptops held postal voter records from 2009. This case highlights a data security breach compounded, or even wholly due to, inadequate data minimisation techniques. The missing information was obsolete and should have been deleted.

In February 2010 the Alzheimer's Society was found to be in breach of the

DPA 1998 when personal data relating to staff was lost following the theft of unencrypted laptops from their offices in Cardiff. In May 2009 the BBC reported that a laptop computer with details of over 100,000 members of six pension schemes had been stolen from offices in Buckinghamshire. The unencrypted data included names, addresses, dates of birth, employer's details, NI numbers, salary details and bank details of pensioners. The data was password protected, but not encrypted.

In October 2008 a laptop with personal data relating to more than 100,000 members of the Network Rail and British Transport Police pension schemes was stolen from Deloitte, while in July 2008 the BBC reported that the Ministry of Defence had confirmed that 121 computer memory sticks and 747 laptops had been stolen in the last four years.

The theft of laptops and loss of memory sticks is shockingly common and given that fact it is surprising how many still hold unencrypted personal information despite the Information Commissioner clearly stating in November 2007 that encryption was the required standard for personal information held on portable data storage devices.

The Information Commissioner used his new powers under the Criminal Justice and Immigration Act 2008 to impose a monetary penalty for the first time in November 2010. A fine of £60,000 was levied on an employment services company for the loss of unencrypted data held on a laptop.

Failures in IT security

In June 2009 the BBC reported that Parcelforce had inadvertently published personal data, including the signatures of recipients, on its delivery tracking website. A flaw in the system also meant that deliveries unrelated to the reference number entered in the system could be viewed.

In January 2009 Monster.com, a recruitment website, reported that hackers had accessed personal information relating to registered users of the website. The information included CVs.

In July 2007 Newcastle City Council admitted that thousands of credit and debit card transaction details were placed on an insecure server in error and had been accessed by overseas computers. The information included payments for council tax, business rates, parking fines and rent, as well as some transaction details relating to use of credit cards for council services.

In September 2007 a credit broker, Loans.co.uk, reported the theft of personal customer data by hackers. In March 2007 TK Maxx reported that hackers had illegally stolen customer data including credit card details from its UK-based accounts processing centre.

Note how few data protection breaches result from failures in IT security; the standard of technical security around computer systems is generally good. The problems normally arise around the interface with people.

E-mails sent to the wrong address

In March 2010 the Highland Council was found to be in breach of the DPA 1998 after personal information relating to members of a family were accidentally sent to an unrelated third party. The information included sensitive data relating to the health of the individuals concerned.

In February 2010 a mortgage company was found to be in breach of the DPA 1998 after an e-mail containing the names, addresses and details of the mortgage accounts relating to more than 15,000 people were sent to the wrong e-mail address. The information was neither password protected nor encrypted.

In the same month, another mortgage company was found to be in breach of the DPA when personal information relating to more than 15,000 mortgage accounts was e-mailed to a member of the public in error. The information included details of arrears as well as other information. It was neither password protected nor encrypted.

Failure to process fairly and in accordance with subject rights

In March 2010 SAS Fire & Security Systems Ltd and Direct Response Security Systems Ltd were found to be in breach of the Privacy and Electronic Communications (EC Directive) Regulations[1] by making cold calls, marketing without consent.

In September 2008, the Information Commissioner chastised the Liberal Democrat political party for using contact details without due authority when making telephone calls to 250,000 householders to play a recorded message about their policies and aims. The automated calls were made for the purpose of direct marketing – promoting the aims and ambitions of the Liberal Democrats – in breach of the Privacy and Electronic Communications (EC Directive) Regulations 2003.

In June 2007 the Information Commissioner announced that mobile phone operator, Orange, was in breach of the DPA 1998 in the way it processed customer personal information. New members of staff at Orange were allowed to share user names and passwords when using the customer information system. In the same month the Information Commissioner's Office (the ICO) found that a home shopping company, Littlewoods, had failed to observe its customers' right to stop the use of their personal data for direct marketing purposes.

Theft and fraud

In May 2007 Cable & Wireless served an injunction on a former executive employee relating to the theft of a customer database. The customers are now being targeted by credit card fraudsters based in Pakistan.

It is noticeable how few data protection breaches are down to malicious intent. Most are the result of either reckless or negligent acts.

Failure to delete or dispose of personal data safely

Following the collapse of Woolworths in 2008 till receipts containing customer credit card details were found in a skip outside one branch as untrained and demoralised staff cleared out the building.

In August 2008 Royal Bank of Scotland plc and other financial institutions were embarrassed by information relating to credit card applications turning up on the hard drive of a computer sold on ebay. The information included account details, signatures, mobile phone numbers and details of family members.

In March 2008 confidential patient care records on paper were found on a roundabout in Dorset. Similarly in June 2007 confidential documents containing information about adults with learning difficulties were found in a street in Lincoln near a social education centre.

In May 2007 a computer sold on ebay was found to contain reports and details about fostering and adopting vulnerable children in Essex. The computer had formerly belonged to Southend Borough Council.

The Waste Electrical and Electronic Equipment Regulations 2006[2] require business users to recycle electronic and electrical equipment, but the cases detailed above underline the importance of making sure that personal data on computer equipment is erased completely.

Failure to keep information secure off-shore

In October 2006, following a *Dispatches* programme on Channel 4, the ICO announced an investigation into the illegal buying and selling of personal information being processed off-shore in India.

Link to breaches of the Data Protection Act 1998

All of these case studies can be linked back to breaches of the data protection principles; failure to comply with these principles is the root cause of information handling problems.

Data security

The Seventh Principle requires that appropriate technical and organisational measures be taken to safeguard personal information from unauthorised access, amendment or deletion, loss or damage. Personal information in transit seems to be particularly at risk of loss.

It was noted how many cases of lost data involved data processors processing personal information on behalf of a data controller. The Seventh Principle makes specific provision for data processors requiring written contracts between data controllers and their processors, including a term requiring the processor to take adequate security measures to comply with the Seventh Principle. Data controllers are also required to undertake security compliance checks on their third-party processors.

In some cases disclosure of information can be accidental or negligent (e.g. where a fax is sent to the wrong telephone number, an e-mail is sent to the wrong address, or the wrong attachment is sent with an e-mail). The accidental disclosure of customer information left accessible in rubbish bins or skips is a fairly common occurrence.

Inaccurate, irrelevant or incomplete records

The Third Principle requires personal information to be adequate, relevant and not excessive. In the credit reference industry there were many issues in the 1990s involving misleading information held on credit reference files. In the CCN case,[3] links between geographical addresses and the names and credit history of former owners or tenants were causing problems for the former residents where current residents (and vice versa) had a bad credit rating. The link with the former resident meant that the poor credit score affected their credit rating even though they no longer resided at that address or had any financial ties to the current resident. In the *Equifax* case,[4] the dispute related to the way in which Equifax responded to requests from customers for credit reference information. Its data extraction technique meant that information was supplied, although it did not specifically relate to the person who had applied for credit and about whom credit reference information was being sought.

The Fourth Principle requires personal information to be accurate and, where necessary, kept up to date. The press has reported on bank statements sent to the wrong address or wrong addressee, as well as the problems noted above with inaccurate e-mail addresses.

Unfair obtaining or disclosure of personal information

This is an offence under the DPA 1998, s 55. It is typified by malicious acts, such as unauthorised hacking into computer records. The Information Commissioner has spearheaded initiatives to investigate 'blagging' techniques: using deceit to obtain information from government agencies[5] by private investigation agents.

Poor record keeping

If good housekeeping measures are not in place to meet the requirements of the Third, Fourth and Fifth Principles then there is a risk that personal information will be inadequate, excessive, inaccurate or out of date. Correspondence addresses may be wrong, meaning that bank statements or other personal information are sent to the wrong address. The longer records are held, the more likely it is that they will become out of date.

In its report *Data Security and Consumer Communications* the FSA reported examples where their research had shown that firms had used personal data unnecessarily, or more frequently than necessary, for example:

- A large fund management firm sent out monthly statements that included answers to the security questions (including the only piece of non-public authentication information) that a caller would need to provide access to the account and effect transactions. In doing this, the firm compromised the security of the client's accounts.
- Annual pension statements that included the consumer's national insurance number, age, date of birth, and current salary – useful information to an identity fraudster.
- A major bank sent out an unsolicited financial promotion for travel insurance that included account holders' credit card limits and part of the card number, both unnecessary for a financial promotion for travel insurance.
- A range of communications (investment bond statements, with-profits plan statements and financial promotions for medical insurance and accidental death insurance) that included dates of birth.
- A firm periodically sent out unsolicited financial promotions for life assurance that included partially pre-filled application forms including the recipient's date of birth.

Transfer of personal information outside the EEA

If personal information is transferred to a territory where there are no or insufficient safeguards for personal information, there is an increased risk that the information will be misused and the rights of the data subject abused. Recent cases have shown that the security of certain data processing centres located in India has been compromised by employee theft, leading to unauthorised marketing cold calls from third parties. The risk of identity theft and fraud is also increased.

Who is likely to suffer from breaches of data protection?

Traditionally, organisations will consider the risk to themselves, to their officers and employees. These vary from committing a criminal offence, which can potentially carry a custodial sentence, to reputational risks, public relations disasters and loss of professional standing. These, in turn, could lead to financial exposure and a deterioration in relationships with clients and customers, regulatory bodies and employees respectively.

When HMRC lost CD-Roms containing the details of 25 million UK child benefit recipients, it suffered a blow to its reputation and the government suffered a public relations disaster. It brought into sharp focus the questions already being asked about the wisdom of several big database projects such as the children's database, the identity card database and the NHS project Connecting for Health.

At HMRC, the Chief Operating Officer resigned or was forced to resign. An individual's career, reputation and professional standing were directly impacted by the breach.

At the time it was reported in the press that low staff morale at HMRC contributed to the issue. Staff morale would have been under further pressure after the media attention around the breach. Generally employees want to be proud of their employer, not ashamed.

All these people were affected by the breach. We now turn to examine the potential impact of data protection breaches on those involved.

Potential impact of breaches on the company, its officers and employees

These are the risks faced by the company, its officers and employees for data protection breaches.

Committing a criminal offence

Under DPA 1998, s 55, it is an offence to unlawfully obtain or disclose personal data. Chapter 3 considered the potential for future custodial sentences for s 55 offences[6] and it was noted that in certain circumstances (e.g. involving police officers who access police databases without authority) there is a risk of a custodial sentence even under current law.[7]

It is important to remember that individual employees can be liable for data protection offences committed at work. In January 2010 it was reported[8] that a detective constable in Cumbria had been charged with an offence under the DPA 1998 after an investigation into allegations of inappropriate conduct and disclosure of information. In a separate report,[9] a doctor in Fife faced charges relating to the misuse of information held on the NHS Emergency Care Summary records. He had accessed the medical records of seven BBC journalists for his own purposes or interest, not through any medical necessity.

Financial risk

Data protection offences carry fines for companies, directors and individual employees. In 2010 the new maximum penalty for a serious DPA offence was £500,000. The FSA has an established track record of levying significant fines on member organisations that breach its rules on data protection.

Risk to reputation

In July 2007, the Information Commissioner made a speech at the launch of his annual report inn which he said:

> How can laptops holding details of customer accounts be used away from the office without strong encryption? How can millions of store cards fall into the wrong hands? How can online recruitment agents allow applicants to see each others' forms? How can any bank chief executive face customers and shareholders and admit that loan rejections, health insurance applications, credit cards and bank statements can be found, unsecured in non-confidential waste bags?

These are all examples of breaches of information security, probably the most damaging reports that an organisation has to make. The Information Commissioner goes on to say that organisations failing to process personal information in accordance with the data protection principles may not only face enforcement action, but also 'risk losing the trust of their customers'.

As a corollary to reputational risk, organisations may find that customer or service user dissatisfaction becomes more of an issue. Data security breaches in particular are often highlighted in the media and, in certain circumstances, regulators will require an organisation to notify their customers or service users that data security has been breached so that they can take action to avoid or mitigate loss or damage. Therefore news of a significant data security breach, and other data protection breaches, tends to enter the public domain. It would make an interesting study to check whether organisations experience an increase in the level of general complaints as a result of the bad publicity surrounding a data handling breach. But there is every chance that, having failed publicly in one aspect of the operation, customer and client relations might also deteriorate in other areas owing to a general level of dissatisfaction over the breach.

A further corollary to reputational risk is the potential for deterioration of the organisation's relationship with its regulators. Many organisations are directly regulated by industry bodies such as the FSA and the British Insurance Brokers Association in financial services, the Tenant Services Authority in the social housing sector, the Charity Commission, the Health Professions Council, the Police Complaints Authority and the Press Complaints Commission to name a few.

Even those organisations that are not directly members of a regulatory framework are regulated in some aspects of their operation: the Advertising Standards Authority regulates advertising, Trading Standards Officers have responsibilities across all industries, similarly the Commission for Racial Equality and the Health & Safety Executive. If an organisation demonstrates a lack of responsibility and worthiness when handling personal information, it may well be in breach of sectoral rules and codes of practice. At the very least it will be held in lower esteem by other regulators.

There is also likely to be an impact on the reputation of an organisation found to be in breach of data protection amongst its peer group. Many commercial organisations are part of a trading group; some operate under the auspices of governing bodies such as strategic health authorities or are departments established within local authorities. A data handling breach can lead to a deterioration in relationships with peer organisations.

Reputational risk is also relevant to individual members of staff and directors of organisations. In individual cases it is probably more accurately described as a professional risk. In 2006, representatives of the 11 banks, building societies and the Post Office were required to sign undertakings that data protection breaches would not be repeated. How would it feel to own up to having presided over that breach? What effect could it have on career prospects within those organisations? It is significant that the Chief Operating Officer resigned over the loss of the CD-Roms by HMRC in November 2007.

Demoralised colleagues

Even where a data protection breach involves customer data there will be an effect on employee morale. The employer's reputation is tarnished, which reflects on their choice of employer. They will also perceive the risk to their own privacy; if the organisation is mishandling customer data it raises the issue that maybe employee data is not being handled appropriately either.

Potential impact of breaches on individual data subjects

Financial

Recent years have seen an increase in identity theft and fraud. Armed with fake or duplicate documents, thieves take out credit cards and personal loans in the name of an unsuspecting individual or empty their savings accounts. With basic personal data to authenticate transactions, thieves have been able to transfer shares from legitimate owners to themselves and then sell them for cash to legitimate buyers. Financial information can be used to 'max out' credit cards over the internet. Bank accounts can be plundered and overdrafts created, leaving victims in debt. Scammers can use personal information to make fake credit cards. This fraudulent activity was the focus of the FSA report into Data Security in Financial Services.[10]

An extract from the FSA report reads:[11]

How lost data is used for identity fraud

The implications of data loss are very serious. Criminals with access to lost or stolen data, particularly highly confidential information such as national insurance numbers, payment card and banking information, can use it to commit identity and other frauds, according to the Serious Organised Crime Agency's (SOCA) Threat Assessment 2006/07. Firms have told us these frauds include false credit applications, fraudulent insurance claims, fraudulent transactions on a victim's account and even a complete account takeover.

There is also has an impact for society at large as the FSA report goes on to explain:[12]

The proceeds of these crimes can be laundered within criminal networks and may be used to fund other criminal activities, including drug trafficking, human trafficking and terrorism. Indeed, identity fraud underpins a wide variety of serious organised criminal activities, according to the SOCA Threat Assessment 2006/07.

To give an idea of the size of the problem of identity theft and fraud in the UK, statistics released by CIFAS,[13] the UK's Fraud Prevention Service, in its report *Fraudscape*[14] show:

Total fraud increased by nearly 10% in 2009 compared with 2008. ...

A 32% increase in identity fraud (where a fraudster applies in the name of an innocent victim or uses an entirely fictitious identity) has been driven by identity fraudsters targeting bank accounts, communications, and mail order products. ...

The 'typical' victim of identity fraud is still the man in his forties, though the increase in women being impersonated, or having their accounts taken over, indicates that now, as never before, anyone can be a potential target.

Findings by CIFAS[15] for the first quarter of 2010 show a 19.86% increase in identity fraud when compared with the same period in 2009; the number of victims of identity fraud has increased by more than 20% compared with the first quarter of 2009.

The impact on the individual is not limited to financial exposure.

Time and effort

Identity theft will impact on the individual in a number of ways including the need to spend time sorting out the resultant problems. Bank and credit cards will be cancelled if they have been compromised and the individual will have to request and wait for replacements to be issued. He or she may experience difficulty in establishing their identity to the satisfaction of banks and other financial organisations.

It will require time and effort on the part of the data subject to correct inaccurate credit reference information. Until a credit record is repaired, an individual may struggle to obtain credit. A poor credit reference history may also impact on his or her ability to obtain a mortgage or find a new job.

Research by CIFAS[16] reveals that it takes between three and 48 hours to sort matters out following the discovery of identity fraud.

Loss of privacy

The unauthorised disclosure of information relating to an individual may have a variety of impacts ranging from potential social stigma for some categories of data subject (e.g. ex-convicts, bankrupts, AIDS sufferers and so on) to personal harm (e.g. where the current address of people under protection such as abused wives or witnesses are disclosed).

Emotional stress

If personal information is disclosed or shared without authority there will be an emotional impact on the individual concerned. This may arise from unwarranted and unwanted publicity, the hassle involved in trying to 'set the record straight', and worry about the likelihood of personal harm or financial loss.

In cases of identity theft and fraud, CIFAS reports that the pyschological impact on victims includes fear, anger, distress and even paranoia.[17] In its report *Number of Identity Fraud Victims Reaches Record Levels* CIFAS includes comments by victims of identity fraud:

'I am at my wits' end.'

'It made me feel sick and afraid, as though I had been stripped of my identity.'

'I worry all the time about what else could happen, that I might not pick up on.'

'I felt complete shock – I couldn't believe this could happen to me. I had to get my daughter to help me deal with it – completing phone calls, etc. And I am an active 65-year old. I hate to think of older people having to deal with it.'

'I feel very anxious at home, and I feel now that I am restricted to my house in case any other documents go missing.'

'I was absolutely devastated because the person who did this to me was someone I know.'

'I am constantly stressed. I can't sleep. I've been conned by a professional. I want to see this person behind bars. She has ruined my life.'

Reputation

The Information Commissioner outlined a case in his 2006 Annual Report involving the Criminal Records Bureau which had incorrectly recorded an offence of driving while under the influence of alcohol against an individual who proved in court that someone else had used his driving licence. An incident like this could seriously impact on someone's career and ability to gain employment, or on their social and family life.

Factors affecting risk

The macro environment

The current macro environment presents a high sensitivity to data protection risks due to the rise in, and rise in awareness of, security issues relating to personal data, frequent media reports of lost or stolen data, the prevalence of identity theft and identity fraud. The incumbent Information Commissioner, Christopher Graham, who was appointed in June 2009, has a background in enforcement with the Advertising Standards Authority and will not be slow to use his enhanced powers to fine businesses that are found to be in breach of the DPA 1998.

As we have seen in earlier chapters penalties for offences under the DPA 1998 have increased. The political message is that enforcement is a key priority.

The sector in which the organisation operates is also a key risk factor. The Information Commissioner is currently taking action to remind estate agents that they should be registered for data protection.[18] In recent years the Commissioner has targeted solicitors, members of Parliament and private investigators regarding notification. The current focus of regulatory criticism is the NHS where so many recent data security breaches have been reported. As all government departments are now subject to assessments (audits) they are likely to be higher risk than commercial organisations, but this may change.

Organisations may also find their risk factors influenced by other sectoral rules and regulations. The Payment Card Industry Data Security Standards set high security targets for debit and credit card information. Any organisation that processes this type of information is subject to these rules as a condition of business with the payment card industry.

Organisational factors

The nature of the operation may have a direct impact on the risk presented by personal data processing activities. Those organisations that routinely process sensitive categories of information, such as the NHS processing information relating to health, solicitors handling information about allegations of criminal offences and political parties processing information about peoples' political views will present a greater risk than say, membership organisations processing member contact details because the categories of personal information are recognised as 'sensitive'.

Those providing third-party processing services to clients also present a particular risk, especially where the clients are reputable organisations of significant size or are UK government departments. These clients are increasingly demanding guarantees of data protection compliance from service providers and will start to seek proof of compliance as time goes by, including requiring audit rights and rights of inspection.

The culture of the organisation massively affects the risk profile it presents. An organisation that genuinely tries to meet its legal obligations and takes great care to comply with the law, industry codes of practice and best practice guidelines presents a much lower risk than an organisation where requirements are labelled 'red tape' and the culture is to do the minimum possible to comply with the law. In my own experience as a data protection auditor one of the most disappointing statements to hear is that an individual employee originally came from a highly regulated environment where data protection was taken seriously and good, compliant data management procedures were in place, whereas the new employer does not have the same level of support for compliance, colleagues routinely follow bad data management practices and the individual starts to follow the crowd, forgetting the discipline that they formerly applied to their working practices.

Intrinsic confidentiality of the data being processed

Some operations process commercially sensitive data, or 'sensitive data' within the meaning of the DPA 1998, which presents a higher risk than applies to those processing less sensitive information. Corporate information is generally lower risk, except where trade secrets and commercially sensitive information is concerned, so companies that trade business to business usually present a lower risk profile than those which trade with consumers.

Some operations require quantities of personal information (e.g. membership organisations are likely to have contact details, basic CV-type information, examination results and records of any disciplinary action against members). Other operations hold very little personal information, possibly simply contact details for customers. It should be remembered, however, that all organisations process information relating to their staff and it is likely that in many organisations this will be the biggest exposure to data protection risk.

The impact of these internal factors is likely to be in respect of the potential number of data subjects likely to be affected if there is a data protection breach or in the resultant degree of damage.

Conclusion

The data protection principles set out standards for good data governance; failure to meet those standards is a risk that can be assessed and addressed like any other business risk. Risk management is a recognised and valued technique, which is easy to understand and which can be used to prioritise resources appropriately however the risk is presented. The standard model is to identify the risk, then decide its severity and how it can be avoided or mitigated.

This chapter has considered the risks inherent in processing personal information and has linked these back to the governance standards set by the data protection principles. It has identified the potential impact on organisations, their directors and managers, their employees and the individuals about whom personal information is held. It concluded by considering the factors that can affect the severity or priority of a risk. All of this feeds into Chapter 7, which explores carrying out a risk assessment.

Notes

1 Privacy and Electronic Communications (EC Directive) Regulations 2003 (SI 2003/2426).
2 The Waste Electrical and Electronic Equipment Regulations 2006 (SI 2006/3289).
3 *CCN Systems Limited and others v the Data Protection Registrar* DA/90 25/49/8 and 9.
4 *Equifax Europe Limited and the Data Protection Registrar* DA/90 25/49/7.
5 See Chapter 3 above.
6 The Criminal Justice and Immigration Act 2008.
7 *R v Hardy* CA March 2007 CA Crim Div.
8 BBC news online 22 July 2010.
9 BBC news website 5 December 2008.
10 *Data Security in Financial Services*, Financial Services Authority, published in April 2008.
11 See para 48.
12 See para 50.
13 CIFAS is the UK's Fraud Prevention Service. It has 265 member organisations spread across banking, credit cards, asset finance, retail credit, mail order, insurance, investment management, telecommunications, factoring and share dealing. Members share information on fraud in the fight to prevent further fraud.
14 The report depicts the UK's fraud landscape in 2009.
15 Press release *Fraud Continues to Pose Problems in 2010*.
16 *The Anonymous Attacker* published October 2009.
17 *Ibid*.
18 Autumn 2010.

7 Conducting risk assessments

Introduction

In his speech to RSA Conference Europe on data breaches,[1] the then Information Commissioner Richard Thomas said:

> The number of breaches brought to our attention is serious and worrying. I recognise that some breaches are being discovered because of improved checks and audits as a welcome result of taking data security more seriously. But the number notified to us must still be well short of the total. How many PCs and laptops are junked with live data? How many staff do not tell their managers when they have lost a memory stick, laptop or disk? How many organisations decide not to tell us? Many losses are simply undetected. Much more worrying is where – in an age of ever-increasing cyber-crime, illegal access and identity theft – organisations are not even aware that personal information which they hold has been stolen, obtained by fraud or otherwise fallen into the wrong hands. Worse still, there are still organisations which are not aware of the risks that they face with any collection of data and have not taken adequate steps to deal with those risks. Worst of all, are those organisations who have simply failed to understand just how much personal information they are accumulating through more and more and ever-cheaper technology. Much is said and written about information being a valuable asset. It is also a toxic liability.

These are the problems that point to serious, high level, systemic failures: many data losses are undetected, organisations are sometimes unaware that personal information has been stolen, that they are unaware of the risk that managing personal information involves and some have even failed to understand how much personal information they are accumulating. Earlier chapters have identified the high-level solution to these problems: organisations need a system of control for data protection compliance. The system of control starts with buy-in at senior management level and continues with a risk assessment of the risks inherent in processing personal information specific to the organisation and its operations.

Identifying the risks

Chapter 6 examined some of the risks against the background of the data protection principles. The principles provide a framework against which to identify risk when conducting a risk assessment, for example when undertaking a Privacy Impact Assessment (PIA) where the full implications of personal data processing can only be guessed at. In practice, in an operational environment, an audit would be required to identify what processing is being undertaken and all the relevant circumstances but even so, the principles form a framework for the audit questions as follows:

Fair processing – First Principle

What processing is being undertaken?
Why is processing being undertaken?
Is the processing both lawful and within the organisation's authority?
Who are the data subjects and any other stakeholders?
What type of information is being collected?
Where is its source?
Who is it shared with?
How have processing activities been communicated to data subjects? And when?
Is the data protection registration up to date and complete?
How are marketing consents being managed?
Are there other aspects of the operation that require consent, for example use of photographs?
Are any 'sensitive' categories of data processed?
Are there policies and procedures to adequately cover the above issues?
Is there any monitoring of the effectiveness of these policies and procedures?

Staying within original purpose description – Second Principle

What processing is being undertaken? Do any secondary activities involve personal data?
Why is processing being undertaken? Are any secondary purposes being met?
How are new initiatives and developments monitored to identify any potential data protection issues?

Information to be adequate, relevant and not excessive for the purpose – Third Principle

How much information is being held?
Is it all relevant?
Are data minimisation principles being observed? How often are application forms etc reviewed to check that questions are still relevant?
Is access to information restricted on a 'need to know' basis?

Are policies and procedures documented to evidence compliance with these issues?

Are policies and procedures monitored to ensure they continue to be effective in practice?

Information to be accurate and, where necessary, up to date – Fourth Principle

What systems are in place to ensure accuracy?

What checks are made on accuracy?

Who is information shared with?

Are policies and procedures in place to cover these issues?

Is any monitoring undertaken to ensure that policies and procedures are effective in practice?

Information not to be retained longer than is necessary for the purpose – Fifth Principle

Is there a data retention policy in place specifying how long information is to be kept?

How long is the information really needed?

How is that justified?

Is data classified (i.e. confidential, commercially confidential, secret etc) Does the classification affect retention periods?

How long is data being retained?

How is information deleted or destroyed at the end of the agreed retention period?

Do the data classifications set standards for data deletion techniques?

Are good housekeeping practices being followed (i.e. is there document management specifying how long documents should be kept, regular purging of files, managed procedure for deleting leaver files on personal drives)?

Are there confidential waste bins accessible to staff who need to destroy confidential documents?

Is there any monitoring of any of the above in practice?

How are changes agreed to documented procedures?

Information to be processed in accordance with subject rights – Sixth Principle

Is there a procedure to manage the exercise of subject rights?

Are the procedures documented?

Have staff been trained to recognise the exercise of subject rights?

Is a log maintained of the exercise of subject rights? Is it monitored to identify trends and problems?

Information to be held securely – Seventh Principle

Is there an IT security policy? Does it contain the standard elements of an IT security policy (e.g. password control, firewall and virus controls, back up, acceptable use)?

Is data classified (i.e. confidential, commercially confidential, secret etc)? Does the classification inform the level of security required for that information?

How is the building secured?

Are individual offices secured within the building?

What security is there for paper files within the building (e.g. locking filing cabinets, clean desk policy, key management policy)?

How is access to the building controlled?

How is access to computer systems controlled?

How is security maintained for information taken out of the office (e.g. laptops, blackberries, home and field workers)?

Are there procedures to control shared working facilities such as hot-desking, shared printers and photocopiers?

Do staff whose role involves confidential discussions face to face or on the telephone have access to a private space to carry out this part of their role, particularly in open plan offices?

How is data moved around, especially outside the organisation? How is it kept secure while in transit?

How is confidential waste paper destroyed?

How is old IT equipment disposed of? Are there adequate checks to ensure that personal information has been deleted from the hard drive before recycling?

Is there an outsourcing policy? Does it cover the data protection points at the stages of contractor selection and entry into formal contract and on a continuing basis?

Does the organisation act as an outsource service provider, a 'data processor' within the meaning of the DPA?

Is there any monitoring of the effectiveness of policies and procedures controlling security management?

Information not to be transferred outside the EEA – Eighth Principle

Are any transfers of personal information made to 'third countries'?

What steps have been taken to authorise the transfer to meet the requirements of the Eighth Principle?

Are there any reasons in practice why the transfers should not be made (e.g. security issues or loss of confidence in the transferee)?

General issues

Have staff received any training on data protection and their obligations under the DPA or risk awareness training?

Do staff know to whom they should refer any queries about data protection within the organisation?

Are staff adequately supported with written data protection policies and procedures?

Are paper files held in a 'structured' filing system within the meaning of the Act as interpreted by the courts in *Durant v FSA*?

Has the organisation had any breaches of security or confidentiality? If so, in what circumstances? What action has been taken to prevent any recurrence?

What are the organisation's biggest concerns in relation to the security and confidentiality of personal information?

Assessing the likely impact of incidents

Risk management means identifying the potential risks, quantifying them and assessing the damage likely to result from an incident. In the last chapter we considered the factors that affect the organisation's approach to risk. These are general factors; there will be more specific risk factors attached to particular data processing activities. The general factors include those in the macro environment such as the current focus of the regulator or the media, which are security and enforcement. So that means security in general is a high priority, likewise any potential for a breach that could be brought to the attention of the regulator.

There are general factors that are specific to the organisation such as its culture, how much risk the senior management is prepared to accept, whether the organisation operates in a regulated environment and whether it is a service provider; increasingly clients are demanding guarantees of compliant data processing.

The questions to consider in relation to the specific risks presented by aspects of data management are: How likely is it that a breach will occur? What is the potential impact of that breach in terms of the number of data subjects affected and the seriousness of the resultant damage?

The remainder of this chapter considers the specific risks presented by aspects of data management in a series of case studies.

Examples of risk analysis in various sectors

Membership records

What processing is being undertaken and why? The focus here is on the processing of personal information relating to members either of an association, a professional body, a charity or even shareholders of a limited company. The processing is necessary to maintain an up-to-date record of current and possibly former members for statutory, regulatory and administration purposes.

Is the processing both lawful and within the organisation's authority? The objective is lawful but it also depends on the conditions of any founding charter or the organisation's articles of membership. For example, there may be a condition that specifies a maximum number of members at any one time; to exceed that number would be outside of the organisation's authority and therefore unlawful within the meaning of the First Data Protection Principle.

Who are the data subjects and any other stakeholders? Data subjects are members, current, former and prospective. Family details may also be recorded (e.g. family membership of the National Trust necessitates providing names of family members). Members may appoint representatives; perhaps they are resident overseas or have powers of attorney in place.

What type of information is being collected? The basic details required are name and contact details, but this may be supplemented with information relating to qualifying criteria such as number of shares held by shareholders, examination qualifications and the examining body for professional bodies and other qualification criteria. Dates of joining as a member and key events and transactions in the lifetime of the membership will also be recorded, together with details of any contact between the member and the organisation. Professional bodies and those involved in regulatory activities will also need to keep details of any disciplinary incidents. Financial information will be collected where membership involves payment of a fee and annual renewals.

What is the source of the information? Most information will be provided direct by the data subject but some may be sourced from third parties (e.g. examining bodies will supply details of examinations passed, or a stockbroker may notify the sale or purchase of shares by a shareholder).

Who is it shared with? This is information that may be shared for legal and regulatory purposes. In the past some membership information has been generally available to other members, say of professional bodies, but this practice has more recently become restricted and usually only the details of those members who speci -fically agree to be contacted by other members are shared. Other optional information is the member's mailing preferences. Although members cannot opt out of receiving mail for purposes of administration in connection with their membership, they can choose whether or not to be advised of 'member offers', goods and services provided by the organisation or third parties which are marketed to members.

Are any 'sensitive' categories of data processed? Potentially there would be; details of criminal convictions and alleged offences will be required by professional bodies in relation to their members, as it is essential information when considering the suitability of the individual for membership on a continuing basis.

Fair processing risks

From the circumstances outlined above risks are:
- The processing may be outside the organisation's authority generally or because it has not established a condition for fair processing per Sch 2 of the Act.

- The processing may be outside the organisation's authority because the privacy notice provided to the data subject may not be complete. The Notice needs to explain how personal information will be used, including the circumstances in which it will be disclosed. It also needs to explain how details relating to other stakeholders may be used.
  - The processing of personal information for direct marketing purposes may be outside the organisation's authority because the data subject has not consented to the activity, or he has consented and then changed his marketing preferences.
  - There is also a risk that individual members may not have access to the privacy notice at the specified time: before any personal data was collected.
  - It is highly likely that the wording of privacy notices has changed over time; there is then a risk that the organisation has not been able to track which version has been given to which member. Where it has tracked the timing of changes the membership database must be subdivided accordingly. This is a priority as this information is likely to be in the public domain, printed on the website, or reviewed by members. If the privacy notice is inadequate it compromises the organisation's authority to hold and use that information. The Information Commissioner and the courts can force data controllers to delete databases on grounds of unfair processing.
- The use of sensitive data needs to be covered by one or more conditions for fair processing set out in Sch 3 of the Act. These are restrictive and the most applicable in these circumstances is consent. If the sensitive data was provided by the data subject then consent can be inferred, but if it was provided by a third party then consent needs to be specifically obtained.
- The data protection registration should mirror the activities of the organisation as described above and to some extent the privacy notice. There is a risk that it is not up to date and complete simply due to passage of time and 'function creep'. This means that personal information is being used for slightly different purposes than previously. This is a high priority risk as the register is in the public domain and therefore easy to check.
- There is a risk that marketing consents are not being managed. Marketing preferences need to be respected and the opportunity provided for members to change them. This is a high priority risk because unwanted marketing material will irritate some data subjects to the point that they will complain to the regulator.
- There is a risk that new processing activity may be introduced without realising that there are fair processing implications, for example sharing member data with local branch chairmen or volunteers.

Proportionality and data minimisation

There is a risk that too much information is being held. Some of it may be irrelevant due to the passage of time or changes in policy. There is a risk that information may be too widely available within the organisation (e.g. the finance team do not require details of examination results or disciplinary action to assess membership fees (although the fact that examinations have been passed or the outcome of disciplinary action may affect member status and ultimately, fees)).

There is also a risk that not enough information is available (e.g. updating details of powers of attorney or posting addresses, or marketing preferences).

Accuracy of information

There is a risk that information is not accurate – members may have moved house, or changed status without informing the organisation.

Data retention

There is a risk that the periods for which personal information is retained in practice do not match the data retention policy. Where possible, automated data deletion facilities should be used. There is a risk that data retention periods are unjustifiable in practice. Data may be at risk of theft or loss when being deleted or destroyed at the end of the agreed retention period. Some databases or spreadsheets may be overlooked when purging electronic files. Files that were created by employees who have left the organisation may still be on the hard drive of their work computers.

Subject rights

There is a risk that the exercise of subject rights may not be recognised by staff who may simply be unaware of the process to manage the exercise of subject rights so that requests are not dealt with correctly or in the right timescale. This is a high priority risk because a data subject who exercises their rights under the DPA 1998 is awaiting a response from the organisation and may take a complaint further if the organisation fails to respond. Many subject access requests are made as part of a general process of complaint therefore it is fair to assume that the data subject is already critical of the organisation and disposed to complain.

Data security risks

There is always a risk that personal information will escape from the control of the organisation due to malicious acts such as theft, or reckless acts such as downloading information to insecure media or sending it unencrypted by e-mail or on

CD-Roms in the post. Data security risks are high priority as lost or stolen data may get into the wrong hands and the ramifications can be significant for both organisation and data subjects.

- There is the risk that the higher standards required by the payment card industry may not be met in relation to financial data. This is a high priority risk as failure to meet data security standards will compromise the organisation's relationship with its sponsoring merchant bank and it may lose its facility to process debit and credit cards.
- There are risks around controlling access to systems and to buildings and individual paper files.
- Data is particularly vulnerable when taken out of the office and when sharing facilities within the office.
- Open plan working brings the risk that confidentiality may not be maintained.
- Recycling old IT equipment carries risks if the hard drives are not adequately processed to remove all traces of personal data.
- Using service providers to process personal data on behalf of the organisation involves various risks:
  - the contractor may fail to provide the service;
  - his security arrangements may not be adequate;
  - he may sub-subcontract the work without authority and without conducting appropriate security checks;
  - the contracts may not meet the requirements of the Seventh Principle;
  - data may be transferred outside the EEA without authority and without meeting adequacy requirements;
  - the data is vulnerable in transit.
- Acting as an outsource service provider or data processor carries the risk of failing to provide the service and failing to meet required security standards.

The transfer of personal information outside the EEA

- Membership records may be accessible worldwide via the website. This needs to be explained to members in the privacy notice.
- Blog sites and other membership websites where input is sought from members again are usually accessible worldwide; there is a risk that the organisation has failed to make members aware of this.
- There is a risk that transfers of information to branch offices located in third countries do not comply with the Eighth Principle.
- There is a risk that transfers of information to third-party processors located in third countries do not comply with the Eighth Principle.

Risks specific to the organisation

The type of organisation, its staff and its culture will present their own risks. For example there may be a risk due to:

- poor leadership and management;
- forceful senior managers who resist change and/or see compliance as 'red tape';
- territorialism, managers not seeing the big picture or refusing to cooperate outside their own 'area';
- low morale among the workforce;
- low risk awareness;
- inadequate staff training on privacy and confidentiality issues;
- poor staff loyalty;
- under spend on IT systems to keep pace with developments in technology or on building security due to pressure on budgets;
- the organisation locating its operations in a rough district.

These risks are common to all the following case studies; only where they present a particular issue are they restated below.

Paper records in the NHS

Maintaining records on paper involves a variety of risks that can be amply illustrated by considering the NHS sector. The NHS is one of the sectors at the forefront of government attention and there are frequent initiatives to improve service delivery and so on. It is also a high-risk sector which is currently experiencing a lot of data security incidents involving patient records. Under the Caldicott rules, data security breaches must be reported to the individuals concerned so many of them reach the press. In April 2010 the ICO said that the NHS had reported more than 30% of the total number of data security breaches since the end of 2007.[2] In June 2010 the ICO issued a press release stating that it had grave concerns about the level of data breaches in the NHS.

What processing is being undertaken and why? Processing involves the administration of patient care records in a hospital and it is necessary to arrange patient appointments, assist in the provision of clinical care of patients and to record any such interaction with the patient. Patient histories may be useful as case studies; these are published by the hospital or its professional contractors.

The processing as described is lawful and within the organisation's authority.

The data subjects are patients. Other stakeholders might include carers and professionals associated with the hospital.

What type of information is being collected? Name and patient contact details, details of medical history and medical treatment provided together with dates. Professional opinions may be recorded and there may be images such as X-rays on file.

What is the source of the information? Very little of the information will be obtained direct from the individual data subject. The referring doctor will supply some information and some information will be in the form of professional opinions.

Who is it shared with? Following treatment, the information may be shared with a variety of other NHS bodies for aftercare and support. From time to time circumstances may require that limited information is shared with the police, either because a hospital worker has been assaulted or because of the circumstances and type of injury treated.

How have processing activities been communicated to data subjects? Most GPs surgeries publish privacy notices. Generally hospitals rely on the fact that their processing of personal information is undertaken for the obvious purpose of patient care.

Are any 'sensitive' categories of data processed? Most of the information processed will be sensitive data.

How much information is being held? There will be significant quantities of information recorded and kept. In the matter of patient care there is a liability issue requiring information to be kept on the basis that it might be relevant to treatment.

Is access to information restricted on a 'need to know' basis? This is a cornerstone of the new electronic patient care records but harder to enforce in respect of paper records.

Data retention policies are likely to be a hot topic in hospitals. There is the liability issue that will make hospital administrators err on the side of data retention, but storage space may also be an issue when considering how long to retain bulky paper files.

Security is likely to be an issue for significant quantities of paper records. Hospital buildings are not secure as they are accessible at most times to members of the public, outpatients and visitors. Individual offices may be secure but records are likely to be in transit around the hospital as they will be required in different departments. Keeping records secure in transit is likely to be an issue.

Fair processing risks

- As hospitals do not generally provide privacy notices their authority to process personal information is restricted to the obvious purposes of patient care and administration. The use of patient histories as case studies would have to be specifically agreed by the data subject. No specific risks here.
- The use of personal information relating to professional contractors may not have been considered and there is a risk that an appropriate privacy notice has not been given. This is likely to be low risk because the use of that information is for obvious purposes around patient care and administration.

Generally data subjects in a professional relationship with the data controller are less likely to be concerned about the use of the professional personal information than say someone in the relationship of patient.

- The type and amount of information recorded increases the likely impact of a data security breach.
- Sharing of patient information is not likely to present risks as it will be restricted to after care and well within the reasonable expectations of the data subject.

Proportionality and data minimisation risks

- Low risks due to the indeterminate nature of how much information is likely to be relevant in deciding on a course of treatment for a patient.
- Due to the nature of paper records it is difficult to restrict access to the information they contain. The records will need to be moved around the hospital, probably by porters and may be left on wards and in treatment areas to which the general public have access at certain times. This is a high priority security risk.

Accuracy of information

- The key risks relate to the accuracy of clinical records for the provision of appropriate patient care. The ramifications of inaccurate information could be fatal for the individual patient and devastating to the hospital's reputation.

Data retention risks

- This is part of the overall security risk. Data kept for longer than is required still has to be kept securely.
- There is a risk that patient files are retained after the death of the patient when there can be no further use for them. This is a low risk as deceased persons are outside the scope of data protection law.
- The secure destruction of patient records on paper is a key risk because the process involves physically handling significant amounts of paper, which has to be physically transferred to a location where it can be destroyed. Data is vulnerable in transit. There have been cases of documents scheduled for destruction being found blowing around the streets after escaping from a contractor's lorry. Most hospitals will outsource the destruction of paper records bringing in risks associated with outsourcing.

Exercise of subject rights

- Unlikely to be a high-risk area due to the relationship between patient and hospital.

Data security risks

- It has been noted that the building in general cannot be secured as the general public must have access most of the time.
- Paper files have to be physically transported to the area where they are required. This presents a security risk as data in transit is more vulnerable than when locked in filing cabinets.
- Data security presents probably the highest risk for this type of processing activity because data security incidents are extremely damaging to the hospital and distressing for the patient.

General factors

The NHS has been in the spotlight for a number of data security breaches over recent years. The Information Commissioner has commented on several occasions about failings in security within the NHS. Therefore any data security breach will receive publicity and ranks as a high-priority risk because the regulator and the press are sensitive to breaches in this area.

Commercial call centres

What processing is being undertaken and why? This will vary with the overall objective of the call centre, but let us assume that the call centre is handling incoming calls from consumers about services provided.

The processing is likely to be both lawful and within the organisation's authority as it is a support function to an overall service delivery operation.

Data subjects will be consumers of specified services which may be provided by the organisation, or the call centre may be operating as a data processor on behalf of a third party organisation. Other relevant stakeholders might include contractors who provide or support the services.

What type of information is being collected? This is likely to include name and contact details and details of the services provided. It will also include details of any complaints and a record of the contact history with the consumer including comments.

What is the source of the information? The information is usually sourced from the consumer when he or she applied for the service. Call centre staff will access the information, usually via a computer. Details of when scheduled work is supplied in connection with the services will be recorded.

Who is it shared with? The information will be shared with contractors undertaking work in connection with the services.

How have processing activities been communicated to data subjects? Most call centres will have an introductory script to recap the activities of the service provider and the basis on which the call centre operates.

How are marketing consents being managed? Where consent to direct marketing is sought, this will be done as part of the call centre script. The marketing preference is updated by call centre staff on the computer.

It is unlikely that any 'sensitive' categories of data are being processed (unless this is a requirement of the service provided such as meals on wheels or disabled transport services). However, call centre staff may record comments to help the contractors when they visit consumer premises to alert them to the fact that a householder is deaf or infirm and may not answer the door immediately.

What systems are in place to ensure accuracy? Call centre staff are generally supported by customised systems and drop-down lists are often used instead of allowing free text entry to avoid typing and spelling mistakes. The comments field will allow any data entry.

The amount of data held and data retention periods are usually outside the control of call centre management as the call centre provides a communication service on behalf of the main service provider.

We will assume that there is an IT security policy in place and a policy on appropriate use of IT including procedures about password control and discipline.

Fair processing risks

- As the consumer contacts the call centre by telephone there is a risk that someone will impersonate a customer either to attempt to access information or for malicious purposes.
- The services provided are usually subject to contract and call centre staff must be sure to identify the caller as a customer before discussing any issue or disclosing any personal information.
- The privacy notice is usually scripted and, in the call centre environment, which is self contained and monitored with supervisors on hand to listen into calls, the provision of appropriate notice of data processing activities is usually low risk.
- The privacy notice needs to explain about data sharing with contractors.
- If consent to direct marketing is sought, there is a risk that call centre staff will not record responses accurately, but this is a low risk.
- Sensitive categories of information may not be sought directly but may be supplied unrequested. There is a risk that call centre staff will record the

reason why someone may be slow to answer the door for example, instead of simply recording that this householder may require a couple of minutes to answer the door. This is part of the overall risk presented by comments screens; there is no way to control entries made except by staff training.

Proportionality and data minimisation risks

- As long as call centre staff have appropriate scripts, this is unlikely to be an issue. Calls follow a script and there is little time for staff to gather extraneous material. Low risk apart from the issue of comments screens covered above.
- There is a risk that scripts will become out of date and feedback on the relevance of information obtained may not be progressed between the data controller and call centre management.
- Access to information should be restricted on a 'need to know' basis but many call centres provide services to multiple clients and the call centre staff have multiple system access. This presents the risk that call centre staff may amass information relating to one particular consumer.

Data accuracy risks

- Again this is relatively low risk as call centre staff are usually supported by a bespoke computer system to prompt questions and provide drop down lists from which to select answers. The risk is in relation to comments entered in free text comments fields and misspelling or mistakes in typing.

Data security risks

- The call centre environment is usually self-contained and monitored appropriately. Supervisors are able to hear calls and are physically present to see when assistance is required. It should be difficult for staff to make unauthorised downloads of information because their workflow is controlled by the telephone system and they are in full view. Those call centres using dumb terminals represent low risk compared to many environments.
- IT will present the only security risks as call centres are usually paper free. The IT security policy may be flawed if does not cover the standard elements of IT or if informal procedures have grown up in the absence of formal, documented procedures.
- Systems access presents a risk to data security. Staff may share passwords or write them down. Staff may have access to data on more than one system if they are cross trained to take calls on behalf of more than one client.
- The call centre may act as an outsource service provider or 'data processor'.

It has service delivery risks and risks associated with proving that it has appropriate security measures in place.

Information transferred outside the EEA

- The call centre may be located in a third country and there is a risk that appropriate authorisation to meet the requirements of the Seventh Principle has not been put in place.

Marketing activity

Marketing departments engage in a variety of activities involving personal data processing. Direct mail and e-mail marketing campaigns are designed and delivered, conferences and events are managed. The customer relationship management (CRM) database may be under the control of the marketing team.

Is the processing lawful? Various rules and regulations applying to marketing activity. Some of these may be subjective, such as decisions by the Advertising Standards Authority (the ASA). An advertisement that is ruled unlawful will impact on the legality of the use of customer personal information for marketing purposes involving that advertisement. Similarly a trademark may be misused in an advertisement and again the processing of customer personal data to send them a copy of that advertisement is unlawful.

Who are the data subjects and what type of information will be processed? Data subjects are likely to be customers and prospective customers. The type of information held is likely to be restricted to name and contact details and details of goods and services provided. The marketing team may however also hold photographs for use in publicity campaigns, customer comments and complaints.

What is the source of the information? Event managers will often have details of bookings made by a third party on behalf of the delegate (e.g. a secretary making reservations for colleagues). So not all information is sourced direct from the data subject. Where the data subject does supply the information, techniques are regularly used to help ensure accuracy, (e.g. tiger's teeth on forms requiring data entry to make writing legible). Marketers also use data cleaning techniques to match addresses and post codes. Sometimes mailing lists are rented from agencies.

Provision of appropriate privacy notices may be an issue. Appropriate wording is required on every competition entry form, every conference booking form, on the website etc and in practice there are often problems with consistency. Marketing consents need to be managed. The use of personal information for marketing by direct mail requires the provision of an opt-out from marketing activity. The use of personal information for marketing by e-mail or text requires an opt-in. Two levels of authority are required on the CRM database.

Best practice for use of photographs is to obtain the consent of the data subject.

However, consent needs to be informed and specific, so the full circumstances of the intended use of the image, the purpose of the publication and potential useful life need to be carefully explained. Many photographers do not have such in-depth knowledge of the intended use of the photographs they are commissioned to take and will use a 'standard' consent form. The usefulness of such forms is questionable.

In the marketing department there will always be new initiatives and developments that need to be monitored to identify any potential data protection issues.

How much information is relevant to the purpose? Wherever possible marketers like to know as much about their customers as possible so that they can sell more products or services to the individual customer and also so that general buying trends can be identified. Information intended for use to profile general trends can quite often be anonymised so that it can be used without identifying individual data subjects.

How long will personal information be retained? Data retention is almost certain to be an issue as marketers like to keep as much historical data as possible. Again anonymisation may be an option where address details are beyond the normal retention period.

How will the exercise of subject rights be managed? There is a right to object to the use of personal information for direct marketing purposes so a procedure is required to identify and action these within, say, 28 days. It is also best practice under the Direct Marketing Association membership rules to check mailing lists against the preference services. There is a Mailing Preference Service for direct marketing by mail, a Fax Preference Service and a Telephone Preference Service.

Data security presents the same problems as the rest of the IT framework. However personal data is likely to be moved around to printers, mailing houses etc and needs to be kept secure while in transit.

These circumstances give rise to the following data management risks.

Fair processing risk

- There is a risk that processing for marketing purposes is undertaken without due authority. This is a high-risk area because marketing material can irritate data subjects particularly if they have indicated that they do not wish to receive it. Therefore they are likely to complain.
  - Privacy notices may be inconsistent in different materials and formats.
  - Appropriate opt-out and opt-in to marketing activity may not have been obtained or recorded accurately.
- There is a risk that processing includes an element of illegality, probably not identifiable before an advertisement is sent out, for example misuse of trade marks, illegal competition terms or advertisements that contravene the Code of Advertising Practice. This is a low risk, the author is not aware of

enforcement action being taken for what is a technical breach and the penalty for the illegal advertisement is usually sufficient.

- There is a risk that photographs are used without due consent.
- There is a risk that new initiatives and developments may be undertaken without adequate assessment of data protection risks.

Proportionality and data minimisation risks

- There is a risk that too much information will be held in the attempt to know more about the customer. Relevance at this time may not be considered by the marketing team if they think it might be useful in the future.

Data retention risks

- As with data minimisation, there is a risk that marketing teams will hold information for longer than data subjects would expect and this has to be justified.
- There is a risk that spreadsheets will be generated to manage a conference or event which are then not destroyed after the event.

The exercise of subject rights

- There is a risk that the right to object to direct marketing may not be able to be actioned within the required 28-day period.

Data security risks

There is always a risk that personal information will escape from the control of the organisation. Data security risks are high priority as lost or stolen data may get into the wrong hands and the ramifications can be significant for both organisation and data subjects.

- There is a risk that information will not be adequately secured in transit between the Customer Relationship Management database and the printer or mailing house.
- There is a risk that competition entry forms are not stored correctly or are not destroyed securely when they are no longer required.
- There is a risk that proper control of an outsourcing policy is not applied when using third party data processors such as mailing houses.

The transfer of information outside the EEA

- There is a risk that marketers will not recognise that the direct recording of customer views and opinions by the customer on a blog site are accessible worldwide and that a deemed transfer of personal information worldwide has taken place in breach of the Eighth Principle.

Outsource service provider

Service providers who process personal information on behalf of other organisations, either third parties or companies in the same group, are defined in the DPA 1998 as data processors and they present a certain risk profile. The data protection principles do not apply to the activities of data processors, only to data controllers. The Seventh Principle requires data controllers to check the security measures the data processor has in place to secure the personal information they will be processing on their behalf.

Clients, in their capacity of data controllers, particularly in the public sector, are increasingly demanding guarantees of data protection compliance from service providers and are starting to seek proof of compliance by requesting contractual audit rights. To demonstrate compliance with data security requirements imposed by the Seventh Principle, a data processor may be required to provide evidence of written policies and procedures.

Arguably a good service provider should recognise the legal environment in which his client operates and could take a positive position on data protection, demonstrating his knowledge of the topic and the organisation's ability to deal with it. Comfort messages could be built into responses to tender and pitches for business.

Data security will be a high priority area for those acting as data processors, particularly in relation to data in transit between controller and processor.

There will inevitably be some personal information held in respect of employees and business contacts but this case study focuses on the data processing activity.

All business processing is undertaken on behalf of clients and the responsibility for data protection compliance rests with the data controller. Therefore it is not concerned with the purposes for which data is processed or whether or not the processing is deemed fair. Data processors need no authority to process personal information except as devolved from the data controller.

The risks inherent in this type of activity are:

Data security risks

- There is a risk that the data processor will not be able to demonstrate a system of control for data security. There are business risks around documenting appropriate security policies and procedures. Without them the data processor may not win contracts.
- Building security and demonstrating the level of security is a risk. The data processor will need to show how access to buildings and individual offices is controlled.

- If any personal information is held on paper, the security of paper files will be a risk. Procedures will be required to control shared working facilities.
- IT security is likely to be a high priority risk. The data processor needs to demonstrate how access to computer systems is controlled and that all the routine IT policies and procedures are in place and being followed.
- If personal information is taken off site, that will present a security risk. The data processor will need to show how security is maintained for information taken out of the building.
- Data in transit is particularly vulnerable and presents a high risk to data processors who will not usually be the originators of the personal information. The information needs to be brought from the client securely. It may also need to be sent on to other data processors or returned to the client.
- Data security measures will be a risk area throughout the processing, including any deletion or destruction of personal information. The data processor will need to demonstrate secure document destruction procedures as well as IT deletion processes.
- There is a risk that the data processor will not observe good housekeeping practices and delete the personal information when the processing has finished. This presents a security risk and would threaten the business if the data controller discovered that information was being retained beyond the time it was being processed.

Transferring personal information outside the EEA

- If the data processor is located, or uses sub-contractors, in a third country there is a risk that the data controller may not be able to authorise transfers of personal data to it in compliance with the Eighth Principle.

Operating CCTV

There is a lot of attention concentrated on the use of surveillance equipment from the media and the regulator. One aspect of the Information Commissioner's work is to help preserve the rights and freedoms of citizens to guard against excessive use of surveillance.

What personal information is being processed? The CCTV operator processes images of individuals by means of closed circuit television cameras. When the images are recorded the DPA 1998 will apply. Usually CCTV is in operation to help secure a building, described as the identification and prosecution of offenders, but it is often used also to promote employee and public safety and it may be used to resolve issues related to damage to property, for example in a car park to identify drivers who damage other cars when manouvering.

Is the processing lawful? The operation of monitored CCTV is covered under the Security Industry Act 2001 (SIA) and operators will need to be licensed for the processing to be lawful. Surveillance activity is also regulated but we will assume that the CCTV operation is a routine personal safety and property protection measure.

Who are the data subjects? Data subjects are employees, visitors to premises and potentially passers-by. The information collected comprises images and behaviour of data subjects, also their associates and friends.

Will personal information be shared with third parties? Sometimes CCTV images are useful to the police in investigating incidents. There is a discretionary power under SIA s 29 for organisations to share personal information with the police to prevent or detect crime.

To communicate processing activities to data subjects, the CCTV Code of Practice published by the Information Commissioner requires appropriate signage. What is appropriate may vary in the circumstances (e.g. large signs above head height are required to notify delivery van drivers that deliveries are monitored by CCTV).

The operation of CCTV is a registrable activity under the DPA 1998 even if other data processing activities are exempt.

CCTV images may also be used to monitor staff, their time of arrival or departure, the length of coffee breaks etc. They may be used to monitor the times of deliveries to provide feedback to courier and delivery firms.

How long will personal information be retained? The CCTV Code of Practice recommends that images can be retained for no longer than 28 days unless the images are required as evidence in a police investigation or prosecution. Data minimisation principles apply. CCTV operators need to take care when siting cameras so that they do not record images of private property.

The principle of proportionality applies; the data controller should have made a reasonable assessment of the security risk the CCTV system is designed to combat before installing it. Also the system must be fit for purpose; the images recorded should be of sufficiently good quality to allow identification of individuals as necessary.

Subject rights apply to CCTV images and requests may frequently be received if the CCTV system is in a high visibility area.

There are security issues, and access to images needs to be controlled. Many systems are digital so IT security is required to control access, provide back up etc. Older video CCTV systems will require building or office security measures to protect tapes and other equipment.

Based on the circumstances outlined above, the following risks have been identified:

Fair processing risks

- There is a risk that signage will be incomplete or inaccurate. This is a high priority risk as the signage should be in view and is therefore easy to check.
  - Images may be used for monitoring purposes without providing appropriate notice to data subjects.
- There is a risk that CCTV images may be monitored live by unlicensed operators in breach of the SIA. The processing is then deemed unlawful.
- There is a risk that the data controller has not registered for data protection or has failed to register that the operation of CCTV is a processing activity.
- There is a risk that there are insufficient policies and procedures to meet the requirements of the Act and the Code of Practice.
  - There is a risk that the policies and procedures may become out of date.
  - There is a risk that CCTV operators may not follow policies and procedures.
- There is a risk that the CCTV images may be used for different processing purposes than those registered and explained to data subjects, for example the use of images to monitor staff or employees of third parties such as delivery van drivers. This is a high priority risk as it impacts on employee relations and may be used against the employer at an employment tribunal.
- There is a risk that CCTV images may be disclosed to the police without them demonstrating due authority to access the information. CCTV operators should ask for minimum information to identify the police officer and the incident under investigation before releasing any images.

Data minimisation and proportionality risks

- There is a risk that cameras may record images from private land adjacent to the monitored area.
- There is a risk that the CCTV system has been installed without justification based on the risk it is trying to combat.
- There is a risk that images will be inappropriately used, for example CCTV images shown in public areas such as a hotel lobby should not include images from areas where guests would expect privacy such as in the hotel corridors outside bedrooms.

Accuracy of personal information risks

- There is a risk that images may not be fit for purpose if they are not clear. Older video systems require tapes to be replaced regularly as they wear out over time, affecting image quality.

Data retention risks

- There is a risk that images will be retained for longer than the recommended period without justification.

Risks related to complying with subject rights

- There is a risk that the exercise of subject rights will not be identified and therefore not dealt with appropriately.
- There is a risk that third-party images will be shared without due authority with data subjects who make a valid subject access request to access their own images.

Data security risks

- There is a risk that images will not be held securely.
  - Access should be restricted on a 'need to know' basis.
  - Where data subjects are allowed to view images on site in response to a subject access request, access should be controlled so that the data subject does not see live image feeds or any material that is outside the scope of his request.
- With older CCTV systems, there is a risk that videotapes will not be disposed of correctly.

Pension trustees

What personal information is being processed? Personal information relating to pension scheme members, both retired and those still working and not drawing down pension benefits, is being processed for purposes of pension scheme administration and, possibly, life insurance policy administration. The data controller is not the employing company but the trustee or trustees of the pension scheme. Trustees routinely outsource pension scheme administration to third party service providers and they rely on employees in human resources (HR) to provide them with support in their role.

What type of information is being processed? In general the type of information held will include name and contact details, employment, salary details and benefit details and information about family members and dependents.

Will the information be shared with third parties? The information may be shared with HMRC and with insurance companies and brokers involved in the provision of life insurance benefits.

How is personal information obtained? The sources of personal information used in pensions administration will be both the employer, which will provide an annual list of those employees eligible to join the scheme, and the prospective member, who will complete an application form on being invited to join the scheme. This form should carry a privacy notice explaining how personal information will be used. The use of personal information as part of the underwriting process for high earners eligible for life insurance cover may not be reasonably foreseeable by applicants so a privacy notice would be essential.

Pension trustees process personal information for purposes of pension scheme administration and, as such, should register for data protection.

What sensitive data is processed? Certain categories of 'sensitive' data are processed (e.g. details of health when underwriting the life insurance risk or when arranging benefits on members' early retirement due to ill health).

Access to personal information should be restricted on a 'need to know' basis but there is an issue with the involvement of the employer's HR staff who may provide support services to pension trustees. These staff may have a conflict of interest between their role representing the employer and the work they do in connection with the pension scheme.

How long is the information to be held? Generally information held for this purpose needs to be retained for very long periods so that pension entitlements can be matched with former employees at retirement. An individual might be a member of a pension scheme at age 25 and have accrued benefits which will not be taken until age 65, some 40 years later.

Pension trustees will hold periodic meetings for which supporting papers will be produced and minutes generated. These papers are likely to contain personal information relating to pension scheme members. Other personal information is likely to be held on computer by the pension scheme administrator, unless the scheme is very small.

The circumstances as described give rise to the following risks:

Fair processing risks

- The processing should be lawful and within the trustees' authority although there may be confidentiality issues arising from the conflict of interest of members of the HR team.
- There is a risk that the trustees are not registered for data protection and that the registration may not have been kept up to date.
- If the privacy notice is not complete there is a risk that the use of personal information for insurance underwriting purposes will be unexpected, compromising the trustees' authority to process the information for that purpose.

The exercise of subject rights

- There is a risk that the exercise of subject rights may not be recognised or that the required response is not made within the required timescales due to pension trustee meetings being intermittent and the fact that the response will have to be collated by the pension scheme administrators and then approved by the trustees prior to issue.

- Where pension trustees include member trustees or independent trustees there are security risks in relation to the control of personal information which is passed to those individuals as part of their role.

Data security risks

- The IT security risks are largely around the use of a data processor and there is a risk that the relationship has not been established in compliance with the Seventh Principle.
- There is also a risk because personal information will have to be transferred from the employer to the pension scheme administrators and information is always vulnerable in transit.
- There is also risk attaching to the paper records that individual trustees may maintain such as copies of minutes and working papers. There is a risk that this paperwork may be retained unjustifiably or may not meet confidentiality standards when it is destroyed.

Data sharing

What is the intended processing activity? Data sharing is the term used to describe a regular or one-off transfer of personal information relating to one individual or a set of individuals between one data controller and another. It is usually part of overall service provision and is undertaken to streamline service provision or improve access to services. It is most common in the public sector where government agencies are under directives to work together for these purposes.

Is the intended processing within the organisation's authority? Each organisation has to address the issue of whether or not the processing is within their authority. For regular correspondents it is good practice to agree data sharing protocols so that staff know that the sharing of personal information within those parameters is lawful. There may also be human rights issues to resolve which may impact to a significant degree.[3]

Is the intended processing lawful? There are aspects of the common law of confidentiality to address. Information provided in confidence may not be used without the specific consent of the individual concerned.

Who are the data subjects? Data subjects will be any service user. There is no limit to the type of information likely to be disclosed and it will include categories of sensitive data from time to time; for example the prison service working with social services and probation officers would disclose details of criminal offences.

What type of personal information will be shared? NHS workers arranging aftercare for patients will disclose information relating to the patient's health. Housing officers at the local council will share information about substance abuse and dependency and criminal records with housing associations and hostels.

Public bodies are constantly required to report on different aspects of their operation and the service users they support to a variety of government agencies. Occasionally this may involve a new initiative or development not foreseen at the time that privacy notices were drafted. Care needs to be taken that the use of personal information for new purposes is identified and due authority sought before any processing can take place. It may, of course, be possible to anonymise personal information for reporting purposes, in which case, it is no longer personal information.

Security aspects need to be considered in the context of data sharing. The personal information being shared needs to be transferred from one body to another, which always carries risk.

From these circumstances, the following risks can be identified:

Fair processing risks

- There is a risk that the purpose of the data sharing is outside of the organisations' authority.
- There is a risk that the data sharing may be unlawful due to duties of confidentiality owed to data subjects.
- There is a risk that the data sharing may be in breach of the Human Rights Act 1998.
- There is a risk that data subjects are not made aware of data sharing activity by an appropriate and complete privacy notice being provided.
- There is a risk that 'sensitive' categories of data are being processed without meeting one or more of the conditions for fair processing sensitive data set out in Sch 3 to the Act.
- There is a risk that new data sharing activities are not adequately monitored to identify potential data protection issues.

Proportionality and data minimisation risks

- There is a risk that irrelevant information may be shared. The incident when HMRC lost computer disks with details of child benefit recipients was compounded by the fact that not all the data held on the disks was required but data minimisation was rejected by management as too costly before the transfer was made.

Data security risks

- There will be data security risks around the physical transfer of the data between the parties.

Moving office

What personal information will be processed? All IT systems and all paper files will have to be packed for the move and transported to new premises.

This is a new initiative, outside of normal data processing activities and the potential data protection issues need to be identified, for example:

- How will access to relevant information be ensured during the move? Procedures may be needed to handle queries during the time that IT systems and paperwork are not available to staff. The move might be handled in stages so that IT systems are duplicated at the new location and then, once all checks and verification processes have been completed satisfactorily, the switch from one system to the other can be made.
- How will security be maintained for information in transit? Back ups of IT systems will be needed.

Using the risk assessment framework the following risks are identified:

Proportionality and data minimisation risks

- There is a business risk that information may not be available to staff during the office move. This may result in personal information being inadequate for the purpose for which it is processed at times. The risk can be avoided by timing the key stages in the transfer to take place at night when the organisation is not providing services.

Data accuracy risks

- During the IT move any problems encountered may have to be resolved by using back-up data. There is a risk that back-up data may not be as up-to-date as the latest live system data. Back ups should be as up-to-date as possible and consideration should be given to introducing extra back-ups during the working day so that the latest possible version of systems is available to restore if needed. Back up and disaster recovery should be tested prior to the planned move to identify any weaknesses.

Data security risks

- The IT move presents security risks as data will not be accessible for part of the time. Also data may be lost and the data restored may not be completely up to date.
- The physical move presents a security risk as files might go astray during the relocation. An inventory of files should be taken prior to the move and files checked on receipt for completeness. The impact of loss of files can be minimised by keeping copies of key documents.

Implementing a new customer relationship management database

What personal information will be processed? The intention is to process personal information relating to existing customers and prospective customers for purposes of marketing analysis of trends and buying patterns and for targeted direct marketing.

Is the intended processing lawful and within the organisation's authority? The processing is lawful provided that the Direct Marketing Association code of practice is followed in respect of opt-ins for marketing by e-mail and opt-outs for direct mail.

Will the information be shared with any third parties? The CRM will only be used by the organisation, personal information on the CRM will not be disclosed to third parties.

What information will the CRM hold and how will it be obtained? For marketing purposes all the information required is name and contact details, details of goods and services provided and relevant dates of contact between the organisation and the individual. Most of the information is provided by the data subject on purchasing goods or services; some information may be collected on competition entry forms, or other initiative to populate the new CRM.

Based on these circumstances, using the risk assessment framework, the following risks are identified:

Fair processing risks

- Processing for purposes of direct marketing carries the risk that marketing consents have not been properly obtained. Without consent (opt-out and opt-in are types of consent) processing is unlawful and unfair.
- There is a risk of unfair processing if processing activities have not been communicated to data subjects. If the new CRM is being populated with new information, then appropriate privacy notices should specify how it will be used and consent sought. If the CRM is to be populated from existing marketing databases, the applicable privacy notices and consents will be the ones given to individuals before any personal information was obtained. The privacy notices may not be consistent and levels of consent may differ.
- There is a risk that the data protection registration is not up to date and complete. It needs to be checked against the specification for the new CRM and amended if necessary.
- Processing will be unfair if individuals are not able to withdraw consent to the use of their personal information for direct marketing purposes by managing their marketing preferences.

- There is a risk that there are no policies and procedures to adequately cover the above issues. Without policies and procedures staff have no support when doing their job and it is difficult to demonstrate compliance to regulators.
- There is a risk that any policies and procedures that are in place are not being monitored. The development of a new CRM could raise new issues not covered by existing policies and procedures.

Proportionality and data minimisation risks

- There is a risk during the development of the CRM that additional categories of personal information will be included in the project.
- There is a risk that some of the personal information obtained either from individuals or from existing databases will not be relevant to the objectives of the CRM.
- There is a risk that access to information will not be restricted on a 'need to know' basis.
- There is a risk that there are no policies and procedures to adequately deal with the above issues. Without policies and procedures staff have no support when doing their job and it is difficult to demonstrate compliance to regulators.
- There is a risk that any policies and procedures that are in place are not being monitored. The development of a new CRM could raise new issues not covered by existing policies and procedures.

Data accuracy risks

- There is a risk that personal information on existing marketing databases is not up to date and accurate. If that information is used to populate the new CRM it will be inaccurate and out of date.
- Again there will be a risk that policies and procedures are not in place to check accuracy and that monitoring of those policies and procedures may not be taking place in practice.

Data retention risks

- There is a significant risk that personal information on the CRM will be held for longer than is required for the purpose. Names and addresses are only current for 24 months or so, but marketers tend to want historical data for research and statistical analysis.

The exercise of subject rights

- There is a risk that the exercise of subject rights will not be recognised by staff.
- There is a risk that the procedure to manage the exercise of subject rights will not be followed.

Data security risks

- There are always data security risks around IT systems, access to systems, ability to download databases or transfer them to third parties with appropriate security.
- There are also security risks around staff who use the personal information as part of their work, for example are password policies being adhered to, clean desk policy followed, care taken when using shared office facilities etc.
- If personal information on the CRM is to be used to send out mailings, an outsourced service provider may be used. There are risks relating to the contract regulating that arrangement and to the security compliance standards of the outsource service provider.

Other risks

- Underspend on the CRM system will restrict its functionality and could impact on compliance functions.
- There is a risk of 'function creep'. What starts as a simple CRM system becomes an overly complex system, which may be capable of more than the organisation has authority to undertake in terms of the purposes for which data is used.

Conclusion

This chapter has identified some of the standard risks posed by routine data processing activities. It is similar, in its way, to the likely findings of a PIA for each of the activities detailed. Note that for most routine projects undertaken by private organisations, this may be an appropriate level of detail for a PIA. It is also worth noting that a PIA may be conducted repeatedly during the course of a project or implementation of a new sales process, for example. It is designed to highlight likely privacy impacts and these may evolve during the life of the development or new issues may arise. A simple PIA process that can be repeated periodically may be of more value to most organisations than a PIA that involves stakeholders such as data subjects by means of surveys and continuing involvement in the project.

Chapter 8 considers the tactics that may be employed to eliminate, or at least mitigate, those risks in practice.

Notes

1 Richard Thomas, the then Information Commissioner in his speech to the RSA Conference, Europe on data breaches, 29 October 2008.
2 BBC news online 28 April 2010.
3 See Chapter 4 for a full explanation of the issues.

8 Avoiding and mitigating risk: tactics

Introduction

Risk management involves identifying the risks and then employing tactics to either remove the risk altogether or, where that is not possible, to mitigate the potential for the risk to occur and/or to mitigate the effect of the risk occurring.

Risks come from the macro environment due to action by government and regulatory bodies and developments within the industry in which the organisation operates. These bodies generate laws, rules, guidance and codes of practice that set benchmarks for the proper conduct of various aspects of business. Pressure from the media increases the severity of a perceived risk as different risks are 'hot topics', increasing the potential for detrimental public relations. It is difficult to employ tactics to avoid or mitigate risks arising from the macro environment. Lobbying for changes in the law consulting on draft guidance and codes of practice are the only tools for this.

The risks arising from the micro-environment are more containable. They relate to the type of industry, the culture of the organisation, the purposes for which personal information is processed, the type and amount of information processed and the number of data subjects concerned. Some of these risks may be avoided, or at least mitigated because they are within the control of the organisation. Various tactics to avoid and mitigate the risks identified in Chapter 7 are considered here with the exception of training; this is a substantial topic and is covered below in Chapter 9.

System-driven controls

Automating processes can significantly improve the accuracy of records, limit their retention and run annual checks.

An IT system can control what data is obtained and how it is entered to the system. Specialist data collection teams such as call centres are supported by systems and scripts that, for the most part, do not allow the collection of irrelevant information. The script mirrors the system and keeps call-centre staff within certain parameters of data collection. Data entry is supported by the system with as few free text entry fields as possible. Misspellings and inconsistency are avoided where there are drop down lists from which to select the data to be entered, or databases to ensure accuracy (i.e. an address retrieved via postcode).

Keeping contact details up to date is a routine task that can be automated.

Many organisations now allow data subjects access to their own records only via a secure website link and encourage them to amend their records to keep them up to date. The system can be programmed to prompt data subjects to do this periodically. Even where automation is not possible, some tricks and tips can still be used. Earlier versions of the DMA's direct marketing code of practice recommended the use of 'tiger's teeth' on paper data collection. This encouraged clear handwriting so that staff employed to enter the details on computer had a better chance of being able to read it correctly.

The security surrounding paper files tends to be less effective than IT security. Computer files are backed up, so it is not easy to 'lose' information in an electronic document. Controlling access to IT systems is a key part of the IT security policy and can be controlled and managed more easily than access to paper files, particularly if buildings and offices where the files are held are not secure. So it follows that moving from paper-based to electronic files offers a number of benefits.

Electronic document management systems can be set up to require a document deletion date to be entered by the person creating the record. IT departments can also delete documents wholesale within parameters they set (e.g. deleting all documents that have not been opened or printed for two years).

Many call centres automate their privacy notice, reminding callers that audio records are made of conversations and that personal information will be used for specific purposes. Some go on to explain that personal information will be used for marketing purposes and that callers who do not want their information used in this way should inform the operator who answers the call. Given the definition of consent, requiring a positive indication from the data subject, it is doubtful that this is sufficient. However the automated system means that every single caller hears the privacy notice before supplying any personal information to the organisation.

IT security can be improved by setting rules for downloading information. Some organisations physically block USB ports so that memory sticks cannot be used; alternatively PCs can be sourced without USB and other connections, forcing employees to follow a procedure which requires authorisation by a manager if they want to download information from the system. Other automated security checks include exception reporting if downloads are of a certain size, or if e-mails are sent with attachments over a certain size.

Data minimisation

As a principle, data minimisation should be the target; obtain and hold only the minimum information required for the purpose. This is clear from the Fourth Data Protection Principle, which states that information should be adequate, relevant and not excessive. The principle should also be applied to user access rights within the organisation's systems. In the same way that different departments within the organisation have their own filing cabinets and access by members of other departments would need to be specifically authorised, so IT systems should allow for access rights to be granted to defined groups of users rather than allowing general access to all information. Only staff with appropriate authorisation and training should be able to access personal information.

Data minimisation should also be included in policies that relate to information handling, particularly downloading. For example, if only the minimum amount of data is downloaded onto a laptop, then only that data is at risk if the laptop is lost or stolen. IT security policies should specify that portable data storage devices such as laptops, BlackBerrys, iPads, and memory sticks are purged weekly to remove files that are no longer required, thereby minimising the amount of personal information held at any one time.

Anonymising data is another way of minimising the impact of loss outside the workplace. IT security and home working policies should remind staff that personal information should be anonymised wherever possible before downloading it to take it out of the office.

Physical security

The tactics that can be used to secure business premises include the following:
- Burglar alarms and CCTV cameras.
- Electronic systems to control access to buildings and individual offices, such as keypad entry and smartcard systems.
- Security guards.

The following tactics can be used to protect paper files:
- providing adequate lockable filing arrangements within the building;
- managing keys to cabinets so that staff only have access to information as required;
- maintaining an up-to-date inventory of files;
- using named markers to identify when a file has been removed from secure filing and by whom;
- checking contract staff and cleaning firms before allowing them access to offices where confidential data may be found;
- the provision of secure document destruction methods, either secure confidential waste bins (including secure recovery of the bins and disposal of the contents) or easily accessible shredders;
- visitor sign-in and out procedures with a manned reception desk;
- a clean desk policy so that information is not visible on desks when staff are absent;
- monitoring the implementation of policies by conducting random work station checks;
- policies to regulate how filing cabinets are locked, perhaps on a last-out locks-up basis, or a designated individual locks up.

IT security

Standard elements of an IT security policy will include:

- firewalls, protection against malware, viruses, worms and trojans;
- restricting access to data on a 'need to know' basis;
- back up arrangements and disaster recovery facilities;
- secure testing environments;
- encryption for portable devices like laptops, blackberries, memory sticks etc;
- secure and complex password policy and control of the process of granting and removing access rights;
- VPN links for staff who work off site together with the security controls for those links;
- housekeeping procedures to allow the managers of employees who leave the organisation a short, specified period in which to access any files created by the leaver to identify those relevant to the operation of the organisation and then delete the remainder from the hard drives of relevant PCs;
- IT policies to highlight that:
  - personal information is confidential, including a definition of 'personal data';
  - the use of the organisation's IT for personal reasons is restricted and outline circumstances when IT may be put to personal use;
  - certain activities (e.g. downloading games, unacceptable material etc) are considered 'improper use' of the IT systems;
  - employee use of company IT is monitored;
  - breach of the policy could result in disciplinary action;
  - e-mail is not a safe transmission facility unless via a secure https link;
  - it is important for security and systems integrity not to download software without prior authorisation, not to use memory sticks unless provided by the organisation;
  - passwords must be kept secure;
  - PC screens should be sited so that they cannot be seen from the street or car park;
  - laptops and other portable data storage devices should be secured in the office by using Kensington cables or similar and stored out of sight in the boot of the car when off premises.

Specific policies can cover the risks associated with the use of laptops and other portable storage devices, highlighting to staff the importance of data minimisation when uploading or downloading files and good housekeeping practices to remove files from laptops etc when they are no longer required. Specific policies can also cover the risks associated with home working and those that arise when sharing facilities such as printers or 'hot-desking' in the office.

Policies and procedures to secure personal data in transit might include:

- a fax policy specifying that confidential faxes must be attended at all times and that someone is there to receive the incoming fax, that it will not be left waiting on the receiving fax machine in an open office;
- a prohibition on sending personal information by CD-Rom in the post;
- a prohibition on sending personal information by e-mail except via a secure https link (a secure form of http link);
- the use of appointed couriers to take paper files or electronic files on memory stick between buildings or to service providers.

Privacy

Privacy enhancing procedures

Organisational measures to maintain privacy include policies and procedures to manage privacy by:
- Putting in place procedures to regulate how photographs are obtained and consent sought and recorded to their future use.

Other procedures such as:
- Putting in place an outsourcing policy which includes:
  - the requirement for written contracts between the organisation and any third parties that process personal information on its behalf;
  - compliance checks on the security provided by the third party for the personal information it processes;
  - clear guidance on what should happen to personal information at the end of the relationship or on completion of a piece of work;
  - clear guidance on subcontracting, particularly when subcontracting to a third party located in a territory outside the EEA.
- Putting in place procedures for the management of any CCTV scheme to cover:
  - an initial assessment of the need for CCTV and the impact of introducing a new CCTV scheme on the privacy of individuals;
  - putting up appropriate signage in a suitable location so that all individuals whose image might be caught on the CCTV cameras will be duly informed of this and the reasons why CCTV is in operation;
  - identifying when SIA licensed operators might be required;
  - notification of the operation of the CCTV scheme to the Data Protection Registrar and procedures to keep the registration entry up to date;
  - keeping policies and procedures up to date;
  - monitoring to ensure that CCTV operators follow the policies and procedures in practice;
  - access to CCTV images to third parties including the police, data subjects making subject access requests and other third parties such as insurance companies;

- the targeting of cameras so that they do not record images from private land adjacent to the monitored area;
- the monitoring of image quality to ensure that records are fit for the purpose;
- the routine deletion of CCTV images to meet data retention standards;
- ensuring appropriate security for CCTV recordings; and
- appropriate use of CCTV images.

Privacy enhancing technologies

The Information Commissioner describes a PET[1] as something that:

- reduces or eliminates the risk of contravening privacy principles and legislation;
- minimises the amount of data held about individuals;
- empowers individuals to retain control of information about themselves at all times.

A PET is:

> ... any technology that exists to protect or enhance an individual's privacy, including facilitating individuals' access to their rights under the Data Protection Act 1998

The Information Commissioner's Office's (the ICO) guidance note *Privacy Enhancing Technologies* describes them as serving a dual role; they can assist compliance within organisations, and can also empower individuals by giving them easier access to and control over personal information that relates to them.

Privacy enhancing technologies probably describe many of the system-driven controls outlined above, but the technical definition of PETs has traditionally referred to pseudonymisation tools which allow individuals to withhold or mask their true identity. This type of technology has been used in services such as PayPal where the individual deals with a trusted intermediary who verifies the identity of that individual to third parties without disclosing personal information. The transaction is undertaken through the medium of the trusted intermediary.

The Information Commissioner encourages a wider approach to the use of PETS. He says they could include:

- encrypted biometric access systems to allow fingerprint recognition to authenticate identity without retaining the fingerprint;
- secure online access for individuals to check their own personal information for accuracy or to make changes;
- software which matches privacy policies on websites with the users browser settings and highlights clashes;

- electronic privacy policies that attach to personal information preventing it being used in any way that is not compatible with the privacy policy.

In practice, technological developments will be made which will facilitate privacy controls as long as systems designers are aware of the need for them and organisations are prepared to pay for their development and application.

PETs have also occupied the Article 29 Working Party. In an Opinion adopted on 23 January 2004 on *Trusted Computing Platforms and in particular on the work done by the Trusted Computing Group* the potential for using trusted computing platforms for security applications was considered to be significant. However PETs have been rolled into the privacy by design programme.

Privacy by design has been designed to encourage public authorities and private organisations to ensure that privacy concerns are identified and addressed from first principles as IT systems are developed.[2]

In the foreword to *Privacy by Design*, the then Commissioner Richard Thomas, said:

At present there is an ongoing lack of awareness of privacy needs at an executive management level, driven by uncertainty about the potential commercial benefits of privacy-friendly practices; a lack of planning for privacy functionality within the systems lifecycle; fundamental conflicts between privacy needs and the pressure to share personal information within and outside organisations; few delivery standards with which organisations can comply; a need for off-the-shelf PETs to simplify delivery of privacy functionality; and a role for an empowered and properly-resourced ICO to ensure that organisations step up to the mark in their handling of personal information.

The privacy by design programme must encourage senior executives to embrace the idea, for Privacy Impact Assessments (PIAs) to be routinely undertaken for new developments and projects to establish stronger compliance. The ICO also needs stronger enforcement mechanisms to employ the principle of Accountability, backed up with stronger powers to investigate and enforce compliance.

Privacy by design

The Article 29 Working Party has recommended that privacy by design is adopted as a new data protection principle.[3] There is a legal way to do this: the Data Protection Directive, Art 17 requires the appropriate technical and organisational measures to protect data. Recital 46 also calls for measures to be taken, both at the time of the design of the processing system and at the time of processing. This all helps promote privacy by design, but in practice it is not sufficiently well executed to make sure that privacy is embedded in IT design and development.

The Working Party set out the general objectives of privacy by design:

- *Data minimisation*: recording and using the minimum amount of personal information required to meet the purpose for which it is processed.
- *Controllability*: data subjects have an effective means of control concerning their personal information.
- *Transparency*: requiring sufficient information to be provided to data subjects about the means of operation of systems.
- *User-friendly systems*: providing sufficient help and simple interfaces to be used by less experienced users.
- *Data confidentiality*: restricting access to personal information to authorised users.
- *Data quality*.
- *Use limitation*: IT systems that can be applied for different purposes must be able to guarantee that data and processes can be segregated securely.

The Working Party gives examples of how privacy by design can contribute to better data protection:

- Biometric identifiers should be stored in devices under the control of the data subject (i.e. in smart cards rather than in databases).
- Video surveillance on public transport should be designed so that the faces of individuals whose images are captured cannot be recognised unless they are suspected of committing a criminal offence.
- Patient names and other personal identifiers in hospital IT systems should be separated from data on their health status and their medical treatment except as is necessary for medical or other reasonable purposes.
- Where appropriate, IT functionality should include facilitating data subjects' right to revoke consent and, where consent is revoked, that should result in data deletion. Too many systems currently do not have the facility for personal information to be permanently deleted.

In essence privacy by design is a series of potential privacy enhancing features that can be developed to help protect the rights of citizens, provided there is the political will and the public finance to see it through. Statements have been made to the effect that privacy by design will be made mandatory. This may be difficult in practice; how can one determine that a system was not following guidelines when the guidelines themselves are so vague? However, IT design remains an issue when some systems do not have the facility to permanently delete records, only to suppress them and then hold the details indefinitely, which is still the case.

Privacy Impact Assessment

A Privacy Impact Assessment (PIA) is the phrase used to describe a risk management technique designed to assess the privacy issues raised by any given set of circumstances (e.g. a new project, development, partnership, or other initiative such as moving office or installing CCTV).

The Information Commissioner says:

> Privacy can be approached as a corporate responsibility, much as ethical and environmental issues are handled. Alternatively, it can be viewed as a risk that threatens the fulfillment of the organisation's objectives.[4]

A PIA can identify fair processing risks such as:
- the risk of processing outside the organisation's authority either generally (particularly key for public bodies) or specifically in relation to the fair processing requirements of the First Data Protection Principle namely:
  - meeting the conditions for fair processing personal data in Sch 2;
  - meeting the conditions for fair processing sensitive data in Sch 3;
  - ensuring that marketing consents are properly obtained initially and maintained thereafter;
  - maintaining an up-to-date data protection registration; and
  - ensuring that all data subjects have been given an accurate and complete privacy notice.
- the risk that personal information may be shared in breach of a duty of confidentiality or in breach of human rights.
- risks related to record keeping – proportionality, accuracy, data retention and data security:
  - ensuring that colleagues are aware of the principle of data minimisation, the need to specify the purposes for which personal information will be processed and that it cannot be held on the basis that it might be useful in future;
  - putting contingency plans in place to ensure that access to vital information is maintained during disaster recovery or even an office move;
  - being aware of the possibility of 'function creep' where the use of personal information evolves into new processing purposes over time;
  - ensuring that appropriate security measures are put in place according to the type and amount of personal information to be processed.
- risks related to the transfer of personal information outside the EEA:
  - identifying any potential for records to be transferred to third countries or otherwise made accessible worldwide, for example via the website or a multinational organisation's internal intranet.

The PIA should be carried out at an early stage of the project and it is distinguished from a compliance check carried out at the end of the project. The process starts with a 'screening' to decide if a PIA is required. The first step is a project outline, accepting that the detail of the project will not be fully determined or determinable, using what there is available to describe the project. The second, step undertakes a stakeholder analysis; this means identifying those parties who have an interest in the project. The third step is an environmental scan, a check on the macro-environment (i.e. to identify if any similar projects have been run before which will have generated information that can advise this project). Have any articles been written which are relevant or research undertaken? This will determine whether or not a PIA is appropriate. Any project that involves using personal information in a way that is new to the organisation will probably benefit from a PIA.

The ICO then recommends that organisations decide if a full PIA is required, or if a small-scale PIA will suffice. Privacy laws are wider than just the DPA 1998 and the ICO recommends that organisations also consider:

- The Human Rights Act 1998;
- The Regulation of Investigatory Powers Act 2000 and the Lawful Business Practice Regulations 2000;[5]
- the Privacy and Electronic Communications Regulations 2003;[6]
- the Data Retention (EC Directive) Regulations 2007;[7]
- statutes that provide authority for organisations to trade or function (e.g. the Insurance Companies Act, statutes creating government agencies and sectoral legislation such as the Financial Services and Markets Act 2000);
- statutory codes (e.g. the Information Commissioner's CCTV Code);
- sectoral codes (e.g. the ABI Code);
- common law duties of confidentiality;
- industry standards, industry codes and professional codes of conduct.

Overview

Projects with substantial privacy implications require a comprehensive PIA process to ensure that the issues are understood and addressed and that the risks are managed. It is a disciplined process involving analysis of technologies and business processes and consultation with stakeholders.

The outcomes of an effective PIA process are:

- the identification of the project's privacy implications;
- that all stakeholders understand those implications;
- identifying and considering alternatives where the privacy implications are severe;
- considering how potential negative implications for privacy can be avoided or mitigated;
- documentation and publication of a PIA report for future reference.

The investment of time and resources in the PIA will depend on the size and complexity of the project and the privacy implications it raises.

Conducting a PIA

There is guidance from the ICO on PIAs, *Privacy Impact Assessment – An Overview* and *Privacy Impact Assessment Handbook Version 2.0*. Part II of the *Handbook* is described by the ICO as 'a practical 'how to' guide on the PIA process.

In general terms the questions to consider when conducting a PIA are those that are set out in Chapter 7 as the elements of conducting a risk assessment. The data protection principles give the structure for the questions and there are examples of the type of risks different processing activities present at the end of that chapter. A final question would be to ask whether any exemptions apply to the proposed processing activity. The exemptions generally apply to exempt the processing from one or more of the data protection principles; very few exemptions apply to the Act as a whole.

Factors affecting choice of tactics

There are a variety of factors that will influence the choice of tactics to avoid or mitigate the risk presented. There will be internal factors to consider such as the type of information held (e.g. there is a significant difference between the following categories of information and one would expect different tactics to secure these sets of information):

- information about corporate clients;
- human resources information about colleagues;
- data relating to vulnerable Housing Association clients; or
- medical data relating to cancer patients.

The nature of the organisation will also affect the choice of tactics. Regulated firms must keep an audit trail of everyone who accesses the trading floor for example, so an access control system would be essential given the nature of such an organisation.

The nature of the processing operation within the organisation may also have an impact. In many organisations, the human resources (HR) department holds the most sensitive information. Many HR departments have restricted or controlled physical access or are laid out in such a way that members of staff can at least be seen when entering the department. Computer screens are carefully sited so that visitors to the department cannot idly read them over someone's shoulder. Paper files are kept out of sight unless someone is actually working on them.

External factors that may influence the choice of tactics to control data protection compliance include government and regulatory activity, also current industry best practice.

Monitoring implementation

Whichever tactics are employed it is important to monitor their effectiveness at controlling the relevant aspect of data protection compliance. It will also be important to leave an audit trail of any monitoring undertaken. This will help to evidence that a system of control is in place and may also help to establish a defence of 'due diligence' or 'reasonable endeavours' to many charges, including some criminal ones.

Conclusion

Consider the question 'What is data protection for?' It tries to control or change organisational behaviour so that organisations take responsibility for information handling. The strategic focus of data protection compliance has to be a robust information management system that allows compliance to be identified and managed. Within the information management system tactics need to be employed to avoid risks or mitigate them where they cannot be avoided.

The benefit of this structured approach is that it demonstrates a commitment to taking genuine responsibility towards the individual data subject. In these circumstances it is unlikely that the regulator will adopt a hard line with any technical breaches and he will, hopefully, adopt a sympathetic approach to any reported incidents.

A variety of tactics to reduce or avoid data management risks have been considered in this chapter with one obvious omission, staff training. This is the focus of Chapter 9.

Notes

1 *Privacy by Design: An Overview of Privacy Enhancing Technologies* ICO, published 26 November 2008.
2 *Ibid*.
3 Joint Contribution to the Consultation of the European Commission on the legal framework for the fundamental right to protection of personal data: *The Future of Privacy*.
4 The Information Commissioner's *Privacy Impact Assessment Handbook*, Version 1.0.
5 The Telecommunications (Lawful Business Practice) (Interception of Communications) Regulations 2000 (SI 2000/2699).
6 The Privacy and Electronic Communications Regulations 2003 (SI 2003/2426).
7 Data Retention (EC Directive) Regulations 2007 (SI 2007/2199).

9   Training and staff awareness

Introduction

The Seventh Principle requires both technical and organisational measures to protect personal information. Organisational measures cover all aspects of security. They can be very diverse but they mainly fall into three groups: policies, procedures and training. (Even technical security measures need policies, procedures, training, or all three to implement them.) Communication of policies and procedures necessarily involves a degree of training.

The Seventh Principle also sets out a requirement for employers to ensure the reliability of staff who have access to personal information.[1] Training, supervision and monitoring, supported by policies and procedures, are the key tools to ensure that employees are reliable in the work context.

There is also a strong argument in favour of risk awareness training in the context of data security. In its report *Data Security in Financial Services*,[2] the Financial Services Authority (FSA) states:[3]

> Data security policies in medium-sized and larger firms are generally adequate but implementation is often patchy, with staff awareness of data security risk a key concern. Training for front-line staff (e.g. in call centres), who often have access to large volumes of customer data, is rarely relevant to their day-to-day duties and focuses more on legislation and regulation than the risk of financial crime. This means staff are often unaware of how to comply with policies and do not know that data security procedures are an important tool for reducing financial crime. In addition, many firms do not test that their staff understand their policies.

Training is essential to raise awareness of the risks inherent in processing personal information. It is also a necessary part of communicating policies and procedures and empowering staff to question the efficacy of those policies and procedures in practice.

Training can achieve more than simple compliance with the law; it can be a useful tool to identify and manage risk. At its most effective it is a major step in establishing personal accountability among those staff whose job involves handling personal information.

Training as a tactic to avoid or mitigate risk

Chapter 8 considered a number of tactics for avoiding risk or mitigating those risks that cannot be avoided. Another key tactic is staff training. There are general issues that are best addressed by staff training (e.g. raising awareness of security risks or handling personal information with respect).

Some risks can only be addressed by training, for example in relation to the exercise of subject rights:

- the risk that the exercise of subject rights may not be recognised; and
- the risk that staff are not aware of the process to manage the exercise of subject rights so that requests are not dealt with correctly or in the right timescale.

The only possible tactic to mitigate these risks is to train staff to make them aware of subject rights and how to identify when they are being exercised (e.g. how a request for subject access might be broached in practice by data subjects). Having identified the issue, staff can follow procedures to ensure that the exercise of subject rights is handled correctly. Without training on how to make an initial identification of the issue, staff will not be able to deal with it appropriately.

Risks specific to the operation can be countered by role-related training. For example in a call centre the following risks might be identified:

- a caller may impersonate a customer either to attempt to access information or for malicious purposes;
- a genuine customer may require help making the telephone call and may enlist assistance from a family member only to be told that personal information cannot be disclosed due to the Data Protection Act 1998 (DPA 1998);
- call centre staff may make inappropriate comments in free form notes areas.

To counter these risks, call centre staff can be trained to follow security procedures to identify callers to their satisfaction before revealing any personal information. They can also be trained to confirm information provided by the customer rather than offering information from the organisation's records (e.g. 'Can you confirm the first line of your address please?' rather than: 'Is it Mr Smith from 1 Acacia Avenue?').

Training can be given to call centre staff on when it is appropriate to deal with a third party on behalf of a customer (e.g. when the customer is able to confirm on the telephone both their identity and the fact that they want a named individual to handle the call on their behalf, where there is a Lasting Power of Attorney in place, or where written confirmation of the arrangements, with appropriate security features to identify the third party, has been provided).

Procedures on how to make free form notes, keeping them professional and factual, can be backed up with training. This may be a general notice to all staff on the niceties of making notes with a reminder that any records they create must be shared with the data subject if they so request, so they should not record anything that they would not wish to share with the subject. Alternatively the training might take the form of 'on the job' supervision where the supervisor addresses a specific issue in notes made by the member of staff on a record, explaining why the notes are inappropriate and advising on how to make them more acceptable. For example, sensitive categories of information may not be sought directly from data subjects but may be supplied without request. There is a risk that call centre staff will record the reason why someone may be slow to answer the door: 'Mr Smith is infirm and takes several minutes to get to the door' rather than 'Allow several minutes for Mr Smith to respond when you call'. This is part of the overall risk presented by free form comments screens; there is no way to control entries made except by explaining to staff that the record could be shared with the data subject and providing guidelines on what should and should not be included in the records they create.

Data security risks

In the *Good Practice Note Training Checklist for Small and Medium-Sized Organisations* the Information Commissioner states:

> High-profile security breaches have increased public concern about the handling of personal information. As some 80% of security incidents involve staff there is a clear need for all workers to have a basic understanding of the Data Protection Act 1998 (the Act).

The fact that such a high proportion of data security risks involve staff means that training is an essential part of data security risk management. A quick look through recent security incidents confirms this:

- In September 2010, the ICO found that PC World (DSG) was in breach of the DPA 1998 following the discovery of consumer credit agreements in a skip near one of their stores. The credit agreements contained personal customer data; they had been kept beyond the period set in DSG's policies and had not been shredded as required by their in-house policies. Policies and procedures were in place but staff had failed to follow them, either because the policies had not been communicated or there was some other block to compliance.
- In another, unrelated incident, also in September 2010, Yorkshire Building Society was found to be in breach of the DPA 1998 following the theft of an unencrypted laptop from one of its premises. The laptop held a 'substantial part of the Chelsea Building Society customer database'. The organisation may have failed to implement a policy of encrypting portable data storage

devices but staff had additionally failed to minimise data. Potentially the download was in breach of company procedures.

- East & North Hertfordshire NHS Trust was found to be in breach of the DPA 1998 when it reported the loss of an unencrypted USB stick used by a junior doctor to record brief details of patients' conditions and treatment to hand over to the next doctor on shift. He accidentally took the USB stick home and lost it on the train. The investigation by the ICO found that the junior doctor was unaware of the Trust's data protection policies. This was compounded by the fact that he had no access to e-mail to receive reminders and updates. The Trust's policy on the use of USB sticks was not clear and there were no technical measures in place to prevent the use of unauthorised portable devices. Although the initial problem, the lost USB stick, was due to action by a member of staff, the incident demonstrates a clear failing of the organisation to put in place unequivocal procedures and to provide appropriate training to those who are meant to follow them.

- Forth Valley NHS Board was found to be in breach of the DPA 1998 after the loss of sensitive data relating to staff and patients. A member of staff had downloaded the information onto a memory stick, which was then lost; the data was unencrypted. Either there was no risk awareness training or the procedures that should have prevented the elements of this breach (downloading information onto an insecure medium and leaving the office) were not adequately communicated to the staff member, or he (or she) chose to ignore the procedures.

Data security risks are high priority because if lost or stolen data get into the wrong hands the ramifications can be significant for both the organisation and the data subject. Training can significantly reduce the risk of security breaches around building and systems access controls, data in transit and office and home working practices.

A key plank in IT security is controlling access to systems and the information that they hold. The IT security policy will usually specify how access rights are authorised and granted and the importance of password protection. Training should reinforce password protection policies: staff should be made aware that computer access leaves an audit trail and that if they share their passwords and there is improper use of the system, they may be accused if it attaches to their log in and password.

Data is particularly vulnerable when in transit. CD-Roms and memory sticks can fall out of pockets, be left on trains or get lost in the post. Staff can be made aware of security risks; for example the IT security policy should remind staff that e-mail over the internet is not a secure medium and should not be used to transfer personal information unless there is a https link. However training should also focus on data minimisation. The employee should go through a series of steps before downloading personal information to a portable storage device or onto an e-mail. The following steps will help staff to recognise the need for the procedure and know how to apply it in practice:

1. Do I need to transfer this information?
2. Does the information need to include personal information or can it be anonymised?
3. Do I need to transfer all of the information or can it be minimised?
4. What are the secure ways it can be transferred?
5. What authority do I need to transfer this information?

Around the office, training can reinforce measures designed to improve confidentiality. Careful positioning of computer screens and use of the screen-lock facility when leaving a workstation make it more likely that personal information on screen is kept confidential. It is a system control to have this functionality, but it relies on training to ensure that the procedure is followed consistently and as a matter of course. Most printers have the facility to 'pull' printing jobs when the user physically enters a code at the printer. This means that staff who share printing facilities can keep their printed documents confidential until they are ready to collect their printing. This function exists on most printers, but is hardly used, either because staff are unaware that it is available, or because they have not been trained to use it.

As well as informing staff about procedures and raising risk awareness, training can also build moral courage and discipline in individual employees. Cases do arise where managers instruct a member of staff to share a password with a new worker so that he or she can access the system and become productive. This usually happens because the manager has forgotten to inform IT that a new employee is starting. The existing employee should refuse to share his password in those circumstances; that takes moral courage and discipline. Ideally staff should be comfortable following disciplines, recommending that others do likewise and challenging colleagues who are not following them. Documents containing personal information do not turn up in skips because one employee has failed to follow the procedures; others would have been aware of the practice.

Special concerns for data processor service providers

Given that the holding and use of personal information carries inherent risks and the Seventh Data Protection Principle enjoins data controllers to make security checks of any outsourced service providers who process personal data on their behalf, it follows that service providers need to pay close attention to security issues. In practice security issues will be no different to those faced by data controllers but the data processor needs to be able to demonstrate to the data controller his security standards; again there is a role for staff training. Staff at a data processor operation should be familiar with security policies and procedures and be able to communicate these to prospective and current clients.

Who needs to know what?

The full technical implication of data protection law is unlikely to be of wide interest, mainly because not all of it will be relevant to all staff. If, however, your organisation has decided upon a strategic approach to data protection compliance, then it will be appropriate to train a designated data protection officer, officers or a committee in all aspects of current data protection law. HR professionals also benefit from training on the full range of technical data protection issues.

The risk management approach to data protection compliance will inform who needs training on which issues. For training to be most effective it should be job specific, which also fits neatly with the managed risk approach. Staff who are engaged in activities other than compliance will find training more relevant if data protection issues are linked to actual workplace scenarios; for example, IT workers who monitor e-mail traffic and content need to know about fair processing and proportionality and understand the procedures around whistle-blowing, reporting other findings and confidentiality aspects such as not discussing monitoring with colleagues or on mobile telephones in public places.

In most organisations staff require a simple training programme to make them aware of the security risks inherent in handling personal information and to guide them towards policies and procedures relevant to their work. This should cover aspects of fair processing (e.g. what to say on the telephone when collecting personal information) and confidentiality (e.g. what you hear at work should stay at work).

Some specialist activities require specialist training (e.g. operating a CCTV scheme and following procedures relating to disclosing images to the police, data subjects and third parties and managing the mechanics of the system so as to produce usable images to meet the objectives of the scheme).

In relation to HR, the Employment Practices Code[4] sets out best practice recommendations including the need for training staff:

> 0.2 Ensure that business areas and individual line managers who process information about workers understand their own responsibility for data protection compliance and if necessary amend their working practices in the light of this.

Those staff involved in marketing will require training on the fair processing elements of data protection to ensure that they understand how to establish authority to process personal information obtained from customers and contacts, what warranties are applicable when renting mailing lists, the contractual and compliance checking requirements of the Seventh Principle when using outsource service providers such as mailing houses and how to safely transfer personal information to those third parties.

The Information Commissioner's approach

The ICO's *Data Protection Good Practice Note – Training Checklist for Small and Medium-sized Organisations* sets out five key areas for staff training:

1. Keeping personal information secure. Do staff know about the following:
   - password security;
   - logging off, or locking computers when away from desk;
   - the importance of using a shredder for confidential paper waste;
   - virus control measures;
   - the clear desk policy;
   - visitor sign-in procedures;
   - how to protect confidentiality by taking care when positioning computer screens;
   - the need to encrypt personal information taken out of the office; and
   - the importance of backing up records containing personal information.
2. Meeting the reasonable expectations of customers and employees by:
   - collecting only that personal information required to meet the business need;
   - explaining new or changed business purposes and obtaining consent where necessary;
   - updating records promptly such as changes of contact details or marketing preferences;
   - information retention and deletion policies so that personal information is held to meet the organisation's business needs but no longer;
   - understanding that it is a criminal offence to release records without the authorisation of the employer;
   - knowing that monitoring will take place, the form of the monitoring and the objectives it seeks to serve.
3. Disclosing customer personal information over the telephone. Do staff know:
   - that malicious persons may use fraud and deceit to try to access information unlawfully;
   - the importance of identity checks to help prevent fraud even with outgoing calls;
   - to limit the amount of personal information provided over the telephone.
4. Notifying under the Data Protection Act. Do staff know:
   - whether the organisation is registered under the Act or relying on an exemption;

- that there is a need to monitor changes in business use so that notification can be kept up to date and accurate.
5. Subject access requests. Do staff know:
  - about the right of subject access;
  - how to recognise when subject rights are being exercised;
  - how to deal with the exercise of subject rights;
  - the applicable time limits and fees for subject access;
  - the importance of being sure of the identity of the person making a subject access request;
  - what to do if the information includes personal information relating to third parties.

This is an overall view of training requirements. In practice, it is crucial to apply the appropriate level of training to the individual role of the staff member; for example most staff do not need to understand notification requirements – this will be appropriate for more senior managers or those who conduct PIAs.

Building a training plan

The first step in developing an appropriate set of training for data protection is to revisit the organisation's strategic approach to compliance. Do data protection officers or committee members need to be trained? Also any specialist activities where staff will require training will need to be identified (e.g. monitors and marketers will require specialist training). There may also be other areas (e.g. staff in HR, payroll and pensions, operational staff in social care or social housing roles) where staff are exposed to significant amounts of personal information, information relating to many people, or to sensitive information.

The second step is to identify and consider the demands of the roles undertaken by different departments and any applicable policies or procedures. Some staff will need to be trained on the confidentiality aspects of their work as well as on security. Administrative staff may handle information about customer arrears and defaults, credit ratings etc and the data protection implications of this need to be outlined.

The findings of these two steps feed into the training objectives. These should be documented so that they can be cross-referenced frequently to keep the training programme on-target and focused. What are you trying to achieve? This will inform the content of the training programme and possibly the style and method of delivery.

Generally if key messages need to be remembered, then training should be kept as simple as possible. Training can be supported with memory aids such as posters on walls, mouse mats with key messages, visual reminders on mugs, pens, notepads etc. This may be particularly important in high pressure environments such as call centres where staff are under pressure to respond quickly to enquiries and issues.

The use of branding to help promote data protection policies should not be overlooked. 'Our Golden Rules for Personal Information' or 'Our Four Steps to Privacy' are tags that give data protection an identity within an organisation and which may make it easier for staff to remember the guiding principles and communicate them to customers and new colleagues.

It is essential to support training with appropriate technical materials such as policies and procedures. The development of the training programme should include a stage checking that appropriate policies and procedures are in place to cover all the aspects being trained and that these are readily understood. Any defects should be remedied before the training is started. Communicating policies and procedures is another aspect to consider. A company intranet is the preferred location for technical material as it is easy to follow links from one area to another, or to conduct a search to find exactly the piece of information required.

A suggested framework to train staff about a specific risk would be to outline the risk, making it as real as possible and explaining the implications of a breach for the organisation, individual staff members and the data subject; then outline the personal responsibility of the member of staff concerned in any breach, explaining about personal liability for certain data protection breaches. For example, sending unencrypted data over the internet by e-mail carries the risk of interception and unauthorised access. It is a real threat; computer hacking programs intercept e-mails and search for keywords such as 'bank account' or 'PIN number' making e-mails with such keywords vulnerable. The implication of such a breach is that personal information will leak out of the control of the organisation. It will face bad publicity, it may have to compensate customers and may face regulatory action. Staff members may face investigation and censure, careers and performance-related pay may be affected. Data subjects may be the subject of identity theft and fraud, face the loss of assets in bank accounts and suffer the stress, worry and hassle of trying to sort out the problem.

Training around fair processing can focus on managing customer expectations. The risk is that a customer will not appreciate the ways in which personal information he supplies will be processed. He may be surprised to receive information about other products or services or to be contacted by a third-party service provider on behalf of the organisation. He may feel that his privacy has not been respected and may complain. The ultimate sanction for unfair processing is that the organisation may be required to delete entire databases if it cannot establish due authority to process that information; deleting only the details of the complainant may not suffice. It will certainly have to devote resources to answering the complaint and any charges laid by the regulator. It may suffer bad publicity with a negative impact on customer trust. Prospective customers may decide that it is not an organisation that they want to do business with and go elsewhere.

Data protection is littered with technical phrases which can be confusing. Training should try to use words like 'privacy' and 'confidentiality' rather than 'data protection', and 'individual' or 'customer' rather than 'data subjects' – these terms are more readily understood. In the NHS 'data protection' has been rolled into the wider initiative 'information governance' – a good example of how an appropriate choice of words can make training more meaningful.

Maintaining organisational awareness

Inevitably data protection cannot remain at the front of all staff consciousness for very long. It will be overtaken by other business or legal needs from time to time. Even when there has been a data protection breach, the focus of managers and staff will eventually move to other topics. Training needs to be constant and ongoing to maintain the right level of awareness and attention.

As mentioned above it is useful to communicate data security as a risk awareness and risk management issue. One approach is to conduct regular risk assessment sessions at team meetings to consider perhaps a privacy related issue in the news and then translate the issue into the workplace. Sometimes staff will already have concerns about privacy or data security, which they will be prepared to share if given the right encouragement. Most people have a basic understanding of the need for privacy and many will have detected areas where security is weak. Staff who handle personal information can brief management on areas for improvement; the ongoing discussion also helps to keep awareness of data protection and data security issues high.

Training materials should be kept up to date by checking what data protection issues are current (e.g. the loss or theft of unencrypted portable data storage devices such as memory sticks and laptop computers is a key compliance issue). Also big data security issues often make the headlines and their inclusion in training materials will help to keep it current.

Imagination and innovation are vital in developing effective training; the FSA report into data security in the financial services industry noted that one building society used a handbag as a training tool; It staff were asked to pick out those items routinely kept in a handbag which could be used to create a false identity. Funny and quirky, but the key training messages will be remembered.

Transparency and communication

One current driver in data protection law is transparency and this may become a new data protection principle in the medium term at EU level.[5] In the UK the Information Commissioner speaks about transparency being a keystone of information law. The Commissioner is responsible for Freedom of Information as well as data protection; he sees transparency as the linking principle between the two.

What is meant by 'transparency' in relation to personal information? Probably the most important aspect of data protection law is the fair processing requirement to keep data subjects informed about the use of their data. It is the basis of authority on which the organisation is entitled to process personal information and it allows the organisation to manage the expectations of the individuals it deals with. This is what has to be transparent and consistent with the purposes recorded on the Data Protection Register.

There are two audiences for communicating policies and procedures. In house there are staff and externally, there are customers and business contacts. Neither audience should be overlooked. Just as the intranet is a good medium to inform staff about any changes in policies and procedures, so the organisation's website is an ideal location for information about how its policies and procedures impact on individuals whose personal information is being processed. The privacy notice is the location for this information. Not all individuals have access to the internet or use it to find out about the organisations with which they have relationships. This needs to be taken into account and alternative means of communicating key messages have to be found. Communicating with some data subjects may involve providing information in different languages or in different styles as well. In Wales, it would be essential to supply details in English and Welsh. In practice, in many parts of the country it is normal to provide details in, for example, Urdu or Hindi. Registered Social Landlords and other organisations who work with vulnerable people sometimes adopt pictorial information for individuals with special needs and educational difficulties.

Sustainability

Many organisations implement training programmes as a one-off exercise without considering sustainability. Staff turnover, as well as the need for refresher training, means that the programme should be designed to be self-perpetuating. The solution will vary depending on the type of organisation. Where staff are closely monitored by supervisors, data protection can become part of the one-to-one training or raised at team meetings. Where the staff are less formally supervised, permanent access to training material may be required, perhaps supported by knowledge testing. Organisations with in-house trainers can include data protection training and security risk awareness as part of their training matrix or skills framework.

Conclusion

There are a number of reasons why training staff on data protection issues is essential. It is a key tactic in risk management and to communicate and explain policies and procedures. It also meets regulatory requirements to ensure that staff whose job role involves handling personal information are reliable in that context.

The development of a training programme should not be undertaken without considering the organisation's strategic approach to data protection compliance as well as risk management (e.g. a strategic approach that involves local data protection champions in operational departments will require technical data protection training to support that role). Developed in the context of the overall strategic approach, training becomes a key part of the system of control for data protection compliance as well as focusing attention on likely privacy issues arising from operational activities, highlighting security risks and contributing to the personal development of the workforce. Just as data protection compliance is an ongoing legal requirement, the training programme should be developed and subsequently refined to keep staff alert to any privacy issues that impact on their work.

Notes

1 Clause 10 of Sch 1, Part II *Interpretation of the Principles in Part I.*
2 Published April 2008.
3 See para 16.
4 Published by the Information Commissioner's Office. *Employment Practices Code – A Quick Guide, Employment Practices Code* and *Employment Practices Code – Supplementary Guidance*. See www.ico.gov.uk.
5 Plans for the development of data protection law.

Part 2

Effective Data Protection: Q&A

Questions and answers

Introduction

With any legal topic it is useful and informative to consider its application in practice to bridge the gap between legal knowledge and what it actually means in the context of real life situations. This section of the book considers some typical questions that arise in connection with applying the data protection standards in marketing or HR, for example. It should provide a reference for managers who deal with records that contain some personal data and help them to balance the rights of individuals against the legitimate business need to obtain and use the data.

A. Fair processing and marketing

What is 'fair processing information?'

For the purposes of the First Principle personal information is not processed fairly unless the individual concerned has been given clear and specific information about the organisation and its intended use of the information.

This is referred to technically as 'fair processing information'. The Information Commissioner urges organisations to refer to it as a 'privacy notice' as this will be more readily understood by consumers.

What should be included in a privacy notice?

The interpretive provisions of the First Principle state that the following information is required:

- The identity of the data controller or his nominated representative.
- The purposes for which the data are to be processed or intended to be processed.
- Any other information which is relevant in the circumstances to allow the processing to be fair.

What is considered 'relevant in the circumstances' is a matter of fact. Guidance from the Information Commissioner suggests that other sources of personal information and likely disclosures of it would be relevant. A useful test is to consider whether there is any information relating to the intended processing of the personal information which, if revealed to the data subject, could affect that individual's decision to provide the information (e.g. if the organisation routinely retains personal information for an especially long period or if it shares information for purposes of national security or fraud prevention measures). These circumstances should be disclosed to the individual before they provide any personal information.

In *Getting It Right: Collecting Information About Your Customers* published by the Information Commissioner's Office in June 2009, the key points to consider were set out as follows: making sure that privacy notices are clear and honest and that they will be understood by the people they are aimed at. Marketers should avoid confusing mixtures of 'opt-ins' and 'opt-outs' and consent boxes should not be pre-ticked. Where customers are to be given a choice (e.g. whether or not to allow their personal information to be shared with another business) that choice should be explained clearly and, when customers make a choice, it should be respected. It should also be made clear to customers what information they need to provide to obtain the goods or services requested, and which information is optional.

In practical terms the requirement is not onerous. Most forms carry the company name and logo, identifying the organisation and the purpose for which personal information is sought may be in the title of the form such as 'Job application form', 'Application to social housing list', 'enquiry form' etc.

Do we need more than one privacy notice?

In practice there may be a need for more than one privacy notice because the organisation may have to inform more than one group of data subjects about the organisation's processing activities and these may not be the same for all data subjects; for example the privacy notice that is appropriate for customers or clients will not be appropriate for potential staff members because the processing activity and the processing purposes are quite different.

In certain printed material lack of space can be an issue so it may be more expedient to outline a full privacy notice in customer brochures and on the website but have a shorter form for specific material, such as advertisements, which outlines the key points of the use of personal information obtained but refers also to the full privacy notice elsewhere.

Who needs to see our privacy notice?

All prospective data subjects need to see an appropriate privacy notice before any personal information is collected from them. The privacy notice is the organisation's authority to process the personal information it intends to collect. If personal information is obtained without first providing a privacy notice then the organisation does not have authority to process the personal information except to the extent that its intended processing was obvious to that data subject at that time.

Where should we include our privacy notice?

A privacy notice should be included at any point where the organisation intends to collect personal information from a data subject. Printed materials such as application or enquiry forms, visitors' books, accident books, competition forms, and so on should all carry an appropriate privacy notice.

Where personal information is obtained face to face or by telephone, then a scripted privacy notice is required and it is useful to have a prompt for staff who speak to customers, either a cue on the computer system if data entry is direct to an IT system or on notepads or posters to remind staff to cover the fair processing elements. Many call centres used automated telephone systems to provide all callers with a recorded privacy notice, in this way ensuring that all data subjects are given the required information in a consistent way.

If personal information is obtained online then a privacy notice is required at the point of data entry or one click away. In any event the website is an ideal location for a privacy notice to provide a written record for data subjects to refer to.

What are the rules about when a privacy notice should be seen?

For processing to be fair, the First Principle requires that data subjects be provided with the information in a privacy notice before any personal information is obtained. So:

- online this means a brief explanation of the purposes for which the personal information will be processed together with a link to a more detailed privacy notice;
- on the telephone the privacy notice should be read to the data subject before any information is requested;
- on forms the privacy notice is required in the same size print as that used elsewhere on the form.

Does it matter if the privacy notice is duplicated in different materials?

The privacy notice will ordinarily be duplicated (e.g. a form will carry the wording and the same wording may also appear on the organisation's website). The privacy notice is the organisation's authority to process the personal information it obtains and the test of whether it has been provided properly is subjective. That means it will depend whether or not that specific data subject had access to a privacy notice. It is not sufficient to show that the majority of data subjects see the privacy notice before they provide personal information; for processing to be fair the specific data subject under consideration must have received the appropriate privacy notice.

As a result it is preferable to adopt a 'belt and braces' approach and possibly duplicate privacy notices in different locations and different formats, rather than to allow a small percentage of data subjects to miss getting the message at all. However ensuring the message is consistent may be an issue in this context.

How prominent should privacy notices be?

The size and prominence of subject information has been debated by the Data Protection Tribunal. In a case involving Linguaphone a notice was given in 6pt type, significantly smaller than that used for other information in the advertisement. The view of the Data Protection Tribunal was that:

> ... the position, size of print and wording of the opt-out box does not amount to a sufficient explanation to an enquirer that the company intends or may wish to hold, use or disclose that personal data....

Guidance from the Information Commissioner's Office (the ICO) states that it would be inappropriate to set down rules about the size, positioning and wording of notification clauses, so it is a matter of judgement; keeping 'fairness' in mind. However, the following are questions the Office would consider when assessing the adequacy of the prominence given to a notice:

- Is the type in the notification of at least an equivalent size to the type used in the rest of the form?
- If not, is the print nevertheless of sufficient size for the customer's eye to be drawn to it?
- Is the layout and print size such that the notification is easy to read and does not appear cramped?
- Is the notification placed at or very close to the place where the customer supplies his/her details or signs the form?
- If not, is it placed in such as way that the customer will inevitably see it in the course of filling in the form?
- If not, is it nevertheless placed where the customer's eye will be drawn to it?
- Is the general nature and presentation of the form such that it conveys to the customer the need to read carefully all the details including the notification clause?

The following are the type of questions the office is likely to consider when assessing the efficacy of notices (text taken from the ICO's web pages):

- Do the words used convey all the likely non-obvious uses and disclosures of the customer's information?
- Do the words properly convey the fact that information about the customer will be passed on to others?
- Do the words convey the full implications for the customer of the use or disclosure (e.g. that he/she might receive telephone marketing calls)?
- Do the words explain the above in a way that would be understood by the great majority of likely data subjects?

On a website the privacy notice should be no more than one click away from the point at which personal information is collected. It is best practice to require the user to tick a box to confirm that he has read the privacy notice before the data collection form can be submitted.

What records should be kept about privacy notices?

Hopefully the content of the privacy notice will not change very often, but version control records are needed so that the privacy notice received by any particular data subject can be identified.

Because the privacy notice seen by a given individual before they provide any personal information becomes the organisation's authority to process that personal information, it is important to know the content of the privacy notice each individual has been given. So, for example, if the marketing database has 50% of data subjects who have received a privacy notice which explains that personal information will be supplied to selected third parties and consent is sought to that, but the other 50% has data subjects who have not received notice of, and consented to, the sharing of their personal information with third parties, then some demarcation will be required to identify those who have not had notice and consented, to prevent the use of their information in that way.

This means keeping a version control record of privacy notices and the dates between which they were in use so this can be matched against the dates when data subjects were added to the database. Many website privacy notices include a term to remind data subjects that the terms of the Notice may change from time to time and to recommend that they read it regularly to keep up to date with any changes.

In practice for most organisations the content of the privacy notice, the identity of the data controller, the purposes for which personal information will be processed and any other information relevant in the circumstances, will not often change although the style may change from time to time.

Do we need consent to use personal information for marketing?

Yes, it is well established that consent is required to use personal information for direct marketing purposes. When planning a marketing campaign the type of consent is critical to the medium that can be used. An opt-out style consent is only valid for direct marketing by mail, telephone or fax, as long as the data subject has not requested that their personal information is not to be used for marketing purposes or registered with the relevant Preference Service. An opt-in style of consent is required to market by e-mail or text message.

The use of personal information to identify marketing trends and for purposes of statistical analysis does not require consent. Normally this kind of processing does not need the level of detail that would be associated with personal information. Customers might be grouped by postcode for example, which does not identify them individually (in most cases), so the information given is anonymised when used for this purpose.

Do we need consent to use photographs for marketing purposes?

The use of photographs and images for marketing purposes is another area where consent should be sought from the data subject. Most photographers are aware that consent of the individuals concerned is needed to lawfully take and use a portrait style photograph of one or two persons, or a small group where the individuals will be identifiable. Best practice is to obtain this consent in writing on a pre-printed form. In practice problems arise because the description of the intended use of the photographs can be too general and not sufficiently detailed. Consent needs to be specific and informed. Therefore there should be some attempt to outline the media in which the photograph will be used, the products or services being promoted and the length of time the image will be in use.

What are the issues around the medium of publication?

If photographs are to be published to a website, it needs to be made clear and an explanation provided of the fact that the images will be available worldwide, in territories where there may be a lower standard of data protection.

To help manage expectations, data subjects also need to be informed if it is intended to use the photograph on posters or other high visibility media. There is a difference between using a photograph on the inside of a brochure and using a large image on the front cover of a brochure.

Are there any restrictions on the products or services promoted using photographs?

In an old, unreported case involving the London Borough of Newham, a photograph had been taken of a young man in a wheelchair using new facilities in the Borough. The photograph was later used on a poster promoting AIDS awareness. The family of the data subject were shocked that the images were used in a way that differed so much from the original context and their expectations. Nor was it helpful that the poster implied that the data subject had AIDS. The case actually went in favour of the Council at the time but it is highly doubtful that would be the decision today.

How long can photographs be retained and used?

If images are to be used for promotional purposes the likely shelf life will be two years in accordance with current best practice. However images recorded on video for training purposes are likely to have a much longer shelf life and this would need to be explained to data subjects as part of the consent process.

Should consent to use of personal information for marketing always be in writing?

Having consent in writing means it can be evidenced, but there are many situations where consent can be inferred from the actions of the data subject; for example, on subscribing to receive a newsletter the data subject is implicitly consenting to a low level of advertising material being included as part of the newsletter. In any situation where processing is not obviously part of the subscription, consent should be sought separately.

What if consent to marketing cannot be established?

If a marketing database has been created without following the opt-in and opt-out rules then its value as a marketing database is seriously flawed. The organisation does not have authority to process the information for marketing purposes. The only use the contact details can properly be put to is a one-time contact to all those named on the database to ask if they would like to be included in future marketing activity. A positive indication of consent would be required at this point, with prospects required to respond either by mail, online or by telephone.

Can a legitimate marketing approach be made to someone who is on MPS?

The Mailing Preference Service (MPS) is a list of consumers who have registered that they do not want to receive marketing information by mail. There are Preference Services for other marketing media, fax and telephone.

Generally the fact that an individual is a customer will override the MPS registration. As part of the initial sales enquiry process the organisation should obtain the prospective customer's consent to receiving marketing material and they may then assume that customers who have already been interested in their products and services will continue to be interested. Those customers have an existing relationship with the organisation. The MPS is a general indication that the individual does not want to receive marketing material from organisations with which he does not have a current relationship.

If the organisation is specifically informed by the customer that he does not want to receive marketing material in future, then this overrides any consent obtained or assumed as part of the sales enquiry process and must be respected.

Business customers cannot register with MPS. However, since 2004,[1] they have been able to register with the Corporate Telephone Preference Service (Corporate TPS).

Can the telephone lawfully be used for direct marketing purposes?

Yes, provided prospective customers have consented to the use of their personal information by the organisation for direct marketing purposes and they have not subsequently notified that they do not wish to be contacted. A telephone preference service allows consumers and businesses to register their preference not to be contacted by telephone for marketing purposes, but an existing relationship with the individual or business overrides TPS.

Cold calling people who have no prior relationship with the organisation is permissible only where there is no TPS registration. This is true whether cold calling consumers or businesses.

There are restrictions on using fax for direct marketing.[2] Consumers and businesses may only be contacted by fax for marketing purposes if they have agreed to it in advance.

Can we approach customers and prospects using SMS/text e-mail?

Yes provided you have specific consent to do so. The standard of consent is the opt-in where an individual gives a positive indication of agreement to marketing contact, for example by ticking a box consenting to receive details of products and services by e-mail or text.

What information must be provided in a marketing message?

The key requirement is to identify the organisation and the fact that it is a marketing message or advertisement. Appropriate contact details should also be provided so that the individual can contact the organisation either by mail, Freephone, or e-mail address. There should be an unsubscribe option when marketing by e-mail or text.

When marketing by telephone, again the requirement is to identify the organisation and provide an address or Freephone number if the person you are calling asks for it.

How long can I keep contact details on databases?

Personal information may be processed for as long as is necessary for the purpose for which it was obtained. The issue about retention depends on how long contact details remain valid. Most marketers would argue that home address details tend to be valid for up to five years but the period for which e-mail addresses continue to be valid may be much shorter. Experience from bounced e-mails and letters returned marked 'gone away' should inform the organisation's policy on retaining contact details.

The life of information on databases can be extended by undertaking database cleansing operations, using a third-party service to verify names and addresses; however if a prospective customer has not been in contact with the organisation for five years then they probably should no longer be viewed as a prospect.

Whatever timescale is chosen it is important to be prepared to justify it both by reference to industry practice and the experience of the organisation. The decision should be revisited from time to time to check that assumptions are still valid and experience of 'gone aways' and complaints continue to support the chosen timescale.

How long can I keep personal information used for marketing research?

Marketers may want to use personal information to analyse trends and predict market behaviour. Information used for statistical analysis may be useful for a far longer period of time than would be useful, or used for direct marketing approaches.

In many cases the personal information can be anonymised without diminution of its value for analysing trends and this policy should be adopted where possible.

The overall retention period for personal information should still be reasonable and within the data subject's expectations, but it is likely that a good argument could be made for retaining personal information for statistical purposes for a longer period than it would be used for direct marketing approaches.

Certain types of research attract exemptions from some data protection requirements, including the Fifth Principle, which restricts the retention of information. Marketing activity is not an exempt activity, but where records have been maintained for historical purposes, they may be able to take advantage of this exemption.

Do we always have to remove people from our mailing list on request?

Yes, there is an absolute right under s 12 of the Data Protection Act 1998 (DPA 1998) to object to the use of your personal information for direct marketing purposes. So if a request to stop mailing or other marketing contact is received it must be actioned within a reasonable period. Twenty-eight days is taken as the reasonable period in which to remove someone from all mailing lists therefore any divergence from the standard 28 days should be supported by compelling reasons.

Is it better to block or erase details when receiving a request to take someone off the mailing list?

It is actually preferable to block personal information when actioning a request to cease direct marketing. A mailing list may be fed from several databases and, if the name and contact details are erased entirely, it is possible that they may be reinstated from another database or that some new contact with the individual may result in them being added back onto the database. Blocking the contact details, on the other hand, retains a record showing that the individual no longer wishes to be contacted for marketing purposes so it is more likely to be complied with.

When we receive a request to remove someone from our mailing list, can we check periodically that they do not want contact with us?

Yes this is allowed but in practice organisations tend to lapse marketing contact completely on receiving a request to stop marketing contact.

In some cases, the individuals who ask to be taken off marketing mailing lists will be customers and there will be a level of contact generated for administrative purposes. However care needs to be taken when making an approach in this context. In 2010, the Advertising Standards Authority found that Virgin Media broke the Privacy and Electronic Communications (EC Directive) Regulations 2003 when it sent marketing material to a customer who had opted out of the use of his personal information for marketing purposes. The company claimed that the e-mail was a service update: the e mail wording referred to the fact that the customer had opted-out and was giving him a further chance to opt-in. The problem appears to be that the e-mail included information about deals, promotions and competitions as well as the reference to changing his or her mind about opting-out of direct marketing e-mail. This shows how careful organisations must be when they decide to contact customers who have opted-out to check that their mailing preferences have not changed.

How is market research conducted in a compliant way?

Using personal information for genuine market research purposes is not the same as using it for direct marketing. All customers may be contacted for market research purposes and so may individuals who have started the purchase process but stopped short of completing a purchase. The aim of the market research must be to find out what the individual thought of the product or service and the sale process and must not be an attempt to resurrect a defunct sale or upsell other products or services ('upsell' is the term applied to the process of inducing a customer who has purchased a product or service to buy other products or services from the same organisation).

A lot of market research is undertaken by specialist organisations and they are usually very clear on the rules for making this type of approach (e.g. they identify themselves clearly at the outset of the call and ask if the individual consents to sharing information about their experience). The Market Research Society has a Code of Conduct 2010[3] which sets out rules covering the use of client databases, lists and personal contact details, respondents' rights to anonymity and designing the data collection process. There are special rules for conducting market research with children too. Organisations carrying out market research on their own behalf need to take great care to remain compliant.

Can we transfer personal information to a third party to carry out market research on our behalf?

Yes, as noted above the market research industry is very professional in its approach and follows an industry Code of Conduct which is enforced by disciplinary action. Outsourcing this type of work to a professional market research company is one way to help ensure the exercise is completed in a compliant way.

When outsourcing work involving processing personal information on behalf of the organisation the Seventh Principle requires that contracts be in writing including two specific terms: that the personal information will be processed only on instructions from the organisation and that appropriate security measures will be taken by the data processor to safeguard the personal information entrusted to it. There is also a requirement to carry out compliance checks both before and during the service to ensure that the data processor is complying with the security requirements. If the intention is to outsource market research to a third party then steps should be taken to check the security arrangements the firm will have in place to safeguard any personal information the data controller may pass to it. The data controller would want assurances that the third party understands its data protection obligations and an overview of how it complies with them.

Personal information is always vulnerable in transit. The contact details of customers to be contacted for market research purposes will have to be transferred to the third party for them to conduct the market research. Investigation should be made into the most appropriate method of transfer which could be by secure https link, encrypted information on a portable data storage device such as a CD-Rom or memory stick or by uploading or downloading the file containing the personal information direct from a secure website. There are even third party websites which provide this capability if it does not exist in-house. The personal information transferred to the market research firm should be the minimum required, that is name and contact details and possibly an explanation of the goods or services provided.

Following the market research exercise it is prudent to either ask for the return or confirmation of deletion of customer personal information held by the market research firm.

What is required to keep information on marketing databases up to date?

The Fourth Principle requires that personal information be accurate and kept up to date where necessary. As the purpose of a marketing database is to facilitate communication with the individuals named on it, it is necessary to keep contact details up to date otherwise that purpose is frustrated. As a rule feedback should be processed from every marketing campaign to change address details and block addresses where letters have been sent back marked 'gone away'. It is also good practice to undertake occasional cleaning or matching exercises to pick up defunct addresses or misspellings in names and addresses.

The longer information is retained the more effort will be required to demonstrate that it is being kept up to date and accurate.

Is it lawful to collect information from customers which is not immediately relevant but which may be useful in future?

No, the requirement is for information to be adequate, relevant and not excessive.[4] Information that is not immediately relevant cannot therefore be collected lawfully.

What are the issues around customer profiling activity and the use of cookies?

Cookies are small files that attach to your computer when you browse a website, under the control of that website. They are an essential part of navigation around a website because they record the pages and the order in which they were viewed. Cookies can be employed to remember your personal selections and preferences on a website. They can also be employed for more furtive activities, reporting which websites have been visited so that a profile can be built of the user's browsing patterns. For this reason the use of cookies is regulated.

What are the information requirements when using cookies?

The Privacy and Electronic Communication (EC Directive) Regulations 2003 introduced information requirements for any website that uses cookies. There must be a disclosure of the fact that cookies are used and an explanation given of how to 'turn them off' in browser settings. Best practice is to include this mandatory information about cookies on website Privacy Policies.

The adoption in the EC of the 'Telecoms Package' presages a change in the law relating to cookies. New information requirements will be set out with the aim of keeping data subjects aware of any monitoring activity.

Is consent needed to use cookies?

Not as the law stands currently, but it may be in due course. There is no requirement to seek consent to the use of cookies under the 2003 Regulations, but the Telecoms package includes provision for consent to be mandatory. There is much industry comment about the difficulty of obtaining consent to the use of cookies as the flow of browsing will be interrupted if consumers are repeatedly presented with consent boxes. Marketers have argued that browser settings could constitute authority to use cookies but, as many individuals simply rely on factory settings and do not alter their browser settings to their own preference, this has been deemed insufficient to establish proper consent.[5]

The Article 29 Working Party (advisory body to the European Commission on data protection matters) recommends that network providers set up prior opt-in mechanisms, that is requiring an affirmative action by the data subject to indicate their willingness to receive cookies and to the subsequent monitoring of their online activities for the purpose of providing tailored advertising.

In addition to the new information requirements, advertising network providers may be required to:

- place a time limit on the scope of the consent rather than leaving it open-ended;

- offer an easy facility for individuals to revoke consent once given;
- create visible symbols to be displayed on the website when monitoring is taking place. In February 2010, a scheme to badge when information is being collected for purposes of behavioural advertising was adopted by some trade bodies in the US.

The Telecoms package must be implemented by EU member states by the middle of 2011.

Notes

1 Privacy and Electronic Communications (EC Directive) (Amendment) Regulations 2004 (SI 2004/1039).
2 Privacy and Electronic Communications (EC Directive) Regulations 2003 (SI 2003/2426).
3 See www.mrs.org.uk.
4 Principle 4 of the data protection principles.
5 Article 29 Working Party Opinion 2/2010 adopted on 22 June 2010.

B. Record keeping

What are the obligations around record keeping?

Data protection law applies to records containing personal information, so the Data Protection Act 1998 (DPA 1998) applies to records held electronically, on computer, on audio or video cassette and to some paper records. The key obligations are set out in the eight data protection principles and the requirements are:

- to keep data subjects aware of the identity of the organisation, the purposes for which personal information is processed and any other information relevant in the circumstances, usually called a privacy notice;
- to stay within the authority of the privacy notice when processing personal information;
- to process only such information as is adequate, relevant and not excessive for the purpose for which it is processed;
- to ensure that records are accurate and, where necessary, kept up to date;
- not to retain information for longer than is required for the purpose for which it is processed;
- to process records in accordance with the rights of data subjects under the Act;
- to ensure that records are secure from unauthorised access, amendment, loss or destruction;
- not to transfer records outside the European Economic Area (EEA) without taking prescribed precautions.

Organisations that obtain, hold or process records containing personal information must be registered on the Data Protection Register unless they are exempt.

How does one meet these obligations?

This book suggests that a strategic approach to meeting data protection compliance requirements is appropriate. If records include personal information relating to many individuals, if they are detailed and include information that is considered 'sensitive',[1] then compliance with data protection obligations will be more onerous than records of say, contact details. Therefore the data protection compliance strategy will need to be more rigorous than if very little personal information is being processed (e.g. a database of business contacts).

A recommended approach would be to identify what personal information is being processed by the organisation and then devote such resource as is appropriate to identifying what the compliance risks are and implementing policies, procedures and training to mitigate or avoid the risks.

How long should records be kept?

The DPA 1998 does not specify how long records should be kept. They may be held for as long as they are necessary for the purpose for which they were created. Many areas of law dictate information retention periods (e.g. accounting records must be retained for seven years to meet tax requirements, records relating to personal injury cases are routinely kept for three years from the date of the incident leading to the injury as that is the relevant period in which a claim may be brought).

For each set of records a decision needs to be made as to how long it is necessary to keep them. The decision needs to be supported with evidence of industry standards and any other information that lends credibility to the retention period adopted.

What exemptions apply to personal information held for research?

There is an exemption[2] from part of the DPA 1998 for records that are used for research, either statistical or historical, provided the information is not used to support decisions taken with respect to individuals and provided that the processing does not cause damage or distress to data subjects.

The exemption operates to remove the data controller's obligations under the Second Principle, which requires processing to be for stated purposes only. It also exempts from the Fifth Principle, the requirement not to retain personal information for any longer than is necessary for the purpose for which it is processed and the subject access obligations are also lifted.

For the purposes of the exemption personal information is still treated as processed for research purposes even if it is disclosed to a third party for research purposes, to the data subject, with his consent or in circumstances where the data controller believes the disclosure meets one of these conditions.

C. Security

Where is the obligation to keep personal information secure set out?

The Seventh Principle states that appropriate technical and organisational security measures should be taken to prevent unauthorised access, amendment, loss or destruction of personal information.

What is the required standard?

The key word is 'appropriate'. The organisation needs to make appropriate security arrangements depending on the type and amount of information being processed and the number of data subjects. It also needs to take account of the state of the art in IT security and ensure that its IT security precautions are appropriate both for it as an organisation and for its industry and the state of the art in technological terms.

As an example of what is considered appropriate, in November 2007 the Information Commissioner issued a statement to the effect that the appropriate level of security for personal information held on portable data storage devices was encryption of the information. What is appropriate will depend on the type of information, the state of the art in IT development, the size of the organisation and the resources available to it and best practice in industry.

Should organisations audit security measures?

Yes. An audit is a way of checking that compliance measures are in place and working effectively. The International Standard for IT security is ISO27001 which requires that organisations adopt an Information Security Management System which will allow management to (among other aspects) adopt an overarching system of compliance to ensure that the information security controls continue to meet information security needs on a continuing basis. The requirement for an overarching system of compliance to ensure that controls continue to meet information security needs can only be achieved by regular audit.

As well as IT technical security, the Seventh Principle requires that appropriate organisational measures be taken to secure personal information. 'Organisational measures' means adopting policies and procedures around office security, the security of individual files and confidentiality. The ICO looks for evidence of a system of control to ensure that policies and procedures are being adhered to in practice which again would necessitate some audit activity to demonstrate that the effectiveness of policies and procedures are checked in practice.

Are there any standard security requirements?

The Seventh Principle simply refers to appropriate technical and organisational measures. In practice access control is a major part of IT security, so standard IT security requirements should include a process for authorising access to the system, restrictions on access on a 'need to know' basis, protection from external interference such as firewalls, virus control, password policies to ensure that users access the system legitimately and disaster recovery procedures to help maintain access in the event of a problem.

Other standard measures one would expect to find in an IT security policy are aspects of work that require information to be encrypted. If payment is accepted by credit or debit card then the Payment Card Industry Data Security Standards will be relevant involving segregation of payment card information from all other information and encryption of payment card details at all times.

Business premises should be secured from unauthorised entry. Standard measures include CCTV, burglar alarms and controlled access systems and should be supported by procedural security measures such as a visitor sign-in procedure.

In areas where personal information is held on paper adequate lockable filing arrangements should be provided, possibly augmented with controlled entry systems for the floor or department if the sensitivity or amount of personal information demands it (e.g. information held in an HR department). Secure document destruction methods will be required, either secure confidential waste bins (including secure recovery of the bins and disposal of the contents) or easily accessible shredders. Supporting the security of paper files in the business environment, a clean desk policy should be enforced so that information is not visible on desks overnight or at weekends when cleaning staff will be on site legitimately, or burglars breaking and entering premises illegally. Procedures may also be required to manage the issue of locking filing cabinets and ensuring that the keys are available to access information in the files when needed (e.g. the last person to leave the department may be required to lock filing cabinets and leave the key with a security officer). Alternatively the manager may lock filing cabinets and keep the key in a key cupboard in the department.

It has been noted that personal information is vulnerable when in transit so procedures to help secure it when in transit should be in place, for example the requirement to keep confidential documents and portable equipment like laptops or Blackberrys out of sight in the boot of a locked car when off premises and to minimise the amount of personal information taken off-site. Policies may also be needed to regulate the use of equipment such as laptops and Blackberrys, and home working to cover the security aspects of personal information taken home and where personal computers and email are used at home. Policies and procedures to regulate the use of faxes, CD-Roms and memory sticks will also evidence that appropriate security measures are in place.

Notes

1 'Sensitive' information is that relating to race or ethnic origin, religious or philosophical beliefs, political beliefs, physical or mental health, sex life, criminal convictions and allegations of any criminal offences.
2 DPA 1998, s 33.

D. CCTV

Is CCTV a data protection issue?

CCTV usually has the facility to make a record of the images on screen and in this case, CCTV raises data protection issues. The Data Protection Act 1998 (DPA 1998) applies to personal information that is held in electronic form covering digital and analogue CCTV schemes where images are recorded onto hard drive, disk or video tape.

What must we do to comply?

The organisation responsible for the CCTV scheme must register with the Data Protection Registrar as a CCTV scheme operator or add 'prevention and detection of crime' as a registered purpose on an existing registration entry. Even where the core business exemption applies, meaning the organisation is exempt from registration in respect of its normal activities, the exemption is lost if the organisation operates CCTV. It is a registrable activity of itself.

In addition to registration, the data protection principles apply to the processing of personal information in the images captured by the scheme. The Information Commissioner has published a Code of Practice for CCTV schemes.[1] This explains how to approach data protection compliance when considering installing a CCTV scheme and the continuing compliance obligations once it has been installed.

The First Principle requires fair processing, which means using personal information appropriately and keeping people informed about your personal information processing activities.

Prior to installing CCTV someone within the organisation should be identified as being responsible for it on a continuing basis. A clear need for CCTV should be demonstrated and then an assessment of the advantages and benefits should be carried out and weighed against any negative connotations, (e.g. whether staff may feel they are being spied upon, or that their privacy is being invaded to an unreasonable degree).

The introduction of CCTV should be a proportionate response to a perceived, real threat (e.g. CCTV cameras are often installed to monitor the activity of sales cashiers in shops or in car parks to detect criminal activity). Consideration should be given to alternative methods to achieve the objective before deciding upon CCTV (e.g. can a car park be locked and intruders kept out of the area rather than monitoring them on CCTV)?

When considering proportionality, think also about the perceived intimacy/privacy of the area being monitored. Is this an area where individuals might expect a greater degree of privacy than the norm? For example the introduction of a CCTV camera in an office reception area is less intrusive than introducing a camera in the staff canteen or rest area. In hotels it is common practice to site CCTV monitors in the reception area where they can be viewed by guests in the hotel foyer, a public space. It has been established that it is intrusive to include views from cameras located in corridors in the more private areas of the hotel on the foyer screens.

Another issue related to proportionality is the use of covert cameras. The Information Commissioner's guidance is that covert monitoring is almost never justified and that police involvement is a fundamental requirement. In practice, domestic problems experienced by businesses will not usually attract police interest so their involvement in covert monitoring is unlikely. So, covert monitoring is inadvisable in most circumstances. Using covert cameras will mean that most staff will not be aware that they are being monitored; this brings us on to another element of 'fair processing' – the need to keep people informed of how and why their personal information is being captured and used. When using CCTV this means publicising that processing by adopting appropriate signage.

Signs indicating the presence of CCTV need to be appropriate to the location of the cameras. In a shopping centre this should be in the welcome area just inside the doors to the retail area. In an office with cameras in reception, it might be at the reception desk, or on a wall nearby. In a bank or building society branch with tills at the far end of the public area, signs should be on the wall or on desks near the doors.

There is also an issue regarding the size of the signs. What is appropriate in a relatively small office reception area (e.g. a small sign on the desk by the visitor sign-in register) would not be appropriate in a 'goods in' yard where lorry drivers are being targeted.

What should CCTV signage say?

The First Principle requires data subjects to be advised of the identity of the data controller, the purposes for which personal information is being captured and used, and any other information relevant in the circumstances.

The CCTV Code of Practice states:

> Signs should:
> be clearly visible and readable;
> contain details of the organisation operating the system, the purpose for using CCTV and who to contact about the scheme (where these things are not obvious to those being monitored); and
> be an appropriate size depending on context, for example, whether they are viewed by pedestrians or car drivers.

The Code also says that it is not necessary to specify the name of the data controller if this is obvious in the circumstances (e.g. where CCTV cameras are inside a shop it will be obvious that the shop owner is the data controller). This is not always as simple in practice as some CCTV schemes are managed by third parties (e.g. retail site owners) rather than individual shops or a security firm. Also there is a risk that local managers of chains of shops will introduce CCTV signs elsewhere in the building where the identity of the scheme manager may not be obvious. If the manager copies existing wording then the new sign may omit the name of the data controller. Finally the name of the shop may be a trading name rather than the legal title of the organisation; this can cause confusion when trying to identify the data controller of the CCTV scheme. For these reasons it is recommended that the identity of the data controller should be stated on any signs.

When can we disclose CCTV images?

There are certain circumstances in which the organisation may disclose, or may have to disclose, CCTV images and other circumstances which it may specify for itself in advance by explaining those circumstances in the privacy notice.

Disclosures required by law cover the situation where a court orders disclosure of images or where a warrant is presented ordering disclosure. Disclosure to the police generally is the subject of an exemption under s 29 of the DPA 1998 which provides that personal information is exempt from the fair processing principle and the non-disclosure requirements when it is processed for the prevention or detection of crime, the apprehension or prosecution of offenders, or the assessment or collection of any tax or duty or similar.

In the Data Protection Good Practice Note *Data Sharing with the Police* from the Information Commissioner's Office (the ICO) the advice is to check the identity of the police officer and his reasons for requesting the release of personal information and consider whether declining to disclose the information would 'significantly harm' the police's attempts to prevent crime or catch a suspect and impede their investigation?

If the decision is to release personal information to the police, data controllers should identify the minimum information that should be disclosed to enable the police to achieve their objective.

The Good Practice Note sets out best practice guidelines. It recommends nominating a person or group of persons within the organisation to whom to refer requests for disclosure of personal information made by the police. As a general rule, any requests from the police should be obtained in writing and signed by someone of 'sufficient authority'. A log should be kept of requests, relevant circumstances and whether or not the decision was made to release images to the police at that time.

Data subjects can also request disclosure of CCTV images of themselves under s 7 of the DPA, the subject access provisions. Subject access requests for access to

CCTV images should be dealt with in the same way as any other subject access request. The request should be made in writing and the organisation has 40 days in which to respond with the required information or to provide an explanation of why the images are exempt from disclosure.

Probably the only grounds for withholding images would be where the police are investigating an incident and release of the images could prejudice their investigations, or where the images of third parties are also captured in the footage and it would be unreasonable and unfair to share those images (e.g. where a subject access request is received for access to images showing a third party who was taken ill, perhaps having a fit or something similar, and access is requested by someone not involved in the incident). The organisation might not be able to seek the consent of the incapacitated individual or may have done so and been declined. The organisation then has to weigh the rights of the incapacitated party against the rights of the onlooker and it is probable that the organisation would decline to share the images of the incident with the onlooker.

Generally the motive behind a data subject making a request for access to CCTV images is not relevant to processing the subject access request. The organisation may, however, seek confirmation of the individual's identity (e.g. by asking for a recent photograph so that the relevant images can be identified).

How long can CCTV images be retained?

The Fifth Principle states that personal information processed for any purpose or purposes shall not be kept for longer than is necessary for that purpose or those purposes. In practice it is up to the organisation to decide how long it really needs to keep the images although the CCTV Code of Practice recommends a 28-day retention period.

There will be circumstances, where an investigation is taking place or a request for access to images as at a specified date has been received, when it will be necessary to keep the images longer than the usual length of time. Normally CCTV schemes have the facility for images to be burned to disk or copied to video or hard drive for retention purposes. Outside of special circumstances, images should be held for no longer than 28 days based on the guidance in the CCTV Code of Practice.

If there are sound reasons for routinely keeping images for a period of time exceeding 28 days, the reasons should be documented and a review undertaken of the reasons for installing the CCTV scheme initially. The retention of CCTV images should be a proportionate response to a real threat. Consider whether alternative methods can be used to achieve the objective of retaining images for a long period. These are aspects of proportionality and the benefit of retaining the images should be weighed against the impact on the rights of individuals to privacy.

Are there any other legal considerations when using CCTV?

Since 2003 certain use of CCTV has been subject to the Security Industry Act (SIA) 2001. Section 3 makes it an offence to engage in licensable conduct without a licence issued by the SIA. Activities that can be licensed include guarding premises, property and persons including carrying out 'any form of patrol or surveillance either to deter or discourage or provide information, if it happens, about what has happened.'

Basically this means that where CCTV images of public spaces are monitored in a live situation by security guards, those security guards should be registered under the SIA. Registration is renewable every three years and is contingent upon attending appropriately accredited training which includes the data protection and privacy aspects of the job.

CCTV is commonly used in the workplace to monitor the behaviour of staff and this also raises data protection issues. Again the Human Rights Act 1998 is relevant here as employees are entitled to respect for their private and family life, home and correspondence per Art 8.

Before commencing monitoring, the general requirement is to consider the likely impact it will have on staff and staff relations and weigh the advantages of monitoring against any adverse impact. The situation where managers inadvertently use CCTV images for monitoring purposes should not arise without this use first being carefully thought through and communicated to staff (e.g. it should not be possible for managers to request details of how long an employee has taken on a cigarette break outside the building which have been captured on CCTV recordings of the outside of the building).

The decision to use CCTV for monitoring should be based on a clearly defined need to reduce a perceived threat or existing problem. It should also be the most appropriate solution to the perceived need. CCTV should not be introduced simply because it is a common practice in business to do so. Once the decision is taken to introduce CCTV as an appropriate monitoring device, it should be targeted when put in place. If, for example, stock is disappearing from the building, it would be appropriate to install CCTV to cover front and particularly rear entrances to the building to ascertain the logistics of the thefts.

Communication of the organisation's policy on monitoring should be clear and made in advance of starting to monitor so that staff know what the position is. CCTV is a deterrent as well as a means of identifying offenders and gathering evidence to support prosecutions, so it needs to be publicised to be effective.

How should we approach auditing our CCTV scheme for compliance?

The CCTV Code of Practice recommends that a senior manager should be responsible for the CCTV scheme. A starting point for an audit is to speak to that manager and check that he or she understands the data protection implications of the scheme and to find out if there have been any problems or issues with the scheme. Check also that staff operating the scheme understand their data protection obligations around security and confidentiality.

Policies and procedures should be checked to ensure that these are consistent with the best practice guidelines in the CCTV Code of Practice. Any deviation from the Code should be queried. Check that operational staff understand the policies and procedures and that they follow them in practice.

Following any audit, document findings and recommendations. Implement recommendations or give reasons why they could not be implemented if that is the case.

What training is needed for CCTV operators and monitors?

Where CCTV is used for monitoring purposes, monitors should be trained on their data protection responsibilities and the relevant policies and procedures. If security or facilities personnel do not undergo SIA training, then training for them should cover the privacy implications of monitoring and the individual's right to privacy and respect for private and family life, home and correspondence etc. In particular, monitors should understand that what they view on CCTV is confidential and must not be discussed except with those people within the organisation who are entitled to know by virtue of their job role. Incidents should not be discussed in casual settings, such as the pub at lunch time or on mobile 'phones on the train and so on.

Monitors should also be briefed on the organisation's whistle-blowing policy as they may be privy to information that could impact on the organisation's prudent management; for example witnessing two members of staff kissing might not appear to be a reportable incident but if those employees are both A list signatories on cheques and bank transfers, then there is a problem that needs to be reported via the whistle-blowing procedure.

What are the implications of outsourcing CCTV?

Where a data controller chooses to outsource personal information processing the Seventh Principle applies to the arrangement. The reason for this is that data processors are not required to comply with the data protection principles, only data controllers are required to comply under s 4 of the DPA 1998. Therefore the contractual and ongoing compliance checks required of the data controller under the Seventh Principle are the only way that data processors are regulated.

When considering outsourcing the exact details of the personal information processing arrangements are key to determining whether or not the service provider will be a data processor within the meaning of the DPA 1998.[2] The service provider must be processing on behalf of the organisation, so the organisation must be the party that decides that it is appropriate to install CCTV and the purposes for which it is installed. The service provider will be following the instructions of the organisation in relation to the CCTV Scheme. In these circumstances the Seventh Principle will apply to require the organisation to put in place a written contract including two specific terms: first, that the data processor will process personal information only on the instructions of the organisation and second, that the data processor will put in place appropriate security measures to safeguard the CCTV images from unauthorised access, amendment or destruction.

In outsourcing arrangements where the Seventh Principle applies, the data controller retains responsibility for the data protection compliance of the processing operation despite the involvement of a service provider.

What are our obligations if the landlord introduces CCTV?

If another interested party installs and manages a CCTV scheme, they will be the data controller in respect of that scheme. In these circumstances compliance with the data protection CCTV Code of Practice is the responsibility of the landlord. If there is any shared access to the images, for example if they are used to monitor staff or deliveries to the premises, then both parties are under an obligation to ensure that the monitoring activity is a proportionate response to a perceived threat and that individuals being monitored are aware of the monitoring.

If the landlord introduces the CCTV Scheme at the request of a tenant and delegates the operation of the scheme to the tenant, it may be that the tenant is the data controller of the scheme because it was the party that decided the purposes for which the images will be processed and is also the party that is making the day-to-day decisions regarding the running of the scheme.

Notes

1 Revised Code 2008.
2 'Data processor', in relation to personal data, means any person (other than an employee of the data controller) who processes the data on behalf of the data controller.

E. Outsourcing

What is an outsourcing arrangement?

Many organisations outsource activities that are outside of their core business activities such as payroll administration or even their entire human resources (HR) function. The rationale for outsourcing is often that a third-party specialist service provider can perform its functions better and at lower cost than the organisation can perform the function in house. Activities that are typically outsourced include:

- payroll administration;
- pension scheme administration;
- share register administration; and
- printing and postage of reports and accounts or marketing material.

Another, less obvious, example of outsourcing arises when activities are split within an organisation between two or more separate legal entities. Some organisations choose a legal framework where one legal entity is supported by other service companies; other organisations have to adopt a group structure for legal reasons (e.g. an insurance company may only transact insurance business, it cannot employ staff therefore staff must be employed in a service company to support the insurance company). Data protection law does not recognise trading groups of companies; each member of a group is treated as a separate entity and its dealings with sister companies are deemed to be at arm's length for data protection purposes. This means that, within a group of companies, one or more of the constituent companies may be considered as a service provider to one or more of the others. Consider the following circumstances:

- A company in a group is deemed to 'own' computer equipment for accounting purposes. The other companies in the group may use the computer equipment although it technically belongs to a third party. The personal information processed on that computer system is being processed by a data processor.
- Staff employed by a service company in a group of companies rather than directly by a trading or operating company. The service company is a data processor for the trading and operating companies which are data controllers.

Can we let a third party process personal information on our behalf?

Yes, outsourcing is a standard business practice but there are data protection compliance issues. Section 4(4) of the Data Protection Act 1998 (DPA 1998) states that data controllers must comply with the data protection principles in relation to all personal data with respect to which he is the data controller. When outsourcing work involving personal information processing to a third party, the data controller retains responsibility for compliance with the principles in respect of the personal information.

185

What are our obligations if a third party processes personal information on our behalf?

The data controller regulates the activity of the data processor pursuant to its obligations under the Seventh Principle. The requirements are set out in Sch 1 to the DPA 1998:

> Where processing of personal data is carried out by a data processor on behalf of a data controller, the data controller must in order to comply with the Seventh Principle –
> (a) choose a data processor providing sufficient guarantees in respect of the technical and organisational security measures governing the processing to be carried out; and
> (b) take reasonable steps to ensure compliance with those measures.

In addition:

> The data controller is not to be regarded as complying with the Seventh Principle unless–
> (a) the processing is carried out under a contract–
>   (i) which is made or evidenced in writing; and
>   (ii) under which the data processor is to act only on instructions from the data controller.
> (b) the contract requires the data processor to comply with obligations equivalent to those imposed on a data controller by the Seventh Principle.

So the requirements are threefold:
- to select a data processor which can evidence it has appropriate security measures in place;
- to put in place a written contract with the data processor specifying that it will only process personal information on the instructions of the data controller and that it will take appropriate security measures to safeguard the personal information from unauthorised access, amendment or destruction; and
- to carry out compliance checks to ensure that the data processor is adhering to its security measures.

What compliance checks should we carry out to meet our obligations when outsourcing?

Both before entering into a contract which involves outsourcing personal information processing and during the term of the contract the data controller should carry out compliance checks to ensure that the data processor has appropriate organisational and technical security measures in place to safeguard the personal information from unauthorised access, amendment, loss or destruction.

As a first step it is always prudent to check that prospective service providers have identified the implications of data protection law for their services and that they understand the legal obligations to which data controllers are subject. They should be able to demonstrate familiarity with the terminology of the Seventh Principle, outline its requirements and show how they impact on the relationship between them and their clients. Draft contracts should include clauses to cover the mandatory sections.

Another key pre-contract enquiry is to find out if any person or group of persons have been designated as responsible for IT security and to ask if there are restrictions in place to control access to your data, create audit trails and to prevent unauthorised amendment or deletion.

In addition, the data processor should be asked to supply such details of its security measures for personal information as it is able to provide without compromising those security arrangements. Technical measures should include disaster recovery, back up, virus protection, firewalls and access controls. IT security standards such as ISO 27001 also demonstrate that information security is being dealt with in a considered and consistent way. Organisational measures should include IT security policy and procedures, policies and procedures to regulate paper records, where necessary, such as clean desk policy and guidelines for using shared office facilities such as fax machines, printers and 'hot-desks'. Building security is another key part of organisational security; find out how buildings and offices are secured against break-ins.

Checks should be made on how personal information will be secured when in transit when it tends to be more vulnerable, on what arrangements the service provider has to ensure secure transfer of personal information between its clients and itself and also how it secures any transfers to subcontractors.

There should be evidence of training for all staff that will be involved in processing the personal information and this should be appropriate and relevant to the tasks they will undertake. Check particularly for evidence of induction training and confirmation that new staff will not be involved in processing personal information until they have undergone training in data protection issues related to their work. The data controller should talk to the staff to find out if they are familiar with data protection terminology and understand their responsibilities when processing personal information.

There is a need to check that staff are monitored and how this is done. This should include information about how new employees are supervised to ensure that the data processor is able to satisfy himself as to their reliability.

It must be clear if all the personal information processing will take place at the service provider's premises or whether any part of the process is outsourced to another third party. If processing is to be subcontracted then a check on the terms of the contract between the data processor and its subcontractors will be required and enquiries need to be made into how the data processor checks the security arrangements of its subcontractors. Ultimately, responsibility/liability remains with the data controller.

Another key issue to check is whether or not the service provider has suffered any data protection breaches, particularly security breaches. Ask for an explanation of the circumstances of the breach and what was done to remedy the situation both in terms of damage limitation and dealing with the immediate effects of the breach and what steps were taken to prevent a similar incident occurring again in future.

In the ICO *Good Practice Note Outsourcing – A Guide for Small and Medium-Sized Businesses* published in 2009, the following good practice recommendations are suggested when using a third party organisation to process personal data:

- select a reputable organisation offering suitable guarantees about their ability to ensure the security of personal data;
- make sure the contract with the organisation is enforceable both in the UK and in the country in which the organisation is located;
- make sure the organisation has appropriate security measures in place;
- make sure that they make appropriate checks on their staff;
- audit the other organisation regularly to make sure they are 'up to scratch';
- require the organisation to report any security breaches or other problems, including requests for information under foreign legislation; and
- have procedures in place that allow you to act appropriately when you receive one of these reports.

What happens when a service provider loses personal information?

Under DPA 1998 it is established in the UK, or another EU Member State, the data controller is responsible for compliance with the provisions of the Act. The data controller is defined as the party that determines the purposes for which data is processed and the way in which it is processed. This means that the data controller is ultimately responsible for the security of personal information, even if it is lost by a service provider.

Data security breaches are often in the news and many of the failings are actually attributable to third-party service providers who are processing personal information on behalf of clients. In practice the media reports headline the security breach as one suffered by the client, while the involvement of the service provider is delegated to the small print. So, in April 2006 it was reported that Marks & Spencer had suffered the theft of a laptop containing employee details relating to 26,000 of its employees and that the data was unencrypted. In fact, the laptop was stolen from an employee of the payroll service provider to M&S.

In November 2008 a memory stick found in a pub car park was found to contain names and confidential sign on information for individuals who use the Government Gateway. The contractor, Atos Origin, was responsible.

In October 2008 the Ministry of Defence revealed that CD-Roms containing personal details relating to approximately 100,000 serving troops had been lost by its contractor EDS.

In September 2008 the Home Office reported the loss of a computer hard drive with details of serving prison officers. The hard drive had been lost by its contractor EDS.

In August 2008 the contractor Mail Source, part of the archiving firm Graphic Data recycled a computer which was found to contain details of NatWest, Royal Bank of Scotland and American Express customers.

Thefts and accidental losses of portable data storage devices will always occur no matter how tight security is or how well staff have been trained to be risk aware. The responsibility of the data controller is to check that appropriate security is in place, which means, among other things, encryption for portable data storage devices. The importance of carrying out security compliance checks cannot be underestimated. In March 2010 it was reported that Zurich Insurance plc had lost an unencrypted back-up tape containing financial details relating to 46,000 policy holders. The tape was actually lost by a subcontractor, another company in the group. Internal investigations revealed failings in the system of control. The subcontractor hid the fact that the data had been lost for over a year. Zurich Insurance had no reporting structure between itself and its subcontractor to allow the incident to be reported and insufficient management controls to identify that a problem had occurred.

The Information Commissioner has published a useful guidance note, *Data Protection Good Practice Note, Outsourcing – A Guide for Small and Medium-Sized Businesses*. This sets out data protection obligations when outsourcing and makes other good practice recommendations when selecting a service provider.

F. Employment

How does data protection impact on human resources?

Data protection is basically about respecting people's privacy and confidentiality so, obviously, there is an impact on creating and keeping human resource (HR) records. For many organisations, HR holds the most records containing personal information and those records contain the most confidential information. So data protection law has a significant impact. In recognition of this the Information Commissioner's Office (the ICO) has published a code of practice for employers, the Employment Practices Code.

What is the status of the Employment Practices Code?

The Employment Practices Code does not have the force of law but it sets benchmarks against which employers' compliance with the Act may be measured. In the introductory section About the Code the following explanation is given:

> The basic legal requirement on each employer is to comply with the Act itself. The Code is designed to help. It sets out the Information Commissioner's recommendations as to how the legal requirements of the Act can be met. Employers may have alternative ways of meeting these requirements but if they do nothing they risk breaking the law.
>
> Any enforcement action would be based on a failure to meet the requirements of the Act itself. However, relevant parts of the Code are likely to be cited by the Commissioner in connection with any enforcement action that arises in relation to the processing of personal information in the employment context.

The Code is the Information Commissioner's view of how data protection law impacts on the records created and kept as part of routine HR activities. It provides a sensible approach to the law and, as such, is taken by Employment Tribunals as being a reasonable standard for employment records and record keeping practices. Therefore the Employment Practices Code should be treated on a 'comply or explain' basis. This means that employers should assume the Code applies to their HR records and should comply with its provisions. In areas where the employer cannot or does not wish to comply with the Code, it should have good, documented, reasons for not doing so.

What is covered in the Employment Practices Code?

The Employment Practices Code is split into four sections covering recruitment and selection, record keeping, monitoring at work and the use of information about workers' health. The publication is split into two: part one explains how the data protection principles apply to HR activities and sets benchmark standards; Part two gives further explanation and provides useful examples of the application of the Code in practice.

What are the key issues around managing data protection compliance in relation to HR?

As with the management of data protection compliance in the operational activities of the organisation, it is important to be able to evidence a system of control in relation to the data protection compliance of HR activities. Either a committee or a senior member of the HR team should be tasked with data protection responsibilities, including overseeing the effectiveness of relevant policies and procedures. There should be a routine review of such policies and procedures as part of the cycle of continuous improvement.

What are the key data protection issues around recruitment and selection?

The principles require openness about intended processing activity, so it is important to ensure that prospective job applicants are given information about the identity of the employer, the purposes for which any CV material submitted will be used and any other information relevant in the circumstances (e.g. any pre-employment checks, or third parties with whom the personal information will be shared).

When carrying out the interviews the personal information must be used in a consistent way between candidates to ensure fairness. Notes made during the interview process should be professional and, where an opinion is given, it should be clear that it is the opinion of a named individual. Interviewers should be reminded that any notes they make will be shared with the candidates on request.

Throughout the process any transfer of CV information, from say agency to employer, or within the employer's organisation between HR department and line managers, must be undertaken in a way that ensures the security of that information. Where individuals are encouraged to make job applications online, steps must be taken to ensure confidentiality (e.g. by using a https link).

Once the recruitment exercise is complete, the records relating to failed applications should only be retained for as long as is necessary to defend the organisation against any potential claims of discrimination in the selection process. Industry best practice is to destroy records six months after the appointment of the chosen applicant. In circumstances where another, similar, vacancy is likely to arise and there are unsuccessful candidates who might be interested in such a position, the situation should be explained and they should be asked if they would like the organisation to keep their details on file.

What are the main data protection requirements for record keeping?

HR records should be kept up to date where necessary and should be accurate. Industry best practice is either to allow employees access to their own personal details on the HR system for purposes of notifying changes of address and status or to conduct an annual review of such details from the HR system to check that records are up to date.

Access to personal information held in HR files should be restricted on a need to know basis to help maintain confidentiality. Paper files should be held securely, locked in filing cabinets out of sight when not in use. Computer systems should have facilities for audit trails to check who has accessed what information.

Any transfers of personal information required for management, administration or payroll purposes should be conducted by secure means. When portable data storage devices are used the personal information should be encrypted and only the minimum information required to complete a task should be provided.

Should subject access requests be handled differently in the employment context?

The same legal provisions (s 7 DPA 1998) apply to requests for access to personal information in the employment context as apply elsewhere. Employees have the right to access information about themselves held in personnel and employment files. They have the right to be informed about the purposes for which personal information is processed and about any automated decision-making processes that might be applied by the employer. The same timescales and procedural requirements apply.

In practice, organisations might choose to respond to the exercise of subject access rights by an employee differently from a request for access from another category of data subject. Given the nature of the relationship between employer and employee the formal process for exercising subject rights might not be deemed appropriate. Checks to confirm the identity of the person making the subject access request will not be required so the need for data subjects to make their application in writing may be disapplied in favour of a face-to-face conversation with a member of the HR team. The HR team can engage with the employee making the request to find out the circumstances of the enquiry, to identify if there is an underlying HR issue. So the whole process may well be handled in a more relaxed way than a subject access request may be by a third party, external to the organisation.

Many employers have an 'open' policy with regard to personnel files allowing individuals to view their own files. Even without such a policy, subject access to information held in personnel files may be facilitated by allowing the employee to read his or her file in a private office, flagging documents that they would like to be copied for their own retention.

The situation will be different where an ex-employee or an employee who is currently suspended from their position at work makes a subject access request. There is a key difference in the relationship, the employee is in dispute (or potentially in dispute) with the employer. He or she may be advised by a solicitor so it will be essential to follow the organisation's subject access procedures carefully. It is likely that the organisation will want to review the content of files to be disclosed in case there is information included that could prejudice the position of the employer and which can be lawfully withheld under DPA exemptions.

What constitutes monitoring in the workplace?

Monitoring is usually undertaken either to check on the activities of employees to ensure that they are working to agreed targets and procedures or to check that their behaviour is within the range deemed acceptable in the workplace. This is an active form of monitoring behaviour and working standards.

Checking the performance of employees and how well they do their job might involve supervisors listening to recordings of telephone calls or checking that administrative work has been completed on a paper file. Monitoring might involve reading e-mail while an employee is absent from work due to holidays, illness or injury to ensure that customer orders are picked up and dealt with. This is a passive form of monitoring, but it is still an intrusion into the activities of the employee.

To check that behaviour is acceptable, monitoring might take the form of electronic scanning of internet usage to ensure that employees follow company policy prohibiting access to the internet for personal reasons during working hours. It might involve CCTV cameras in public areas such as the company car park or targeted on cash tills to check for theft.

What are the key data protection issues around monitoring workers?

Monitoring employees is by its nature intrusive so someone senior should be responsible for the decision to introduce monitoring techniques. They should be able to demonstrate that monitoring has been introduced to achieve a specific objective and that it was the right system to achieve that objective, describing the benefits expected to result from the monitoring. In particular they should consider whether other systems would achieve the same objective (e.g. if there is a risk of damage to property or personal attacks in a car park, rather than introducing CCTV as a deterrent, would improved lighting achieve the same objective?).

They should also be able to show that they have taken the rights of employees into account, particularly Art 8 of the Human Rights Act 1998, the right to respect for private life and family, home and correspondence. Consideration needs to be given to the impact of the proposed monitoring on workers' autonomy and on the relationship between employer and employee.

The legal environment needs to be checked; the interception of e-mail is regulated by the Regulation of Investigatory Powers Act 2000, and the Lawful Business Practice Regulations 2000,[1] while manned CCTV schemes fall within the remit of the Security Industry Act 2001. As a final check, it is essential to ensure that the monitoring will address the need identified. For example if e-mails are to be checked to identify any orders addressed to employees who are on holiday, then only those e-mails arriving in the period that the employee is on holiday should be checked; any e-mails which obviously do not relate to the purpose should be ignored.

Monitoring will necessarily involve some degree of worker involvement to assess the output of the monitoring scheme. Monitors need to be trained in their data protection responsibilities. They will need training, policies and procedures around the need for confidentiality in the conduct of their work and the findings of the monitoring scheme, when information resulting from monitoring should be shared and how to use the whistle-blowing scheme where reports are made outside the normal operational channels.

To meet fair processing requirements employees should be informed about monitoring, why it is being introduced and what form it will take. It is good practice to inform workers how they may obtain personal information that relates to them under the right of subject access, setting out the procedure and whom to approach in the first instance.

The period of retention for information obtained by monitoring needs to be set at a reasonable length of time; the Employment Code recommends a period not exceeding six months, except where the information is required as part of an ongoing police operation or to support a prosecution.

What are the key data protection implications around the use of information relating to workers' health?

Information relating to health is defined as 'sensitive personal data' under the Act and there are special obligations when using it to make sure that it is only processed for legitimate and restricted purposes. Generally this means that, with the exception of routine HR processing of details of illness or injury to meet Health & Safety requirements and arrange statutory and contractual sick pay, information relating to workers' health should only be processed in cases where their health can impact on whether or not the employee can undertake his job safely.

Schedule 3 to the Act sets out conditions to meet when processing sensitive personal information. One of these more or less covers routine HR activities; processing information for health and safety purposes is necessary to meet statutory obligations on the employer and to help in the discharge of his duty of care towards employees. Arranging the payment of sick pay is another legal obligation. However processing sensitive information for work planning and management purposes does not meet a Sch 3 condition unless the specific informed consent of the worker is sought. Generally this is to be avoided and the Information Commissioner strongly recommends identifying those activities where actual detail of illness or injury is required to achieve the employer's objective and where simply recording the employees' absence is all that is required. For example an employee may confide in the HR team that they will be undergoing surgery later in the year. That information is required by the HR team to instigate the payment of sick pay, to confirm to line management that the employee is taking authorised sick leave and, when the return to work is imminent, to arrange for an ergonomic assessment of the employee's needs in the workplace for health and safety purposes. The line manager does not need to know the details of the illness or injury afflicting the employee unless he/she chooses to share that information. Neither does the payroll team need to know the medical details; they simply need to know the dates when the individual is absent from work, any special sick pay arrangements and that the sick leave was authorised.

Where specific information is required regarding an employee's health (e.g. pre-employment questionnaires, routine drug or alcohol testing or other monitoring) then a senior member of the HR team should be designated to undertake an impact assessment before introducing any collection and use of information. The Information Commissioner describes an impact assessment as a process involving:

- identifying clearly the purpose or purposes for which health information is to be collected and held and the benefits this is likely to deliver;
- identifying any likely adverse impact of collecting and holding the information including the intrusion into the employee's private life and the potential impact on his relationship with the employer;
- considering alternatives to collecting and holding such information;
- taking into account the obligations that arise from collecting and holding health information, for example when medical testing reveals a health issue that the employee was not previously aware of;
- judging whether collecting and holding health information is justified in all the circumstances.

How do we ensure that our occupational health scheme meets data protection requirements?

Having outlined above the ramifications of processing information relating to workers' health in all but the most routine HR activities, it is understandable that many organisations choose to outsource occupational health activities. Generally service providers understand the legal environment in which they work and their clients operate and the arrangement is usually that the service supplier will provide the minimum information required by the organisation. The usual reason for referral of an employee will be to determine fitness to work. The occupational health scheme will carry out a medical examination and will advise the organisation whether or not the individual is fit to work and, if so, whether any special needs have to be accommodated, such as special seating or lighting or access to lifts rather than stairs etc.

The pitfalls of using an outsourced service supplier generally arise when using, say, a designated doctor to carry out the occupational health review. Smaller service providers may not understand the legal environment in which the employer operates and may provide more detail of medical conditions than is required to ascertain whether the individual is fit for work. The organisation must make it clear that an indication of fitness to work and the nature of any necessary modifications to the workplace is all that is required.

This is not a relationship where the occupational health adviser is processing personal information on behalf of the employer. Rather it is processing personal information as a data controller for the purpose of giving a professional opinion. Therefore the contractual requirements and compliance checking generally required when outsourcing work involving personal information processing do not apply to the employer in these circumstances.

Note

1 The Telecommunications (Lawful Business Practice) (Interception of Communications) Regulations 2000 (SI 2000/2699).

G. International transfers

Can I transfer personal information internationally?

The Data Protection Directive[1] created a standard for the handling and use of personal information in all EC member states. It also established a prohibition on the transfer of personal information outside the European Economic Area (the EEA), subject to a range of exemptions. The EEA comprises the EC Member States, Norway, Iceland and Lichtenstein.

This raises an issue when proposing to transfer personal information to a territory located outside of the EEA (known as a 'third country'). The prohibition is set out in the Eighth Data Protection Principle, which also provides derogations from the prohibition. When considering a transfer to a third country, the order of exemptions is as follows:

- transfers within the EEA are authorised;
- transfers to countries approved by the European Commission for that purpose are likewise authorised (currently[2] Andorra, Argentina, Canada, the Faroe Islands, Guernsey, the Isle of Man, Israel, Jersey, Switzerland, and Uruguay);
- transfers to the US to companies which subscribe to 'safe harbor' are approved;
- transfers where the adequacy test has been met (of which more below) are approved;
- transfers subject to a Sch 4 condition are authorised (again, covered in more detail below).

What are the Schedule 4 Conditions?

Transfers:
- made with the consent of the individual;
- in the performance of a contract entered into at the request of the data subject or which is in his or her interests;
- pursuant to legal proceedings (e.g. to establish, exercise or defend legal rights);
- in the vital interests of the data subject, which is interpreted restrictively, meaning literally in a 'life or death' situation;
- of information held on a public register which is open to inspection and any conditions attaching to the register are complied with;
- on approved terms. There are standard, approved, terms for the transfer of personal information to data controllers and data processors located in third countries available for incorporation into international contracts;
- which are specifically authorised by the Information Commissioner. The Binding Corporate Rules (BCR) regime falls into this condition. Multinational

organisations may apply in standard format to the Commissioner to seek approval for a suite of internal policies and procedures around personal information management which are applicable to all the organisations offices and locations worldwide.

How do we establish that a transfer is made with the consent of the data subject?

In general, the processing of personal information does not require the consent of the data subject but transfers of personal information to third countries may be authorised by consent. Consent is defined in the Data Protection Directive as a freely given indication of agreement to a specific course of action. This means that it is difficult to show that consent has been given to a clause built into terms and conditions that the data subject is unlikely to be able to challenge.

Where an organisation chooses to rely on consent to legitimise processing activities it must be able to clearly show that there was no duress. This makes it even harder to establish consent in relationships such as that between an employer and an employee because there is a fundamental inequality in the relationship, with the employee more likely to agree with conditions attached by the employer.

The fact that consent must be an 'indication of agreement' means that silence cannot be construed as consent. There must be a positive action to indicate agreement. The Information Commissioner has stated that seeking the consent of the data subject to process personal information constitutes an attempt to pass responsibility for fair processing which the organisation itself should be carrying. Therefore the guidance on this point is that consent as an authorising condition should be considered as a last resort when all other options have been exhausted.

When is consent a useful condition to authorise international transfers of data?

This condition is useful when publishing information about individuals to an internet site which is available internationally. Guidance from the Information Commissioner is that the publication of information to a website constitutes a worldwide transfer of that information because it is accessible worldwide. Informed consent is the appropriate Sch 4 condition for authorising the publication of information by a data subject on a website (e.g. when participants in a discussion website post comments or blogs). Because their comments may be accessible worldwide, there is a deemed worldwide transfer of the personal information in their comments and name.

Similarly an organisation located within the EEA but which allows its managers to work (or take holidays) outside the EEA and access their e-mail account and other intranet facilities while abroad, is deemed to be transferring the personal information to third countries. This is something that needs to be brought to the attention of employees at the time they complete their online profile for the intranet so that they can give implicit consent to the publication of their profile worldwide.

Within the HR context there may be occasions when consent to a transfer of personal information outside the EEA is appropriate (e.g. where a senior manager is applying for an international post in a multinational organisation). His experience and employment details may have to be shared with executives located in territories outside the EEA as part of the selection process. This should be made clear to the applicant at an early stage of the recruitment process and the manager's decision to proceed may be taken as implicit consent to the transfers outlined.

Does consent always have to be explicit?

No, as the last example in the preceding section demonstrates, in certain circumstances it is possible to establish implicit consent. Consider the case where an individual makes a personal liability claim against an organisation; the individual is likely to commence the claim with full details of medical conditions resulting from the incident complained of. This information will be submitted to the organisation without any prior warning, so the organisation has no opportunity to explain its fair processing or privacy notice policy or to obtain consent to the processing of medical details which comprise sensitive personal information. In these circumstances the claimant has given implicit consent to the organisation processing the personal information by virtue of having submitted it to the organisation.

What is the 'adequacy test'?

If none of the Sch 4 conditions apply, then the data controller must assess the adequacy of the protection for data subjects' rights and freedoms both in the third country and as offered by the transferee organisation.

The adequacy test is a legal test concentrating on the level of data protection in the third country and the ease with which a data subject can enforce his or her rights. There are also issues around the stability of the current political regime and whether or not it is likely that the regime would interfere with data protection rights or overrule them.

There is a more general aspect to the adequacy test relating to the type of data being transferred, the origin of the data, its destination, the safeguards in place at the transferee organisation, the understanding of privacy and confidentiality issues at the transferee organisation and its attempts to train staff appropriately etc.

Having investigated all these aspects it is the decision of an individual or group of individuals at the transferor organisation to decide whether the situation provides adequate protection for the specific transfer of specific personal information to the specific transferee organisation and document the reasons why.

What, if any, sectoral rules apply to the international transfer of personal information?

There are specific regimes regulating the transfer of Passenger Name Records (PNR) to the US in connection with the Patriot Act in the US (prevention of terrorism and anti money laundering legislation).

For similar reasons there are also special sectoral rules applying to the transfer of financial information. The Society for Worldwide Interbank Financial Telecommunication (SWIFT) transfers bank data for purposes of carrying out secure financial transactions and to identify money laundering and fraud.

Notes

1 Directive 95/46/EC.
2 As at October 2010.

H. Websites

Are there any data protection considerations when setting up a new website?

Yes, there are several. If a website is to be used to obtain personal information overtly from visitors, perhaps an enquiry form, comments or blog spot, then a privacy notice is required to set out the intended purposes for which the information will be processed. Where information is collected covertly by using cookies then a notice is required explaining how cookies are used by the organisation and how they may be disabled by changing browser settings.

If the website will be used to publish personal information (e.g. photographs or profiles of employees) then the employees must first be consulted and their consent obtained to the publication based on clear information about the circumstances of the publication (e.g. are they being put forward as a contact in relation to specific enquiries or as a general point of contact and so on).

As websites are accessible worldwide, the publication of personal information on a website is a deemed international transfer of the information worldwide. Therefore action needs to be taken to authorise the transfer of personal information outside the European Economic Area (the EEA) which is otherwise prohibited under the Eighth Data Protection Principle. The most likely condition to satisfy the legal requirements is to seek the informed consent of the individuals whose personal information is being published explaining that their personal information will be available worldwide in jurisdictions where there will not be the same level of data protection as they enjoy within the EEA.

Some organisations promote their services by way of case studies and care needs to be taken where the services are personal services illustrated by case studies involving personal information. Even where a set of circumstances is anonymised in a case study, it may still be sufficiently singular to allow identification of the individual concerned. In general it is advisable to make up case studies and inform readers that the details of the case study are typical rather than actual circumstances.

What are the issues relating to intranets or in-house websites?

Even where a website is designed for a restricted audience, as is the case with intranets, any personal information published there may be deemed to be transferred outside the EEA if staff access the information internationally. This may arise not only where an organisation has an international presence, but also where managers are encouraged to access the intranet site when travelling abroad.

An intranet site is more likely than a website to hold personal information relating to employees. Most will have telephone directories, an overview of the work carried out by different departments and contacts within each department for enquiries. This publication of personal information about an employee must be done with the consent of the individual concerned, not just in outline, but consent to the actual wording and appearance of the information on screen, so that they can judge the overall effect.

Many organisations encourage staff to undertake voluntary work in the community and they may promote this by posting photographs related to different projects. A photograph is personal information and the publication of photographs should be dealt with in the same way as the publication of contact details. Where third parties are also involved (e.g. children and teachers in schools) consent should also be sought from those third parties to the publication of their personal information on the intranet (or in hard copy on company notice boards).

I. Enforcement

How is data protection law enforced?

The regulator for data protection in the UK is the Information Commissioner. The Information Commissioner is the national data protection supervisory authority and there are corresponding Commissioners in other EC Member States. There is an Assistant Commissioner for Wales, another for Scotland and a third for Northern Ireland.

The Information Commissioner's Office (the ICO) is responsible for investigating complaints, a process known as 'assessment' and enforcing the data protection principles. The role also involves the promotion of good practice, including developing and assisting in the development of codes of practice, encouraging the observance of the requirements of the Data Protection Act 1998 (the DPA 1998) by data controllers, and advising the public about their rights.

Part V of the DPA 1998 sets out the enforcement tools at the Commissioner's disposal. These include:

- enforcement notices, where a course of action is set out for the organisation to follow or specific actions are prohibited;
- assessment notices, which set out the details of a failure to observe the data protection principles;
- information notices and special information notices, which require specific information to be provided to the Commissioner as part of an ongoing investigation.

Failure to comply with one or more of these notices is an offence under s 47 of the DPA 1998.

What approach does the Information Commissioner's Office take on enforcement?

The ICO has adopted a risk-based approach.[1] Action is more likely to be taken where a potential failure to observe the principles would affect many data subjects or where the consequences of a failure would be significant and affect a large number of data subjects.

The Commissioner has frequently stated that the objective of the ICO is to encourage compliance and best practice by educating organisations in their data protection obligations rather than taking a heavy-handed enforcement approach. However the ICO is not unwilling to take enforcement action.

This approach to enforcement was set out in the ICO document *Data Protection Regulatory Action Policy* published in April 2010. It describes the overriding imperative of the ICO as to 'take a practical down to earth approach – simplifying and making it easier for the majority of organisations who seek to handle personal information well and tougher for the minority who do not', further described as a 'carrot and stick approach'.

The policy says that the ICO is prepared to take 'a tough and purposeful approach on those occasions where that is necessary'. In particular enforcement action will be taken where obligations are deliberately or persistently ignored, or where the ICO thinks that examples need to be set or issues clarified.

The initiation of regulatory action is likely to be driven by issues of general public concern, including those raised in the media or where the intrusive nature or novelty of particular processing activities raises concerns. Consumer complaints may raise issues that the ICO considers should be targeted for regulatory action and so may its other activities (e.g. visiting a data controller to discuss their compliance arrangements).

In practice enforcement of data protection law and freedom of information is likely to be the keynote of the activities and publications of the ICO for the next few years. The direction of the ICO can be inferred from the background and experience of the individuals who have held the position of Information Commissioner. The last Commissioner, Richard Thomas, was a public lawyer. He oversaw the implementation of the Freedom of Information Act 2000, which impacted so significantly on public bodies. The current Commissioner, Christopher Graham, was formerly the Director General of the Advertising Standards Authority (the ASA); his background is in enforcement with a powerful regulator. Failure to comply with a ruling from the ASA quickly results in all the organisation's advertisements being effectively banned. On the Information Commissioner's website there is a list of undertakings given by organisations found to be in breach of data protection law. Until recently the list was quite short, but it has noticeably lengthened since Mr Graham took over. This is anecdotal evidence, but is indicative of the ICO's current focus.

What type of regulatory action might be taken?

The ICO can choose from a number of courses of action. These are not mutually exclusive and can be applied as seems most appropriate for the circumstances, the likely educational effect on the organisation and on industry in general. These are:

- criminal prosecution for offences under the Act;
- a caution, described as an alternative to prosecution where a criminal offence is admitted but a caution is considered a more appropriate reaction than prosecution;
- issue of an enforcement notice;
- the newly introduced monetary penalty notice: maximum fine set at £500,000;
- an order made under s 159 of the Consumer Credit Act 1974 requiring a credit reference agency to add a 'notice of correction' to a consumer's file;
- making an application to the court for an injunction to prevent the continued

use of an unfair contract term (application is made under the Unfair Terms in Consumer Contracts Regulations 1999[2]);

- making an application for an enforcement order under s 213 of the Enterprise Act 2002, requiring a person to cease conduct harmful to consumers.

A more generally available power is the power to generate publicity around a data protection breach. Given that the sanctions for data protection breaches have historically been limited and ineffectual, previous Commissioners have clearly stated their strategy of seeking publicity as an enforcement tool.[3]

When is compensation payable?

The ICO cannot order an organisation to pay compensation to data subjects who have suffered damage or distress as a result of a data protection breach. If a breach has occurred and the organisation decides that it should be reported to the ICO,[4] then the ICO will want to know what action has been taken (or planned) to alleviate any damage or distress to data subjects. This may include the payment of compensation.

Where a data protection breach is suspected from circumstances described by a data subject in a complaint to the ICO, it will 'assess' the processing, giving a view on whether or not it the complaint is in breach of one or more of the data protection principles. The complainant then has recourse to the courts to seek compensation for any damage or distress caused to him as a result of any breach.

Can I make a complaint on behalf of the company?

In cases where employees take customer lists either for their own or another's benefit they are in breach of data protection law as well as their contracts of employment and any duty of confidentiality. These were the circumstances when T-Mobile employees allegedly sold customer lists, including their mobile phone contract expiry date, to brokers for onward sale to other mobile 'phone operators. In the past the general policy adopted by the ICO has been that organisations have rights and remedies to take action against employees who breach confidentiality, employment contracts or copyright and the Office has not generally got involved further. The T-Mobile case however was handled differently. The Information Commissioner stated in a press release in November 2009 that he had investigated the incident and had discovered that the information had been sold on to several brokers in exchange for 'substantial amounts of money'. He also said that the Office had obtained 'several search warrants and attended a number of premises', concluding that a prosecution file was being prepared.

The main thrust of the November 2009 press release was to repeat the perceived need for custodial sentences for offences under s 55 of the DPA 1998 (unlawful obtaining and disclosure of personal information) but it marks a change in approach. In this new climate it may be worthwhile enlisting assistance from the ICO when investigating employee theft of customer lists comprising personal information.

Notes

1 ICO Data Protection Strategy.
2 Unfair Terms in Consumer Contracts Regulations 1999 (SI 1999/2083).
3 In the ICO Data Protection Strategy it says the Office will 'recognise the role of reputation, consumer pressure and market forces in delivering good practice particularly with reputable private sector businesses'.
4 See Chapter 4 for guidance on when to report a breach.

Glossary

Article 29 Working Party
An advisory body to the European Commission on data protection and privacy issues, constituted under the Data Protection Directive and made up of representatives from the national data protection authorities and the European Data Protection Supervisor.

Binding Corporate Rules
Set of internal policies and procedures adopted by multinational organisations and approved by the national data protection supervisory authority to provide a framework for compliant handling of personal data throughout the organisation. Approval of Binding Corporate Rules authorises the transfer of personal data to the organisation's offices worldwide, even where the office is located in a country outside of the European Economic Area.

Caldicott Guardian
Nominated individual within an NHS Trust with responsibility for safeguarding the confidentiality of patient information.

CCTV Code of Practice
Code of practice on data protection for CCTV operators published by the Information Commissioner's Office.

Data Protection Act
UK Act of Parliament, the Data Protection Act 1998.

Data Protection Directive
Directive 46/95/EC passed by the European Commission in 1995.

Data protection principle
One of eight standards set out in the Data Protection Directive for personal data processing and incorporated into the UK Data Protection Act 1998 under the First Schedule to the Act.

Data security breach notification requirement
Mandatory self-reporting of data security breach incidents to the authorities and/ or the individuals whose personal data has been compromised.

Employment Practices Code
Code of practice on data protection for employers published by the Information Commissioner's Office.

European Data Protection Supervisor (EDPS)
An independent agency responsible for protecting personal data processed by bodies and authorities of the European Commission and encouraging best practice among them. It monitors the EU administration's processing of personal data; advises on policies and legislation that affect privacy; and co-operates with similar authorities to ensure consistent data protection. The EDPS is a member of the Article 29 Working Party.

European Economic Area (EEA)
European Union Member States together with Norway, Iceland and Lichtenstein.

First-tier Tribunal (Information Rights)
This tribunal hears data protection issues, formerly the Information Tribunal.

GRC software
Software to facilitate the management of governance, risk management and compliance issues.

Lisbon Treaty
A treaty of the European Union that aims to streamline EU institutions. It amends the 1992 Maastricht Treaty and the 1957 Rome Treaty. It replaced the vexed European Constitution, which was rejected by several Member States and it contains some of the changes the constitution intended to introduce. Its importance in data protection law is that it amended the EU three 'Pillar' structure.
- First Pillar: The Single Market.
- Second Pillar: Common Foreign and Security Policy.
- Third Pillar: Police and Judicial Cooperation in criminal matters.
The 1995 Data Protection Directive only applies to the Single Market, the First Pillar and the Lisbon Treaty therefore highlighted that European data protection law needs to be amended to include former Third Pillar activities.

Madrid Resolution
The Joint Proposal on International Standards for the Protection of Privacy approved by the 31st International Conference of Data Protection and Privacy in Madrid in November 2009. The Madrid Resolution is a set of standards for data protection with wider international application and appeal than the European Data Protection Directive. It was approved by data protection authorities from more than 50 countries, spanning all five continents and a group of top executives

from 10 large multinational companies: Oracle, Walt Disney, Accenture, Microsoft, Google, Intel, Procter & Gamble, General Electric, IBM and Hewlett-Packard.

Marketing Preference Service
A list of individuals who request not to receive marketing material by specific media and maintained by independent bodies, for example the 'Mailing Preference Service' allows individuals to opt out of receiving marketing material by direct mail, the 'Telephone Preference Service' allows individuals to opt out of receiving telephone calls made for the purpose of marketing.

National data protection authorities
National supervisory authorities for data protection established pursuant to the Data Protection Directive. The Information Commissioner in the UK is the national data protection authority.

Payment Card Industry Data Security Standards (PCI DSS)
Standards set by the payment card industry for the security of customer credit and debit card information.

Phorm
Internet behaviour mapping technology which allows internet service providers to target advertising based on internet usage.

Privacy by Design
The concept of incorporating a data protection compliant framework into systems developments.

Privacy Enhancing Technologies (PETs)
Technology which protects or enhances privacy rights.

Privacy Impact Assessment (PIA)
The identification of the likely implications of a project or development on the privacy of individuals carried out at an early stage of project planning and development.

Privacy notice
A statement which satisfies the fair processing requirements of the First Data Protection Principle.

Safe harbor
A protocol to which US-based organisations can subscribe. It involves adherence to a set of principles similar to the data protection principles to regulate and

safeguard personal data. Adoption of Safe Harbor by an organisation authorises the transfer of personal data to its premises in the United States, even though those premises are located in a country outside of the EEA.

Senior Information Risk Owner (SIRO)
Person designated with responsibility for confidentiality and security of personal data within an NHS Trust.

Directory

Websites

Data Protection Consulting	www.dp-smart.co.uk
European Commission – Justice and Home Affairs	http://ec.europa.eu/justice
Diect Marketing Association	www.dma.org.uk
FEDMA	www.fedma.org
HMSO	www.hmso.gov.uk
Information Commissioner	www.ico.gov.uk
NHS Information Centre	www.ic.nhs.uk/
Vice-President of the European Commission, Viviane Reding	http://ec.europa.eu/ commission_2010-2014/ reding/index_en.htm
UK legislation	www.legislation.gov.uk

Publications from the Office of the Information Commissioner

Introductory

Data Protection Act overview
Data protection myths and realities
It's your information – How to access your information (Welsh)

Practical application

A report on the surveillance society
A report on the surveillance society – Appendices
A report on the surveillance society – Public discussion documents
A report on the surveillance society – Summary report
Advice for the elected and prospective members of local authorities
Advice to local authorities on disclosing personal information to elected members
CCTV data protection code of practice – Consultation response form
CCTV in pubs – FAQs
Code of Practice on Telecommunications Directory Information Covering the Fair
    Processing of Personal Data
Credit agreements – Data sharing
Credit explained

Data protection – When and how to complain

Employment Practices Code – A quick guide (PDF)

Employment Practices Code – Supplementary guidance

Getting it right: A brief guide to data protection for small businesses

Getting it right: Collecting information about your customers

Getting it right: Small business checklist

Good Practice Note – Buying and selling customer databases

Good Practice Note – Calling customers listed on the Telephone Preference
    Service

Good Practice Note – Charities and marketing

Good Practice Note – Corporate Telephone Preference Service

Good Practice Note – Data sharing between different local authority departments

Good Practice Note – Disclosing information about tenants

Good Practice Note – Disclosure of employee information under TUPE

Good Practice Note – Disclosure of personal information under the Taxes
    Management Act 1970

Good Practice Note – Electronic mail marketing

Good Practice Note – How does the Data Protection Act apply to recording and
    retaining professional opinions?

Good Practice Note – Individuals' rights of access to examination records

Good Practice Note – Outsourcing: a guide for small and medium-sized businesses

Good Practice Note – Publication of examination results by school

Good Practice Note – Security of personal information

Good Practice Note – The use and disclosure of information about business
    people

Good Practice Note – Tied agents and independent financial advisers

Good Practice Note – Training checklist for small and medium-sized
    organisations

Good Practice Note – Use of violent warning markers

Guidance on data security breach management

Health data – Use and disclosure

ICO view on CCTV in pubs

It's your information – Claiming compensation (Welsh)

It's your information – Radio frequency identification tags (Welsh)

It's your information – Sharing information about you (Welsh)

It's your information – Unwanted marketing (Welsh)

It's your information – Using social networking sites safely (Welsh)

It's your information – Your rights to police information (Welsh)

New rules on e-mail marketing

Notification fee changes

Notification of Data Security Breaches to the Information Commissioner's Office

Pension trustees and their use of administrators

Personal information online: Small business checklist

Personal information promise

Personal information toolkit

Privacy Impact Assessment – An overview

Promotion of a political party

Protecting your personal information online

Registration officers – Right to inspect local authority records

Taking photographs in schools

Technical Guidance Note – Access to information about public authorities' employees

The collection and use of identity information in pubs and clubs

The exemption from notification for 'not for profit' organisations

The guide to data protection

The sale of information relating to planning applications to local traders by local planning authorities in England and Wales

Use of ID scanning devices in pubs and clubs

Use of personal information available on the electoral roll

When can I disclose information to a private investigator?

Detailed specialist guides

A Surveillance Society: Qualitative Research – Presented by Oliver Murphy, Diagonostics Research

Article 29 Working Party Opinion on the European Court PNR ruling (WP 122)

Barrister's chambers notification

Binding corporate rules – Applying BCR for international transfers (WP74)

Binding corporate rules – Cooperation procedure

Binding corporate rules – FAQs related to BCR

Binding corporate rules – Framework BCR (WP154)

Binding corporate rules – Standard application form

Binding corporate rules – Table of BCR requirements (WP153)

Binding Corporate Rules Authorisation

CCTV Code of Practice 2008

Commentary by the Information Commissioner on Government amendments introduced in the House of Lords – July 2009

Coroners and Justice Bill – Additional commentary by the Information Commissioner 17/02/2009

Coroners and Justice Bill – Memorandum submitted by the Information Commissioner to the Public Bill Committee 30/01/2009

Coroners and Justice Bill Committee – Memorandum submitted by the Information Commissioner

Coroners and Justice Bill: Memorandum submitted by the Information
  Commissioner to members of the House of Lords
Crime mapping advice
Data Protection Legislation – Presented by Gareth Crossman, Liberty
Data Protection Regulatory Action Policy
EC model clauses – controller to controller
EC model clauses – controller to controller revised 2004
EC model clauses – controller to processor
Employment Practices Code
Employment Practices Code – Supplementary guidance
Evidence submitted by the Information Commissioner to the All Party Group on
  junk mail – investigation into data management
Exploiting engineering ingenuity to protect personal privacy – Presented by
  Martyn Thomas CBE
FIPR Report – Protecting children's personal information
Framework code of practice for sharing personal information
Good Practice Note – Automatic renewal of policies or membership by credit or
  debit card
Good Practice Note – Checklist for handling requests for personal information
  (subject access requests)
Good Practice Note – Releasing information to prevent or detect crime
Good Practice Note – Subject access and employment references
Good Practice Note – Subject access requests and local authority housing
  records
House of Lords' Constitution Committee Surveillance Society report
How the revised schedule 12A of the Local Government Act 1972 interacts with
  DPA
ICO Data Protection Strategy
ICO evidence to the House of Lords' EU Home Affairs inquiry into the
  Framework Decision on Passenger Name Records (PNR)
ICO further evidence for the inquiry into 'The Impact of Surveillance and Data
  Collection upon the Privacy of Citizens and their Relationship with the State'
ICO Personal Information Survey by ICM
ICO response to the House of Commons Home Affairs Committee report 'A
  Surveillance Society?'
Information Commissioner's guidance about the issue of monetary penalties
  prepared and issued under section 55C (1) of the Data Protection Act 1998
International transfers – legal guidance
Issues paper – Protecting children's personal information
Monitoring under section 75 of the N. Ireland Act 1998 – Good practice note
New approaches to identity management and privacy
Notification handbook – A complete guide to notification

Notification of barrister's chambers

Notification of pension scheme trustees

Personal information online code of practice

Privacy and security in road pricing – Presented by Phil Carey, Department for Transport

Privacy by Design conference – Building trust through effective guardianship of personal data

Privacy by Design conference – Conducting a PIA

Privacy by Design conference – ICO PIA Handbook one year on

Privacy by Design conference – Introduction by Jonathan Bamford, Assistant Commissioner

Privacy by Design conference – Lessons learned in the first year

Privacy by Design conference – Privacy Engineering White Paper

Privacy by Design conference – Programme

Privacy by Design conference – Promoting data protection by privacy enhancing technologies

Privacy by Design conference – Report presented by Toby Stevens of the Enterprise Privacy Group

Privacy by Design conference – The MoD data loss inquiry and the lessons learned on information assurance

Privacy Impact Assessment Project – Presented by Adam Warrens

Privacy impact assessments around the world – Presented by Colin Bennetts

Privacy notices code of practice

RAND Europe review of the EU data protection directive

RAND Europe review of the EU data protection directive: summary

Research into young people's views and use of social networking sites (data protection topline report)

Response of the Information Commissioner to the Ministry of Justice's Consultation Paper of 16 July 2008

Surveillance Society Follow Up Report (May 2007)

Technical Guidance Note – Access to information about public authorities' employees

Technical Guidance Note – Access to personal information held by schools in England

Technical Guidance Note – Access to personal information held by schools in Northern Ireland

Technical Guidance Note – Access to personal information held by schools in Scotland

Technical Guidance Note – Access to personal information held by schools in Wales

Technical Guidance Note – Access to personal information held by schools in Wales (Welsh)

Technical Guidance Note – Dealing with subject access requests involving other people's information

Technical Guidance Note – Determining what is personal data

Technical Guidance Note – Disclosures to members of Parliament carrying out constituency casework

Technical Guidance Note – FAQs and answers about relevant filing systems

Technical Guidance Note – Filing defaults with credit reference agencies

Technical Guidance Note – Privacy enhancing technologies

Technical Guidance Note – Radio frequency indentification

Technical Guidance Note – Subject access requests and health record requests by members of the public

Technical Guidance Note – Subject access requests and legal proceedings

Technical Guidance Note – Subject access requests and social services records

Technical Guidance Note – The use of personal information held for collecting and administering council tax

The ICO position on the Government Data Handling Reviews

The ICO's view of the proposals for the retention of DNA profiles contained in the Crime and Security Bill

The Information Commissioner's response to the House of Lords Constitution Committee report 'Surveillance: Citizens and Society'

The privacy dividend: The business case for investing in proactive privacy protection

The use of biometrics in schools

What is personal data? – A quick reference guide

ICSA publications

For a full and up-to-date list of ICSA publications, visit www.icsabookshop.co.uk

Index

Accountability principle 27–28
  likely impact 69–71
    suggested wording 70
Article 29 Working Party 29–31
  data controller 30–31
  Privacy by Design 30
Audit
  definition of 78
  delivery of 79
    ICO 78–79
    practicalities of 79–80
    review 80–81
    'system of control' 77
Avoiding and mitigating risk 132–143
  data minimisation 133–134
  factors affecting choice of tactics 142
  IT security 135–136
    policies and procedures 135–136
  monitoring implementation 142–143
  physical security 134
  privacy 136–143 see also Privacy
  Privacy Impact Assessment 139–142
    conducting a PIA 141–142
    definition 139
    Information Commissioner 140–141
    organisation 141
    overview 141
  system-driven controls 132–133
    privacy notice 133
  training tactics 145–146

Binding Corporate Rules 63–64
Breach of confidence
  data sharing, and 58
British Standard on Data Protection
    71–77
  elements of system of control 71–77
    appointing data protection officers
      74–75
    Caldicott Report 75

'common accountability measures'
    72–73
  governance, risk management and
    compliance software 76–77
  job-related risk management 76
  managing data protection compliance
    in projects 77
  PIMS 71–72
  register of personal information
    75–76
  senior accountability 73
  SIRO, and 73, 75
BT
  Phorm 17

Call for evidence 28
CCTV
  Code of Practice 22–23
  controls on use of 6
Consent 52–54
  fair processing, and 53–54
  freely given 54
  marketing activity, and 54
  privacy notice incomplete, where 53
  when needed 53–54
Criminal Justice and Immigration Act 2008
    19–20
Current themes 28–32
Custodial sentences 45–46

Data controller
  new definition 59–60
Data processor
  new definition 59–60
Data Protection Act 1998
  breaches 90–92
    data security 90–91
    Data Security and Consumer
      Communications 92

Data Protection Act 1998 *continued*
    inaccurate, irrelevant or incomplete
        records 91
    poor record keeping 91–92
    transfer of personal information
        outside the EEA 92
    unfair obtaining or disclosure of
        personal information 91
Data Protection Directive 3–4
    globalisation, effects of 32–33
    legislative change, and 18
    lobbying power 18–19
    strengths of 23–24
    UK legislation, and 15–16, 17
Data protection principles
    consent, and 52–54 *see also* Consent
    data sharing 55–58 *see also* Data
        sharing
    Eighth Principle 61
    Fifth Principle 58–59
    First Principle 50, 52
    Human Rights Act 1998, and 57–58
    keeping people informed 52–53
    retention of electronic records 58–59
    Seventh Principle 59–61
    summary of 50–52
        accuracy 51
        adequate, relevant and not excessive
        51
        EEA, and 51–52
        fair processing 50
        individual's rights 51
        length of time 51
        measures 51
        purposes 50
    when to report breaches 64–65
Data sharing 55–58
    breach of confidence, and 58
    Code of Practice, proposed 55–56
    data protection issues 58
    Ministry of Justice guidance 56
    reasons for 55
    ultra vires, and 56–57
Data Sharing Review 18–19

E-mail
    backup 59

European Commission 32–35
    Communication 34–35
    consultation on data protection law
        32–35
        embedding data protection in
            organisations 34
        empowering data subject 34
        globalisation 32–33
        harmonisation 34
        one legal framework 32
        technological changes 33
    effect of globalisation 33
        Madrid Resolution 33
    embedding data protection in
        organisations 34
    empowering the data subject 34
    legal framework of 32
    regulatory structure 6–9
European Union
    driving force, as 14
        European Data Protection Supervisor
        7–8
        legislative changes 14, 33
    regulatory structure 6–9
        Article 29 Working Party 8–9
        Commissioner 6–7
        National Supervisory Authorities 8,
        22–28
    technological changes 33

Fairness
    meaning 50
Financial Services Authority
    action by 25–26
Fines 46–48
    level of 46–48

Globalisation
    effects of 32–33

Human Rights Act 1998 4–6
    Article 8.4–6
    Article 8.2 5
    data protection principles, and 57–58

Influencing interpretation 20–26
    courts, and 20–21

Influencing interpretation *continued*
  Durant, and 20
  Financial Services Authority 25–26
    companies, and 25–26
  Information Commissioner, and 22–24
    Data Protection Directive 23
    Durant 23
    Information Tribunal 21–22
    Police National Computer 21
  media pressure 24–25
    celebrity confidentiality cases 24
    ICO, and 24–25
Information Commissioner 9–12
  audit *see* Audit
  Data Protection Strategy 11
  duties 9–10
  enhanced powers of 11–12
  framework, on 28–29
  influencing interpretation 22–24 *see also*
    Influencing Interpretation
  lobbying for powers to audit without
    consent 20
  media pressure 24–25
  principle of accountability 29
  privacy 140
  risk management 88, 94
    supporting departments 10
  training 146, 150–151
  website 10
Information Tribunal 21–22
International Conference of Data Protection
  and Privacy 26–27
  Madrid Resolution 26–27
International transfers 61–64
  adequacy criteria 62–63
  Binding Corporate Rules 63–64
  legal guidance 61–64
  step 1 62
  step 2 62–63
  step 4 64

Jersey
  criticisms of 14–15

Lawfulness
  meaning 50
Legislative change 14–18

BT, and 17
Data Protection Directive 18
Durant case 15–16
EU, and 14
European Commission 16–17
forces behind 14–18
Jersey, and 14–15
Letter of Formal Notice 17–18
Lobbying power
  UK, in 18–20

Madrid Resolution 26–27
  Data Protection Directive, and 27
  principle of accountability, and 70–71
  privacy groups 48
Marketing activity
  consent, and 54
Media
  pressure from 24–25
Monitoring 81–83
  clinical information assurance 83
  confidentiality and data protection
    assurance 81–82
  corporate information assurance 83
  definition of 81
  Information Governance Management
    81
  Information Security Assurance 82–83

National Supervisory Authority in UK
  Information Commissioner 9–10 *see*
    also Information Commissioner
Norwich Union
  fining of 25
Notification 38–44
  definition of 38
  next developments 41–43
    accountability principle 42–43
    Data Protection Register 43
    NHS East of England Strategic
      Health Authority 41
    Orbit Heart of England Housing
      Association 42
    transparency of 41
  penalties for failure of 43–44
    fines 43–44
  requirement of 38–39

Notification *continued*
  business activities 38–39
  exempt businesses of 39
  who can notify 39–40
    ICO, and 40
    online registration 40

Obtaining or disclosing personal
    information unfairly 44–45
Offences
  obtaining or disclosing personal
    information unfairly 44–45
Operation Motorman 44

Penalties 45–48
  fines 46–48
Pension trustees 123–128
  data security 125–126
  data sharing 127
  exercise of subject rights 124–125
  fair processing 124, 126
  moving office 127–128
  proportionality and data minimisation
    126
Phorm 17
Privacy 136–143
  by design 138–139
  CCTV schemes 136–137
  enhancing procedures 136–137
  impact assessment 139–142
    conducting 141–142
    fair processing risks 140–141
    overview 141
  privacy enhancing technologies (PET)
    137–138
Processor
  definition 60–61

Retention of electronic records 58–59
Risk assessments 101–131
  assessing the likely impact of incidents
    105
  commercial call centres 113–116
    data accuracy 115
    data security 115–116
    fair processing 114–115

  information transferred outside the
    EEA 116
  proportionality and data
    minimisation 11
  examples in various sectors 105–109
    accuracy of information 108
    data retention 108
    data security risks 108–109
    fair processing 106–108
    membership records 105–106
    privacy notice 107
    proportionality and data
      minimisation 108
    'sensitive' categories of data 106
    subject rights 108
    transfer of personal information
      outside the EEA 109
  identifying the risks 101–105
    fair processing – First Principle 102
    general issues 104–105
    information not to be retained longer
      than is necessary for the purpose
      – Fifth Principle 103
    information not to be transferred
      outside the EEA – Eighth
      Principle 104
    information to be accurate, and,
      where necessary, up to date –
      Fourth Principle 103
    information to be adequate, relevant,
      and not excessive for the purpose
      – Third Principle 102–103
    information to be held securely –
      Seventh Principle 104
    information to be processed in
      accordance with subject rights –
      Sixth Principle 103
    staying within original purpose
      description – Second Principle 102
  implementing a new customer
    relationship management
    database 128–130
    data accuracy 129
    data retention 129–130
    data security 130
    exercise of subject rights 130
    fair processing 128–129

Risk assessments *continued*
    proportionality and data
      minimisation 129
    marketing activity 116–119
      data retention 118
      data security 118
      exercise of subject rights 118
      fair processing 117–118
      proportionality and data
        minimisation 118
      transfer of information outside the
        EEA 118–119
    operating CCTV 120–123
      accuracy of personal information 122
      CCTV 120–121
      data minimisation and
        proportionality 122
      data retention 123
      data security risks 123
      fair processing 122
      risks relating to complying with
        subject risks 123
      Security Industry Act 2001 121
    organisational risks 110–113
      accuracy of information 112
      data retention risks 112
      data security risks 113
      examples 110
      exercise of subject rights 113
      fair processing 111–112
      general factors 113
      NHS 110–111
      paper records in the NHS 110–111
      proportionality and data
        minimisation 112
    outsource service provider 119–120
      data security 119–120
      transferring personal information
        outside the EEA 120
    pension trustees 123–128 *see also*
      Pension trustees
Risk management 86–100
    avoiding and mitigating risk 132–143
      see also Avoiding and mitigating
      risk
    breaches of Data Protection Act 1998
      90–92 *see* Data Protection Act
      1998

    'big picture' approach 86
    data lost in the post 86–87
    e-mails sent to the wrong address
      88–89
    factors affecting 98–99
      macro environment 98
      organisational factors 98–99
    failure to delete or dispose of personal
      data safely 90
    failure to keep information secure
      off-shore 90
    failure to process fairly in accordance
      with subject rights 89
      failures in IT security 88
    inherent risks 86–90
    intrinsic confidentiality 99
    lost and stolen laptop 87–88
    potential impact of breaches on
      company, its officers and
      employees 93–95
      committing a criminal offence 93
      demoralised colleagues 95
      financial risk 93
      risk to reputation 94–95
    potential impact of breaches on
      individual data subjects 95–98
      emotional stress 97
      financial 95–96
      loss of privacy 97
      reputation 98
      time and effort 96–97
    reasons for 86
    theft and fraud 89

Section 55 offence 44–45
Staff awareness *see* Training
Strategic approach 66–85
    audit 77–80 *see also* Audit
    British Standard on Data Protection
      71–77 *see also* British Standard
      on Data Protection
    recommended for data protection
      compliance 67–69
    Data Sharing Review Report 69
    FSA 68
    risk management 67
    systemic failures 68–69

Training 144–155
building a plan 151–154
fair processing 152
policies and procedures 152
technical phrases 152–153
data security risks 146–148
data in transit 147–148
recent security incidents 146–147
Information Commissioner 150–151
maintaining organisational awareness
153
Seventh Principle Data Protection
Principle 144
special concerns for data processor
service providers 148–150
Data Protection Principle 148–149
Employment Practices Code 149–150
technical implementation of 149–150
sustainability 154

training as a tactic to avoid or mitigate
risk 145–146
transparency and communication
153–154

UK
lobbying power in 18–20
National Supervisory Authority
9–12
Ultra vires
data sharing, and 56–57
Unsolicited marketing
freedom from 6

Websites
publication of material on 61

Zurich Insurance plc
fining of 25–26

Part Two – Questions and Answers

Section A: Fair processing and marketing 160–172
Conduct of market research 169
Consent in writing to use of personal information 165
Consent not established 165–166
Consent to use of photographs 164
Cookies 171–172
    consent 171
    customer profiling activities 171
    information required 171
Customer profiling 171
Definition of fair processing160
E-mail 167
Information in marketing message 166
Information which may be useful in future 170
Issues around medium of publication 165
Keeping information on marketing databases up to date 170
Mailing Preference Service (MPS) 166
Marketing
    blocking or erasing details 168
    compliance 169
    consent 164, 165
    contact details 167
    future information 170
    information, provision of 167
    issues around customer profiling activities 171
    MPS 166
    personal information 165, 167
    removal of content 168
    removal of people 168
    SMS/text or e-mail 167
    telephone, use of 166
    third partner transfer 169–170
    up to date database 170
Privacy notice 160–164
    consent 164
    contents 160–161
    duplication 162
    more than one 161
    number of 161
    prominence 162–163

    prospective data subjects 160
    records of 163
    rules of 162
    where to be included 161
    who needs to see 161
Removal of people from mailing list on request 168–169
Restrictions on use of photographs 165
Retention and use of photographs 165
SMS 167
Telephone, use of 166
Time for keeping contact details on databases 167
Time for keeping personal information 167–168
Transfer of personal information to third party 169–170

Section B Record keeping 173–174
Exemptions 174
Obligations 173
    meeting 173
Time for keeping 174

Section C Security 175–177
Audit 175
Obligation 175
Required standard 175
Standard requirements 176–177

Section D CCTV 178–184
Auditing 182–183
Compliance 178–179
Data protection issue 178
Disclosure 180–181
Implications of outsourcing 183–184
Legal considerations 182
Obligations of landlord 184
Retention 181
Signage 179–180
Training for operations and monitors 183

Section E Outsourcing 185–189
Arrangement 185
Compliance checks 186–188
    checks 185
    Outsourcing – A Guide For Small And Medium-Sized Businesses 189

Section E *continued*
Definition 183
Loss of personal information 188–189
Third-party processing 185, 186

Section F Employment 190–196
Data protection issues 191
Data protection requirements 192
Employment Practices Code 190–191
Key issues 191
Handling subject access requests 192
Impact on human resources 190
Monitoring in the workplace 193
Monitoring workers 193–194
Occupation health schemes 195–196
Recruitment 191
Selection 191
Sensitive personal data 191–192
Worker's health 194–195

Section G International transfers 197–200
'Adequacy test' 199

Authorisation 198–199
Consent of the data subject 198
Eighth Principle 197
Explicit consent 199
Schedule 4 conditions 197–198
Sectoral rules 200
Standard for handling 197
Transfer of personal information 197

Section H Websites 201–202
Data protection considerations 201
In-house websites 201–202
Intranets 201–202

Section I Enforcement 203–206
Approach of ICO 203–204
Complaints 205–206
Compensation payable 205
Enforcement of data protection law 203
Regulatory action 204–205